Magical Feminism in the Americas

Resisting Female Marginalisation and Oppression through Magic

Md Abu Shahid Abdullah
East West University

Series in Literary Studies

www.vernonpress.com

In the Americas:
Vernon Press
1000 N West Street, Suite 1200
Wilmington, Delaware, 19801
United States

In the rest of the world:
Vernon Press
C/Sancti Espiritu 17,
Malaga, 29006
Spain

Series in Literary Studies

Library of Congress Control Number: 2024937430

ISBN: 979-8-8819-0110-3

Also available: 979-8-8819-0025-0 [Hardback]; 979-8-8819-0090-8 [PDF, E-Book]

Cover design by Vernon Press with elements from Freepik.

Table of Contents

Preface

At one time a predominantly male-dominated literary world tended to view the advent of magic realism in fiction mainly as a phenomenon starring a few major Latin American male novelists. Most literary critics went as far back as Jorge Luis Borges to locate the origins of this kind of narrative where the lines between fiction and realism could and would blur in the hands of adept writers of fiction. They viewed magic realism almost always as the Latin American literary efflorescence of male authors excelling in narrating the lives of people in fictional worlds who, despite being immersed in the quotidian, were going through events that would seem magical to everyone but themselves. Moreover, most of these critics agreed that it was the generation of male Latin American novelists led by Colombia's Gabriel Garcia Marquez who had made a noteworthy movement out of such unique blending of the quotidian and the magical. True, every once in a while they would place a woman novelist or two among the writers excelling in the form. But no doubt these critics felt the example of someone like Isabel Allende was another case of the exception validating the rule.

It is the great merit of Md. Abu Shahid Abdullah's *Magical Feminism in the Americas: Resisting Female Marginalisation and Oppression through Magic* to illustrate how, far from being an exception, Isabel Allende is one of many distinctive Latin American female writers of recent times producing quality fiction in this unique mode. Abdullah is able to prove convincingly in the course of his work that women writers of the whole of North as well as South America have been depicting the lot of women negotiating a path for themselves compellingly by depicting situations where the real and the magical are fabulously intertwined. He also stresses that they have been making use of their female-centred narratives to write persuasively about and against male domination and patriarchal tyrannies.

Indeed, Abdullah's book title clearly indicates his intentions in this regard. *Magical Feminism in the Americas: Resisting Female Marginalisation and Oppression through Magic* is a critical work of importance because of the way it showcases the phenomenon of women writers—stretching all the way from Chile to Canada, on the one hand, and from Cuba to Hawaii, on the other—making creative use of their experience of life in male-controlled societies that inevitably tend to repress and marginalise women's voices. As well, Abdullah is able to show how these women writers make impressive use of their novelistic license to reveal women finding ingenious ways of overcoming the shackles patriarchy tends to impose on their sex.

Abdullah first analyses Isabel Allende's *The House of the Spirits* in some detail to reveal how the Chilean novelist depicts some of his women characters forging bonds to resist male tyranny. He emphasises the way Allende resorts through her clairvoyant protagonist to a non-linear and unconventional narrative mode to forge an alternative to dominant male ways of writing. Abdullah then features the Nicaraguan novelist Giaconda Belli's work, *The Inhabited Woman,* to portray what he perceives to be its rendering of "the double victimisation of women" by male-induced systemic pressures. Belli is seen by him as a writer deploying magic as a means for his fictional women of empowerment and resistance against patriarchal forces, as if to provide an alternative national history. Abdullah next discusses the Hawaiian-American Kiana Davenport's novel *Shark Dialogues.* Here too Abdullah features a contemporary American female novelist able to give voice to marginalised and repressed females ingeniously. Abdullah finds in the book the use of an imaginatively structured polyphonic narrative that blends myths with recorded history. Once again, he details the way this representative of the new generation of women writers goes beyond conventional male modes of story-telling to devise alternative methods of narration absorbingly.

Abdullah's next exhibit in his gallery of women magical realist writers is the USA's Louis Edrich. To Abdullah, her novel *Tracks* fuses myth and magic with the lives of Chippewa Native American women's lot in postmodern ways. He sees Edrich deploying the supernatural to counter the colonising impositions of white male supremacy. Interestingly, Abdullah argues that the carnivalesque manner is applied and the Native American trickster figure put to use in Edrich's fictional work to depict subversive but indigenous ways pursued to cope with white male colonisers/ exploiters of Native American land and peoples.

Abdullah next deals with two women writers of the Americas who too in their unique styles use their works to protest as well as challenge white male tyrannies. The first of these writers is the Cuban novelist Cristina Garcia. Abdullah focuses on her use of the phoenix myth in her novel *Dreaming in Cuban* and notes how she uses a dialogic narrative where multiple points of view are juxtaposed to undermine Eurocentric perspectives. The critic sees Garcia highlighting immigrant Cuban-American women's endeavours to cope with the sort of double marginalisation they are subjected to as exiles in the

United States. Abdullah then discusses at some length the Chicana writer Ana Castilo. To him, her novel *So Far from God* is another instance of a magical realist women writer of the Americas using ingenious and magical situations to represent women's bid to empower themselves against patriarchal systems that tend to downgrade them. To Abdullah, Castilo plots her narrative to showcase native healing traditions and beliefs. Communing with dead ancestors, Abdullah writes, is, for Castilo, a pathway for women looking for ways out of the sufferings they undergo.

In the final section of *Magical Feminism in the Americas: Resisting Female Marginalisation and Oppression through Magic,* Abdullah spotlights the works of two more noteworthy female novelists of the Americas—Canada's Gail Anderson-Dargatz and the United States's Gloria Naylor. He sees both applying magical realist devices in depicting women ingeniously tackling racist and sexist abuses. In the process they also highlight the importance of countering such abuses through female solidarity and empowerment. He shows how Anderson-Dargatz's novel *The Cure for Death by Lightning* portrays the traumas caused by sexually abusive males on their female relatives. As for Naylor, Abdullah emphasises how she describes females bonding with each other to contend with male dominance, utilising magic and native healing means to deal with male aggression. To him, Naylor seems to be bent on depicting women healing each other's wounds in such situations, finding this route to be the best way out of the trauma and wounds that have been inflicted on them.

Abdullah's *Magical Feminism in the Americas: Resisting Female Marginalisation and Oppression through Magic* is thus a book drawing attention to a phenomenon in contemporary writing that is well worth paying attention to for anyone interested in magic/magical realism, quality contemporary female writing branching out of South and North America, or feminist fictional works of note for all us interested in recent developments in fiction, especially in the Americas, and in quality feminist writing. His is a persuasive account of representative women writers of the region who have taken recourse to magic realist modes to articulate not merely the plight of their sisters but also to illustrate ways out of a situation induced by their double marginalisation by patriarchy as a whole and colonial domination in particular.

What is remarkable to me is that Abdullah is a male critic and teacher of literature who has spent most of his life in Bangladesh. To have developed expertise to such an extent that he can write a book like *Magical Feminism in the Americas: Resisting Female Marginalisation and Oppression through Magic* is an amazing feat. Moreover, he appears to have read the books written in

Spanish on his own, as the extracts he has quoted from them in the language reveal. His book seems to have mastered the critical literature on the subject fully. His writing is also lucid. The book is comprehensive in its coverage and organised effectively to encompass representative women writing in the magical realist mode from all across the Americas. I feel that the book will be useful to students of fiction, feminist writing and comparative literature. It is a work that will surely be referred to for any of these areas as well as anyone wanting to know about contemporary women's writing of distinction from the Americas that have relevance for all of us—east or west, north or south.

Fakrul Alam is Bangabandhu Chair Professor, Department of History, and Professor (retired), Department of English, University of Dhaka

Chapter 1

Introduction

Human beings have been in contact with trauma or traumatic events either directly or indirectly and have found their experiences too horrible to express. Women have also been oppressed and marginalised throughout the world in multifarious ways without having any voice of their own. In giving a literary representation of female marginalisation, these traumatised women find it extremely difficult to express their thoughts or emotions. Due to the increase in the number of women's writing in the past few decades, the plight of oppressed women has come under focus. Female characters of these novels live in shamelessly patriarchal societies which shun and oppress them, relegating them to a miserable life. In depicting their victimisation, female authors have resorted to magical realist techniques. They have employed magical realism in their writing based on female involvement and experiences and have attempted to describe the strength and experience of women in a male-dominated society. When incorporating feminist elements, this mode of writing/narrative technique becomes a means for female emancipation and empowerment. This is when the term magical feminism, which refers to the use of magical realism from a feminist viewpoint, comes to the scene. Magical feminist works are written by female writers with female protagonists, mainly dealing with the subjugated position of women in society.

In the simplest terms, magical realism is the blending of the realistic and the fantastic without one dominating over the other, which dissolves the differences between the two in such a magnificent way that the real seems fantastic and the fantastic seems real. In magical realist novels, magical events happen in the midst of reality, creating a narrative which has the potential to distort the traditional understanding of history, culture, and reality, and thus helps the author to reverse all sorts of hierarchical orders in a subversive manner and to reshape dominant orders of the society. It is because of its ability to deconstruct present ideologies through social and political commentary and the transgressive and subversive aspects that magical realism becomes an apposite means to voice the 'other'. According to Zamora and Faris, "Magical realist texts are subversive: their in-betweenness, their all-at-onceness encourages resistance to monologic political and cultural structures, a feature that has made the mode particularly useful to writers in postcolonial cultures and, increasingly, to women" ("Introduction" 6). Although, over the years, the contexts under which magical realism originated and flourished have changed, the need for forms of representation of both privileged and un(der)privileged authors remains the same. Magical realism is no longer limited to a non-Western sphere but, over time, has found a place in the Western mainstream domain; however, it continues to be used from a marginalised perspective.

The term 'feminism' refers to a group that works to define, develop, and protect women's equal chances in the political, economic, and social spheres. Its ideas are similar to those of women's rights. Feminism mostly addresses issues affecting women, but because it aims to achieve gender equality, some feminists opined that men's freedom is also a significant element of feminism and that men are negatively impacted by sexist and gender stereotyping. In addition to advocating for women's rights to autonomy and bodily integrity, as well as the right to procreate, feminist activists have fought for women's rights in contract, property, and voting. They have been against sexual assault, harassment, and domestic abuse. In the field of economics, they have fought for rights at work, such as fair compensation and chances to advance professionally and launch businesses. Art history and modern art, aesthetics, prejudice, stereotyping, objectification, oppression, and patriarchy are some of the themes that are examined in feminism. According to Barker, feminism may be viewed as a social and political movement as well as a varied body of theoretical work. He mentioned that "feminism has sought to examine the position of women in society and to further their interests" (68).

When magical realism attempts to give a voice to marginalised women and to help them challenge or fight patriarchy, it can be labelled magical feminism. Magical feminism can, therefore, be the combination of magical realism and feminism, explicitly operating from a female/feminist context. Again, when feminist authors use magic (or magical realism) to serve their purpose, i.e., to provide equality between men and women, to empower women, and to challenge patriarchal authority, this can also be called magical feminism. The term magical feminism, which was introduced by Patricia Hart to explain the narrative of Chilean author Isabel Allende, refers to "magical realism engaged in a female-centered work" (30). Concurring with Hart, Wells considers magical feminism a type of writing that "reacts to specific feminist concerns to subvert homogeneous patriarchal dominance" (20). Magical feminist literature poses a challenge to patriarchal hierarchy and male dominance, providing agency and empowerment to women. Unlike magical realism, which employs its magical features and elements to discover various social, political, and cultural issues, magical feminism, using myth and magic, attempts to particularly explore the subjugation and marginalisation of women under racial, political, cultural, ethnic, and colonial contexts, highlighting or demonstrating a type of empowered women in a realistic world and thus unsettling the binary oppositions. Magical feminism foregrounds gender, which ultimately clarifies society's perceptions about women. This particular genre also teaches and normalises authoritative women and thus identifies the capability for power existing in traditionally vilified household chores.

The research project aims to show the way magical feminism resists female marginalisation and oppression in the Americas. Dealing with multiple victimisation of women in the Americas who have suffered not only because of their gender but also their race, ethnicity, political ideology, social status, financial insecurity and such, magical feminism provides a voice to them so that they can speak about their marginalisation and victimisation. In other words, by using magical feminism, these female authors attempt to give a voice to the oppressed women, enabling them to resist and challenge the traditional female role and to raise their voices against various social and political issues. The subversive and transgressive power of magical feminism enables the oppressed women to break patriarchal constraints and to reverse the traditional power structure. By creating an imaginary realm through traditions, local beliefs and rituals, myth, magic, and the spirits of the dead ancestors as guides, magical feminist technique functions as a survival strategy for women in traumatic and oppressive situations and provides them consolation. The project includes a total number of eight novels from African American, Latin American (Chile), Native American, Chicana, North American (Canada), Central American (Nicaragua), Hawaiian American and Cuban American backgrounds.

The introductory chapter gives an overall idea about the book and introduces its main arguments. It links issues like female marginalisation, feminism, magical realism, and magical feminism. It talks about how, by using magical realist techniques, female authors across the Americas attempt to give a voice to oppressed women and enable them to fight patriarchy. The second chapter titled "Magical Realism, Feminism, and Magical Feminism: History, Features and Functions" includes the definition and types of magical realism. It also deals with the increasing use of this narrative technique or genre of fiction across nations and cultures. It shows that although earlier this particular narrative was used only from a non-Western and postcolonial standpoint, authors are now using it from a Western perspective while writing from a marginalised standpoint. It also highlights the ability of magical realist techniques to represent both individual and collective trauma in a more graspable way.

The third chapter, "Magical Feminism and Female Marginalisation in the Americas", limits itself to the suffering of women in the Americas and advocates the role of magical feminism in alleviating their suffering. Dealing with multiple victimisation of women in the Americas who have suffered not only because of their gender but also their race, ethnicity, political ideology, social status, financial insecurity and such, magical feminism provides a voice to them so that they can speak about their marginalisation and victimisation. In other words, by using magical feminism, these female authors attempt to give a voice to the oppressed women and enable them to resist and challenge the traditional female role and to raise their voices against various social issues such as patriarchal constraint, social injustice, social hierarchy, and class conflict. This chapter shows how female authors in the Americas employ magical feminism from African American, Latin American (Chile), Native American, Chicana, North American (Canada), Central American (Nicaragua), Hawaiian American and Cuban American backgrounds. For example, in *Mama Day*, by questioning white supremacy with the help of supernatural power and magical healing ritual, Gloria Naylor provides an alternative oral narrative form and empowers black women; in *The House of the Spirits*, Allende enables Chilean women to foresee political upheaval through female clairvoyance, having the potential to empower women's understanding of the hidden human reality and to transform destructive patriarchal system; in *Tracks*, by giving Native American women magical power and by incorporating native belief and rituals, Erdrich enables them to free themselves from both patriarchal and colonial constraints and to assert their gender identity; by creating and rewriting myths, featuring Chicana women, Ana Castillo in *So Far from God* attempts to write against marginalisation of non-Western cultures and exclusion of women in male-centered stories, showing the misunderstood, marginalised and demonised condition of women. She also shows the way women's magical connection with nature equips them to fight patriarchy; in *The Cure for Death by Lightning*, Anderson-Dargatz shows how both traumatic realism and magical realism converge in Beth's lightning arm, which is magically connected with her trauma of sexual violence, resistance and protection in the Shuswap region, Canada, performing as silent witness and a defence mechanism; in *The Inhabited Woman*, Belli breaks the silence of the marginalised native women in the history of Nicaragua and creates an alternative history capable of voicing the untold stories of female suffering.

Magical realism enables Belli to bring back the magical Itzá from the past, symbolising the significance of the memory of other rebellious women as a source of empowerment; in *Shark Dialogues*, Davenport shows the feminisation of Hawaii in the backdrop of native cultural recuperation and identity formation and attempts to establish a relationship of women with social, cultural and political frameworks and resistance against environmental destruction with battle against socio-political marginalisation; and in *Dreaming in Cuban*, through telepathic communication between three generations of female family members of a Cuban family (del Pino family) and the presence of the spirit of a dead family member, Cristina García helps them overcome physical boundaries and provides them with the sense of togetherness and empowerment.

The entire analysis of the eight novels is divided into four parts, each of which contains two novels, covering two chapters. Part I, Attacking Dictatorship and Transforming Destructive Patriarchal System, analyses Isabel Allende's *The House of the Spirits* and Gioconda Belli's *The Inhabited Woman*. Chapter 4 titled "Resisting Patriarchy and Challenging Dictatorship in Isabel Allende's *The House of the Spirits*" shows the way Allende employs magic to empower female understanding of the veiled human reality, having the potential to alter the vicious patriarchal system. Instead of playing the traditional roles found in masculine writing, female characters in the novel form a female bond, thus a female force, which challenges patriarchal repression, social and sexual prejudices, tyranny and political repression. Allende shows how the political upheaval is seen through female clairvoyance: Clara's power of prophecy constructs a lens through which to observe the nature of the Chilean coup d'état. The move from spirits and predictions is a sensible feminist development. Allende's attempt to write in a circular style undermines the conventional, linear version of history, enabling women's history to overtake (or, at least to run parallel to) men's history. Chapter 5, "Reconstructing Personal Identity and Creating an Alternative National History: Magical Realism and the Marginalised Female Voice in Gioconda Belli's *The Inhabited Woman*", shows the way Belli blends personal stories of Nicaraguan women over centuries with the social and political reality of Nicaragua in the 1970s. Her novel attacks both patriarchy and dictatorship, where Belli adopts a gendered standpoint, depicting the double victimisation of her protagonist Lavinia—a rebel and a woman. By magically attaching Itzá—an indigenous female warrior who died centuries ago—to Lavinia's body and by giving her a voice, Belli breaks the silence of the marginalised native women in the history of the nation and allows her to create an alternative history capable of voicing the untold stories of female suffering. By magically connecting Itzá and Lavinia, Belli connects both the past and present of Nicaragua, and shows how they end up being one and the same since both die for the sake of liberating their own people. Lavinia's magical association with Itzá and, thus her memories of the past empower her on her way to being a new woman who seeks to be liberated from the patriarchal constraints of the society.

Part II, Resisting Colonial Constraints and Asserting Female Identity, contains Kiana Davenport's *Shark Dialogues* and Louise Erdrich's novel *Tracks.* In Chapter 6, "Relating Women with Cultural and Socio-Political Framework and Highlighting the Issues of Marginality in Kiana Davenport's *Shark Dialogues*", by including Hawaiian women with complex identities as having a strong role in the history of the nation and describing their participation in the wellbeing of the descendants, Davenport attempts to investigate the colonial and neocolonial (postcolonial) history of Hawaii. She also shows female resistance against both patriarchal and colonial systems, thus confirming cultural and environmental unity. By linking bodies, lands, and languages, she attempts to establish a relationship of women with social, cultural, and political frameworks and resistance against environmental destruction with a battle against socio-political marginalisation. By blending magical realism and proven facts (history), linking present realities with ancient myth, and disrupting traditional concepts of time and space, Davenport allows the multiple perspectives of the marginalised voices to surface. Chapter 7, "Resisting White Supremacy and Constructing Ethnic and Female Identity: Magical Resistance in Louise Erdrich's *Tracks*", focuses on native people in a Chippewa reservation, covering twelve years from the winter of 1912 to the summer of 1924 and depicting white invasion which causes huge loss of the Native American regarding their lives and lands. The chapter shows the way by giving the Native American women a voice by the means of magic, the novel revolves around alternative version(s) of history and/or reality and the postmodern notion of understanding the past and memory. By giving women magical power, Erdrich enables them to free themselves from both patriarchal and colonial constraints and to assert their gender identity.

Part III, Protesting Cultural Domination and Challenging Nationalist Male Politics, includes Cristina García's *Dreaming in Cuban* and Ana Castillo's *So Far from God.* In Chapter 8, "Linking Magical Realism and Transnational Feminism: Developing Female Identity in Cristina García's *Dreaming in Cuban*", through the remembrance and reimagination of three generations of women of del Pino family, which is made possible by the help of myth, magical occurrences and traditional healing practices, Cuban American author Cristina García attempts to recover, reconceive, and to create and develop awareness of Cuban women and cultural heritage that might have been erased. By highlighting the heritage of Cuban women who strongly endured the volatile time during the Revolution, García admits a history of female protest to the mainstream male politics. Magical feminism in the novel combines multiple voices and alternative viewpoints on past and present, making it an apposite vehicle for investigating transnational spaces and issues, and thus attempts to render marginal voices (read female voices) and realities and to subvert and deconstruct Eurocentric notions of identity, reality, and truth. Chapter 9, "Political and Gendered Magical Realism in Ana Castillo's *So Far from God*", writes against marginalisation of non-Western cultures and against the exclusion of women in male-dominated narratives, and attempts to link the novel's most magical realist character to its political-activist sensibilities. The novel depicts damaging American influences on the lives of Chicano who are marginalised and forced to integrate into American culture to be successful. In the novel, Castillo creates a new *mestiza* myth to show the negative treatment of Chicana women in the US society and to show female empowerment by refusing to follow the patriarchal rules imposed on women. Castillo also criticises the brutal patriarchal forces that attacked Caridad through the Mexican folk healing process and a magical healing which comes from the love and prayer of her female family members and women around her. Castillo also emphasises women's magical connection with nature to fight patriarchy. Again, Caridad's establishing a magical and harmonious relationship with nature symbolises an essential bond between women and nature and provides her magical strength to threaten patriarchy.

Part IV, Questioning Racial and Gendered Supremacy and Empowering Women, contains Gail Anderson-Dargatz's *The Cure for Death by Lightning* and Gloria Naylor's *Mama Day*. Chapter 10, "Healing Trauma of Sexual Abuse and Rejecting Patriarchal Authority in Gail Anderson-Dargatz's *The Cure for Death by Lightning*", deals with the trauma of sexual abuse of Beth and her mother Maud. Maud's scrapbook and Beth's autobiography depict family stories of sexual violence, and work as the main instruments of healing. Just like the way the butterfly on the first page of Maud's diary is associated with her healing, the cure for death by lightning symbolises Beth's therapeutic journey. In the novel, both traumatic realism and magical realism converge in Beth's arm to voice and cure her trauma. Therefore, her lightning arm is miraculously connected with her trauma of sexual violence, resistance, and protection, performing what the scrapbook has done for Maud—silent witness and a defence mechanism. Beth's healing can be considered an act of imagination where she creates her own world and takes refuge there. In Chapter 11, "Challenging White History and Emphasising Female Solidarity in Gloria Naylor's *Mama Day*", Naylor focuses on female empowerment through the supernatural power and magical healing ritual of a black character, Mama Day, who floats on the border between the natural and the supernatural. Through Mama Day's magical 'fertility rite', which helps Bernice to conceive, Naylor shows the way women heal other women, and thus emphasises female empowerment. By giving the African American inhabitants of the fictional Willow Springs, a woman-centred island controlled by a woman with magical power, a voice, Naylor attempts to create an entire world for the black people, devoid of many of the facts or facets of the racial history of the US. Again, through the depiction of the matriarch Sapphira Wade, who has the power to draw magical power from nature and who is believed to be a divine woman, Naylor seems to question the reality based on written evidence and advocates an alternative oral reality, which is subjective. Naylor shows the way the Willow Springers defend themselves against the White exploitation, Western education system and the loss of cultural memory through their oral tradition and fostering the memory of the past. The concluding chapter reiterates the logic and arguments and connects all the texts and their contexts together. It also focuses on the challenges of employing magical realism in a female context, and therefore provides the scope for future research.

Female suffering in the Americas, which has directly been associated with colonial ideology, is infused with social, political, racial, cultural and many other reasons why men have the upper hand. In depicting female marginalisation and oppression and providing a voice to women to challenge patriarchy, female authors in the Americas find magical realism an appropriate technique and/or narrative style due to its subversive and transgressive potential. The blend of the real and the magical from a female perspective unsettles the traditional gender binary, helps women find their own voice, and enables them to deconstruct the West vs. non-West discourse. Again, due to its hybrid and polyvocal narrative, magical realism has been an empowering strategy for women who have been dominated by patriarchal, rationalistic voice of the phallocentric discourse. It also enables women to create a space for themselves and to search for an individual and cultural identity. The magical realist/feminist novels of these female writers in the Americas question the official history, which is patriarchal, nationalist, and colonial, and advocate an alternative one, emphasising female subjectivity and freedom.

Chapter 2

Magical Realism, Feminism, and Magical Feminism: History, Features and Functions

Origin and Development of Magical Realism[1]

The term 'magical realism' has been defined and applied by authors and researchers from different parts of the world in a complex and paradoxical way. It was German art critic Franz Roh who first coined the term 'magic realism' in 1925 to depict a trend in German painting, namely the post-expressionist painting movement. Bowers states that this type of painting was characterised by clear, cool, delicately painted, and sharply focused images, consistently portraying the fantastic in a realistic manner (9). Irene Guenther notes precisely: "The juxtaposition of 'magic' and 'realism' reflected far more the monstrous and marvelous *Unheimlichkeit* [uncanniness] within human beings and inherent in their modern technological surroundings [...]" (36). 'Magic realism' was later re-termed 'magical realism' when the focus shifted from paintings to literature, especially to fiction. Since then, the term has been applied mainly to describe literary works rather than paintings. According to Spindler, the meaning and the application of the term varied substantially from Roh's formulation when it was later applied by commentators such as Arturo Uslar Pietri to European and Latin American literature in the 1930s and 1940s, and by Angel Flores to the works of Latin American authors like Gabriel García Márquez and Carlos Fuentes in the mid-twentieth century (75-76).

According to Adams, the term developed to refer to an assimilation of real and magical elements with Alejo Carpentier's coinage of the term 'lo real maravilloso'—approximately, 'the marvellous reality'—in his book *The Kingdom of the World* published in 1949, "producing a specifically Latin American reading of this shift from a unity to duality of ontological codes" (3). Various definitions

---

[1] A part of this chapter is taken from my book *Traumatic Experience and Repressed Memory in Magical Realist Novels* published in 2020.

and applications of the term have shown its ability to analyse the artistic and literary representations of reality and history. Magical realism is no longer confined to Latin America but rather has been used by writers from all over the world from the perspectives of the marginalised and oppressed. Magical realist technique possesses the outstanding ability to represent traumatic historical events in literature by turning traumatic memory into a narrative memory.

Although the Venezuelan Arturo Uslar Pietri persuaded others with his magical realist short stories during the 1930s and 1940s, it is Alejo Carpentier who is considered the most crucial person in forming a Latin American understanding of magical realism. Can argues: "By claiming the sole right of a distinctly Latin American magical realism, [both Carpentier and Pietri] shifted the emphasis Roh placed on the aesthetic and stylistic features of the mode to political and cultural issues" (29). The subversive ability to deal with critical social and political issues has made the magical realist narrative one of the most sought-after narrative techniques from the perspectives of the oppressed. Carpentier coined the term "lo real maravilloso" and suggested "marvellous reality to be the heritage of all of America" ("On the Marvelous Real in America" 87). The evolution of the concept from Roh's definition to Carpentier's formation through the Latin American scholars has resulted in texts where two opposing interpretations of the world, namely the natural and the supernatural, are presented in such a way as to convey the notion that they are not contradictory. I would like to say that the simultaneous existence of the magical and the rational worlds in the magical realist narrative is far from being opposing but rather is harmonious and complementary.

Angel Flores is another influential figure in the discussions of magical realism in Latin American literature. Although he mostly agreed with Carpentier and Pietri, he disagreed with them on certain aspects. For example, Flores offered particular names and dates which are significant for the development of magical realism in Latin American literature and took on a more comprehensive approach in order to identify the sources of magical realism (Flores 113). Jorge Luis Borges is often considered the pioneer of magical realism, but it is actually Flores who first regarded Borges to be a genuine magical realist, and his *A Universal History of Infamy* as the earliest sample of magical realist writing in Latin America.

With Borges's translation of the short stories of Franz Kafka into Spanish just a few years before the publication of *A Universal History of Infamy*, magical realism reached the other side of the Atlantic. In Latin America, the colonial legacy, dictatorship, failed revolutions, capitalism (neocolonialism) and economic dependency—all paved the way for magical realism to enter the region's literary domain. Flores strongly believed that the sense of the marvellous found in magical realist texts was an artistic outcome produced through narrative technique rather than the magnification of Latin American culture (Flores 115). He believes that texts from any historical, social, political, or cultural background can be considered magical realists if they accomplish a "transformation of the common and everyday into the awesome and the unreal" (114), and if they have a narrative structure where "[t]ime exists in a kind of timeless fluidity and the unreal happens as part of reality" (115). By strongly arguing that magical realism does not necessarily have to possess a cultural, social, political, or historical origin, Flores freed the term from Latin American confinement and made it available for all. In response to Flores' essay, Mexican art critic Luis Leal disagreed with his definition of magical realism as the blending of the real and the supernatural and the writers he considered magical realists. Leal notes: "[...] magical realism does not use dream motifs; neither does it distort reality or create imagined worlds, as writers of fantastic literature or science fiction do [...]. In magical realism the writer confronts reality and tries to untangle it, to discover what is mysterious in things, in life, in human acts" (121). Leal also emphasises the comparative analysis of magical realism and other bordering literary genres or modes, such as fantasy and science fiction, in terms of their artistic and stylistic characteristics.

Although it is a misconception that magical realism is a distinct feature of Latin American literature, it is also true that it is the Latin American writers who were mainly responsible for making this particular literary mode a part of the established literary canon. The globalisation of magical realism is also paralleled by the change in its theoretical discussions. Stephen M. Hart recapitulates the change in the understanding of magical realism in three phases: firstly, the initial works of Angel Flores (1955) and Luis Leal (1967) mainly focused on the formal features of the mode (Hart 5); secondly, critics started to transfer the attention to social, cultural and ideological topics related to the mode after the initiation of postcolonial studies in the 1980s, and the most influential figure of the phase was Stephen Slemon with his 1988 essay "Magic Realism as Postcolonial Discourse" (5-6); and thirdly, in the 1990s, a new paradigm appeared after the publication of Lois P. Zamora and Wendy B. Faris's *Magical Realism: Theory, History, Community* that distinguished magical realism as a universal literary phenomenon and attempted to analyse the narrative technique in its historical background through existing theories (6).

The use of magical realism has been considered a strong protest against the social, cultural and political hegemony of imperial thought; it is also considered a regional alternative and a protest to the Eurocentric categorisation of the world. The direct allusions to history and the history of the margins have strengthened the postcolonial identity of magical realism, which, by questioning the usual conflict between real and fantastic, completes the postmodern task of challenging the view of genre and questioning the convention of realism. Stephen Slemon has contributed largely to connect magical realism and postcolonialism. In "Magic Realism as Postcolonial Discourse", he considers magical realism the instrument of "the silenced, marginalized, or dispossessed voices [in their fight against] the inherited, dominant modes of discourse and cognition in colonialism's 'phenomenal legacy'" (414). According to Slemon, it is an instrument to address social and political issues while turning away from the Western style of narration and literary tradition and thus asserting own sense of identity (414). Many critics have closely associated magical realism with postcolonialism and postmodernism because of their certain similarities. The way postmodernism is characterised by scepticism and pluralism is quite the same way magical realism questions the notion of a singular version of truth and reality and advocates multiple approaches and alternative truths. Just as postcolonialism attempts to depict colonial life or colonial history from the perspectives of the colonised people, magical realism also gives a voice to the oppressed, and allows them to rewrite the official reading of the dominant history. Subsequently, magical realism becomes an instrument for authors to convey a non-dominant and/or non-Western standpoint (from a feminist, postcolonial and anti-racial perspective) in resisting dominant cultural discourse. Brenda Cooper opines that magical realism and its features and tools are "alternatively characterized as transgressive mechanism that parodies Authority, the Establishment and the Law, and also as the opposite of all of these, as a domain of play, desire and fantasy for the Rich and Powerful" (29).

Again, magical realism can be associated with postmodernism regarding their common characteristics. Both magical realism and postmodernism question traditional ideas of time, space, and reality (history) and doubt established authority and absolute knowledge, narrative, and language. Magical realist narratives go beyond the limit of what is understandable and are postmodern in the sense that they refuse the binary and fixed ideas imposed by Western modernity. Both terms show reluctance to speak from a specific centre as Theo D'haen considers "the notion of the ex-centric, in the sense of speaking from the margin, from a place 'other' than 'the' or 'a' center, [...] an essential feature of that strain of postmodernism we call magic realism"

(194). According to D'haen, it is the rejection of magical realism to speak from a specific centre which makes it a powerful instrument to challenge and attack the governing discourse through decentering (195). By dealing with history as an untrustworthy idea, magical realism, through the insertion of magic or unrealistic means, recuperates those marginalised voices silenced by the dominant history, which always speaks the language of the rulers and is victorious. Concurring with D'haen, Anne Hegerfeldt also considers magical realism a challenge against the Western rationalist and empiricist mindset. She argues that magical realism has the ability to "further challenge the hegemony of the Western worldview by unsettling received notions about literary genres, the use of language and the objectivity of science and history, about who can be regarded as reliable, and what can assuredly be accepted as real" (Hegerfeldt 346). By dissolving the boundary between the real and the magical, magical realist narratives question the Western notion of an absolute truth and thus advocate the existence of multiple realities and subjective interpretation of events or issues.

Features and Types of Magical Realism

Magical realist writers present everyday happenings along with magical elements and materials originated from myths and rituals. Bowers states: "The variety of magical occurrences in magic(al) realist writing includes ghosts, disappearances, miracles, extraordinary talents and strange atmospheres [...]" (21). According to Luis Leal, authors of magical realism do not construct imaginary worlds where we can escape from mundane reality. We should not forget that in their works, authors need not validate the enigma of events the way fantastic writers have to (121). Leal further states that, in magical realism, "the principal thing is not the creation of imaginary beings or worlds, but the discovery of the mysterious relationship between man and his circumstances" (122) and that magical realism tries "to seize the mystery that breathes behind things" (123). Regarding magical realism, it can well be asserted that it does not create any separate world of fantasy devoid of the elements of our own world. It rather shows the coexistence between two worlds which cannot be doubted or separated.

Chanady states that in magical realism, we find two conflicting but consistent perspectives; the first one provides the logical observation of reality and the second one the unquestioned recognition of the magical as part of a daily reality (21-22). It is quite clear from Chanady that magical realism includes logical observation and that it is not completely devoid of reality. According to

Anne Hegerfeldt, the fundamental feature of magical realism is "the fusion of realistic and fantastic elements" or "the co-existence of elements from traditionally incompatible codes" (50). Some characteristics of magical realism are identified as the coexistence of the real and the imaginary, dexterous time shifts, complicated narratives and stories, various uses of dreams, myths, magic, rituals, folk and fairy stories, orality, and the use of the opposite or duality. The repetitive narrative in a magical realist novel parallels with a distorted sense of time, space and identity. The use of the opposite or duality analyses any given event from more than one point of view and thus leads the reader closer to the truth or reality.

In "Scheherazade's Children: Magical Realism and Postmodern Fiction", Wendy B. Faris identifies some prime features of magical realist fiction: "an 'irreducible element' of magic, something we cannot explain according to the laws of the universe as we know them" (167); "descriptions detail a strong presence of the phenomenal world—this is the realism in magical realism, distinguishing it from much fantasy and allegory" (169); "the reader may hesitate (at one point or another) between two contradictory understandings of events—and hence experiences some unsettling doubts" (171); "the closeness or near-merging of two realms, two worlds" (172); and "these fictions question received ideas about time, space, and identity" (173). All these different statements share one aspect that is very crucial for magical realist narrative: a complete blending of the supernatural and the ordinary or the simultaneous existence of two opposing realities.

William Spindler has divided magical realism into three types based on the meaning of 'magic': metaphysical magical realism, which introduces a notion of unreality and the uncanny but does not clearly deal with the supernatural; anthropological magical realism, which considers popular culture and magical beliefs as important as Western science and rationality; and ontological magical realism, which presents magic in a mundane way without any conflict with reason. In *Magical Realism and the Postcolonial Novel: Between Faith and Irreverence*, Christopher Warnes identifies two types of magical realism based on the way(s) they respond to causality: faith-based magical realism, which functions "synecdochically or metonymically" (14); and irreverent magical realism, which operates "metaphorically" (14). Warnes's first type of magical realism considers reality as something not absolute, but rather something which can be manipulated. Thus, it advocates the notion of an alternative truth or reality. It challenges the official reading of traumatic history and replaces it with a subversive one from the perspectives of the victimised. The second type of magical realist text employs the supernatural for the purpose of defamiliarisation or estrangement, which is a method normally supported by other metaphorical and metafictional devices. This sense of defamiliarisation or estrangement is evident in Márquez's *One Hundred Years of Solitude* where ordinary objects like a magnet and ice are imbued with a magical aura and are thus made unfamiliar.

Again, Roberto Echevarría classified magical realism as ontological magical realism, which takes the source material from the social and cultural background of the place(s) where the story is set, and epistemological magical realism, which does not necessarily depend on the social and cultural background of the fiction or of the writer for the source elements. Jeanne Delbaere-Garant pointed out a quite related difference between what she named 'folkloric magical realism' (which is similar to Roberto Echevarría's ontological magical realism), where magical realism derives from a domestic or folk tradition, and 'scholarly magical realism' (which is similar to epistemological magical realism) where magical elements are collected and assimilated from various traditions and cultures to create a specific narrative effect.

For this research project, I would like to focus on magical realism from three different perspectives: conceptual, structural, and functional. From a conceptual or thematic point of view, magical realism is characterised by the coexistence of magical and realistic elements, the presence of ghosts (most of the time those of the ancestors), folklore, oral culture, rituals, myths, fairytales, the grotesque and the carnivalesque. Authors of all the texts I will analyse in my book exercise boundless freedom and use their source materials from their geographical and cultural context. From a structural standpoint, the magical realist narrative is a repetitive and non-linear one, which includes flashback and flashforward. From a functional perspective, this non-linear narrative questions the accepted notions of time, space, identity, history and truth. It is by distorting the traditional understanding of history, culture, and reality that magical realism helps the author to reverse all sorts of hierarchical orders in a subversive manner and to reshape dominant orders of society. Although there are different traditions of magical realism, and different ethnic traditions (many of which are covered in the book) have very different associations with magic, it is always used from the point of view of the oppressed and marginalised in their fight against the dominant where the authors emphasise indigenous oral tales, and individual and cultural memory as strong weapons. By using narrators who are unreliable, many magical realist novels disrupt the notion of a singular version of truth and provide an alternative version of event and history. The subversive and transgressive power of magical realism enables marginalised and oppressed women to reverse the power structure. By penetrating the rigid wall of the story of their victimisation, the magical realist technique gives them an accessible literary representation. Last but not least, by creating an imaginary realm, it provides the characters with consolation.

According to Abdullah, "Magical realism is the very opposite of [...] the absolutist and the traditional. Through magical events, writers can find new viewpoints and can open new windows through which they can see the world differently and thus provide us with a different perception of reality" ("Heavy Silence and Horrible Grief" 31). Magical realist works help us think differently about the ordinary events or issues we come across daily and thus provide us with a different perception of reality. Simpkins says apart from presenting the supernatural in mundane ways, an ordinary object, through the process of 'defamiliarisation', becomes unrealistic and magical. This interplay between the supernatural and the ordinary turns magical realism into a unique narrative technique which produces more realistic texts (150).

Because of its inherent transgressive and subversive qualities, magical realism has become a common narrative style for novels written from the point of view of the politically, socially or culturally powerless, such as native people living under a colonial system, Native Americans and African Americans in the US, women living in a patriarchal society, or people living with different cultural and religious beliefs in another country where they are the minority. These transgressive and subversive aspects of magical realism have been used, for instance, in Angela Carter's writing to subvert the authority of the British ruling classes; in Toni Morrison's writing to express the cruelties and traumatic experiences of slavery and the female subjugation which was largely ignored in the white slave-owners' history; in the writing of Jeanette Winterson to write from the perspectives of homosexuals; in Gloria Naylor's *Mama Day*, to provide an alternative oral narrative form and to empower black women; in Allende's *The House of the Spirits*, to foresee political upheaval through female clairvoyance, and to transform destructive patriarchal system; in Erdrich's *Tracks*, to free Native American women from both patriarchal and colonial constraints and to assert their gender identity; in Ana Castillo's *So Far from God*, to write against marginalisation of non-Western cultures and exclusion of women in male-centered stories; in Anderson-Dargatz's *The Cure for Death by Lightning*, to magically connect Beth's lightning arm with her trauma of sexual violence, resistance and protection in the Shuswap region, Canada, performing as silent witness and a defense mechanism; in Belli's *The Inhabited Woman*, to break the silence of the marginalised native women in the history of Nicaragua and to create an alternative history capable of voicing the untold stories of female suffering; in Davenport's *Shark Dialogues*, to show the feminisation of Hawaii in the backdrop of native cultural recuperation and identity formation; and in Cristina García's *Dreaming in Cuban*, to help three generations of female family members of a Cuban family overcome physical boundaries and to provide them with the sense of togetherness and empowerment. It is clear from the remarks above that magical realism is a strong blow against a dominant culture and a singular version of truth. It is also a subversive and "alternative form of writing which is used to challenge dominant writing (official history) by representing traumatic events from the standpoint of the oppressed" (Abdullah, "Heavy Silence and Horrible Grief" 31). Magical realism has been employed by female authors from both Western and non-Western viewpoints, highlighting the marginalisation of women all over the world. In the Americas, female authors employ myth, magic and various rituals to enable women to fight not only their gendered subjugation but also the social, cultural, racial, and ethnic marginalisation. It also gives them a voice and thus helps them create an alternative history and reality, challenging dominant discourse.

Feminism: Definition, Waves and Types

Because of patriarchal gendering, which views women as men's property both inside and outside the home, women are linked with feminine roles and men with male ones. Thus, the social system that defines male and female roles is predicated on men's activity and superiority compared to women's passivity and inferiority. The notions of heterosexual hegemony, patriarchal gendering, and submissive female roles are linked to the alienation of the repressed women. Feminist thinkers such as Virginia Woolf, Betty Friedan, and Simone de Beauvoir might be used while discussing women's roles in patriarchal societies. Feminism stands out among philosophies that critique societal influences. The goal of this conversation is to provide women with equal rights and legal safeguards. Feminism's primary issue is the gender gap in society, which promotes the notion that women are less valuable than men.

The feminist movement advocates for women's equality and freedom from males. It opposes misogyny and views women as subjects and human beings rather than as objects. Feminism now encompasses more than simply women's issues; it also addresses economic, social, religious, racial, and transgender issues. Kunjakkan wrote that the women's liberation movement is known as feminism. It is created by Western society, and it is depicted rather than stated

(87). Feminists seek to provide an explanation for why women experience oppression, repression, and suppression in ways that men do not, as well as to offer ethically sound and politically viable solutions for granting women the same freedom, equality, and justice as men. Barker went on to say that feminists contended that women's subordination occurs throughout societal structures and behaviours, making it a structural reality. According to him, it is patriarchy which institutionally subjugates women, and it has its roots in the male-headed family, mastery, and supremacy (68). The historical process has led to the development of feminism as an ideology. Feminism can be regarded as a) a comprehensive theory that examines the types and features of female oppression by men all over the world; b) a socio-political concept and practice that seeks to liberate women from female authority and mistreatment; c) a social movement that strategically confronts the sex-class system; and d) a philosophy that opposes all misogynistic ideologies and practices. Feminists fought for equal rights with white males during the twentieth century, largely unconcerned with racial injustice and the plight of women of colour. The split between liberals and radicals, as well as a rising recognition of the necessity for many feminisms, typified feminism in the twentieth century and contributed to the Movement's propensity for doctrinal and/or tactical divisions.

The concept of feminism can be divided into three waves or phases: the first wave, the second wave, and the present wave. The feminists themselves are clueless about the beginning and finish of every given wave. However, throughout the phases of feminism, the notion that "women are unequal to men because men created the meanings of equality" persisted (Kunjakkan 91). The first wave of feminism started with the Seneca Falls Convention in 1848 in New York by a group of women who actively worked to end slavery in the US and to advance women's political and legal equality (Chrisler and McHugh 37). Jenainati and Groves stated that the first wave began as organised feminist activism in the USA and Britain throughout the second part of the nineteenth century. They do not identify as feminists; instead, the injustices they experienced were their main focus. Among their accomplishments were the passage of the Married Women's Property Act of 1870, the reformation of secondary education for girls, and women's access to higher education. They were active until 1914, when the First World War broke out (20-21). According to Dickens and Fontana, the first wave of feminists examined women's rights through the lens of traditional liberal theory, emphasising equality (14) because women were viewed as objects and because women's bodies allowed men to dominate women (Kunjakkan 91). The initial wave of support for women's suffrage and political equality was led by white middle-class and upper-class women.

The phrase "second wave" was first used to refer to the surge in feminist movements in America, Britain, and Europe. The Women's Liberation Movement (WLM) and the Women's Right Movement (WRM) helped to create second-wave feminism. The illusion of a universal feminine experience was a point of contention for second-wave feminists, who argued that women's opinions differed depending on factors such as age, race, class, and education. The notion of femininity as defined by society and the belief that women are associated with nature and the "body" and men with the "mind" were contested (Jenainati and Groves 86-87). The second wave tried to combat the social and cultural injustices with which women had to deal. Equality in salary, education, and opportunity, use of free contraception, and abortion on demand were the key causes of the second-wave feminist movement in the Western world; in contrast, third-world women, including tribal women, prioritised access to food, fuel, and water. In general, the second wave focused on comprehending and accounting for the oppressions that were thought to be experienced by every woman. It also emphasised the interactions that women have with one another and with the male social order. As second-wave feminism gained traction in the late 1960s, the term "glamour" was demonised and linked to the exploitation of women's bodies for sexual purposes (Dyhouse 4). Second-wave feminists saw glamour as undignified and women who invested in their looks as having "false consciousnesses" or engaging in politics of appearance that were supported by capitalism and patriarchy (Dyhouse 123-124). Glamour was no longer connected with female autonomy. Second-wave feminists stressed more the exclusive biological and cultural distinctiveness of women which to some extent made them superior to men (Dickens and Fontana 14).

Sondra Farganis divided the American second wave of feminism into three stages. Gender disparities didn't really matter in the initial phase of establishing gender equality through anti-discriminatory laws as long as people were treated equally. The focus of theoretical literature on women changed in the second phase, with a greater emphasis placed on exploring the experiences, sensations, and emotions of women. During this era, women's attributes were celebrated, and feminists contended that adopting a female perspective would not only result in a fresh outlook but also a markedly improved one. They demanded parity between genders and elevated feminine ideals to a level comparable to that of male principles. Third-phase feminists worked in tandem with postmodern feminists, stressing the diversity of women and the idea that gender is a continuum rather than a binary (103-104). The second wave demanded the necessity of communal solidarity and an awareness of discrimination and injustice.

In response to the perceived flaws in the second wave of feminism as well as in opposition to the initiatives and actions led by that wave, the third wave of feminism arose in the early 1990s. This wave continues to address social and cultural inequities in addition to promoting women's participation in politics and the media. In order to assist young ladies and transgender youngsters, the third wave was developed. During the third wave, objectification of women was a significant problem. The primary goals of the third-wave feminist movement included defining gender identity, empowering sexuality, combating violence against women, and addressing women's health concerns (Chrisler and McHugh 42). The third wave saw the emergence of postmodernist discourse, and the women's viewpoint approach was replaced by a more radical analysis of the racial, religious, and socioeconomic disparities that exist among women (Dickens and Fontana 14).

In her work, *The Variety of Feminisms and their Contributions to Gender Equality,* Sociologist Judith Lorber divided the feminist viewpoints and ideologies of the past years into three main groups. These three types of feminisms are "*gender reform feminisms, gender resistant feminisms, and gender revolution feminisms*" (8).

Gender Reform Feminisms: The second wave of feminism began with the feminisms of the 1960s and 1970s. They are liberal feminism, and Marxist and socialist feminisms. Their roots were liberal political philosophy of the eighteenth and nineteenth centuries, which produced the concept of individual rights; Marx's critique of capitalism and class consciousness in the nineteenth century; and ideals of national development and anti-colonial politics in the twentieth century. Women are positioned in these viewpoints by gender reform feminisms.

Gender Resistant Feminisms: As gender reform feminisms gained traction in the 1970s and women began to attend previously all-male schools and workplaces, they became increasingly conscious of the daily and persistent criticism they were receiving from coworkers and bosses, teachers and students in the classroom, other activists in social and political movements, and, most importantly, from male counterparts at home. Issues such as being overlooked and interrupted, not receiving praise for skill or excellent work, and being passed over for positions requiring leadership, combine to build a pattern that gradually depletes women's strength. Even earlier, young girls had come to the realisation that their male coworkers saw them only as handmaidens, bed partners, and coffee makers. The 1970s saw the emergence of gender-resistant feminisms as a response to the realisation that brotherhood did not have any place for sisters. These feminisms include "*radical feminism, lesbian feminism, psychoanalytical feminism, and standpoint feminism*" (Lorber 16).

Gender Revolution Feminisms: In the 1980s and 1990s, feminist theories began to take shape. These theories challenge the prevailing social order and dismantle the complicated hierarchies of privilege and power. They also examine the ways that cultural outputs, particularly those seen in the media, legitimise subjugating behaviours and inequality. Therefore, these feminisms possess the revolutionary capacity to upend the principles and framework of the established social order. According to Lorber, they are "*multi-ethnic feminism, men's feminism, social construction feminism, post-modern feminism, and queer theory*" (25).

Terms like magical realism, magical feminism and feminism possess a common aim or characteristic: to emancipate women from patriarchal constraints. Women started to take an interest in writing because they believed it had the revolutionary potential to fight injustice. Furthermore, the fact that feminism finds it necessary to restore and revive the natural environment, harmonious and spiritual connections between men and women as well as with their natural world, is another thing that unites feminism and magical realism in one text. Additionally, it seeks to eliminate obstacles to connectivity, which is essential for the growth of social structures that prioritise equality and acceptance of all diversity. Feminism has changed women's image from being passive and subservient to being active and empowered in their society. Female authors thus rewrite and modify the earlier ideology found in literary works written by men to explore feminist themes, and therefore, to include women in the process of social production. Simone de Beauvoir argues that a woman will not be able to emancipate herself "unless she takes part in production on a large social scale and is only incidentally bound to domestic work" (85). In line with this, feminist literary works have dealt with topics connected with male dominance over female, the male/female relationships, and women's constant struggle to get rid of violence. Just like feminism, magical realism also attempts to overthrow the obstacles between men and women and to turn the traditional customs upside down. They both show their doubt about the authority of the patriarchal system where, by employing magical realist elements, female authors encourage women to use their potential power.

Magical Feminism: Magical Realism in a Female Context

In the simplest terms, magical feminism refers to the employment of magical realism from a female or feminist context. What makes the combination of magical realism and feminism, termed by Patricia Hart as Magical feminism, suitable is that "feminism seeks the necessity for restoration and revival of the natural environment, harmonious, non-violence, and spiritual interactions between female and male and also with their natural world" (Zobaie 27). Feminism also aims to destroy the hurdles to interaction, which is required for the development of social and cultural systems, emphasising equality and tolerance. It is the female writers who attempt to rewrite previous male-dominated philosophy found in literary works created by male authors to investigate feminist issues and to provide an alternative and marginalised version of their reality. By taking readers a step outside their reality and own experiences, magical feminism, just like magical realism, enables us to examine our own reality from the standpoint of fantasy or unreality but at the same time reexamines the notion of normality in the male-dominated society where this normal experience(s) can be relegated to as ordinary 'female issues'. Attempting to liberate women from stereotypical ideologies and representations, magical feminism attempts to provide alternative viewpoints through duality and subversion, and thus to critique repressive depiction of women. Magical feminist texts also question received ideas about female identities and thus make the reader (re)examine the biased notions of what gender identity really stands for.

By situating dominant official history in terms of patriarchal, nationalist, colonial, racial and ethnic marginalisation, magical feminist authors search for the means through which female subjectivity and liberation may be achieved. Magical feminism, as a political tactic, focuses on gender, an act which sheds light on society's views about women. It normalises powerful women, considered abnormal and thus a threat by the patriarchal society, and therefore addresses the presence of potential power and seemingly mundane activities. Again, by placing women in the traditional domestic sphere and by turning their mundane domestic elements—culinary, herbalism, gardening, old wives' tales, witchcraft, power of nature and such—into a magical source of agency, magical feminist authors connect magic with domesticity and with women empowerment. By having the potential to change the concept of normality in the world, magical feminism brings alternative stories of power where women are no longer passive and subservient but rather are active and makers of their own destinies. Apart from showing the victimisation of women and giving them the necessary power to defy dominant authority and to change their fate with the help of myth and magic, magical feminism also challenges the stereotypical depiction of powerful, patriarchy-defying women as evil. Elizabeth Plummer argues that since "the powers which women have been afforded has been restricted to the power of the impossibly perfect or good woman, the power of the evil temptress, or the power of the scapegoat, women need their new mythmakers to open the portals to a more complex vision of what their femininity can mean" (82). "Magical feminist witches [can be] the metaphor of those new mythmakers" (Wells 31) where it rewrites the old rules for women, avoiding "an endless succession of *eithers* and *ors*: virgin or mother, nurturer or amazon, wife or whore, daughter or mother, angel or temptress" (Plummer 183).

Women's power of magic and/or witchcraft and the connection with the world of spirits isolates them as they go against society's traditions and expectations but, at the same time, helps them to find a voice and space for themselves in the antagonistic society, since people are afraid of and intimidated by them, and to assert their own identity. Magic is thus an empowering means for women to challenge their oppression and to find agency. Rebecca Gordon opines that the women's practice of magic emphasises the changing of one's perception, which includes the understanding that reality is constructed, and thus can be manipulated and rewritten subjectively (10). By opining that women's desire to liberate themselves from patriarchal oppression, in both psychic and institutional levels, requires that the boundaries of real(ity) must be transgressed, Gordon highlights the role of magic in the life of marginalised women to tackle the multifarious modes of oppression. Gordon also draws a connection between politics and religion or spirituality and ultimately identifies the need for a specifically "female spirituality, which she terms "Goddess worship" (9). She considers "Goddess worship [...] a celebration of female power [which] has attracted many women whom traditional western religion, with its patriarchal codes, has left disempowered, spiritually void, and in many cases, outraged and angry" (9). Sharing Gordon's ideas, Jan Berry uses the term "women's ritualizing" to refer to the practice through which women make and develop their own rituals (279). According to Berry,

> [Ritualizing] is common to women in many cultures and times, it has a particular relevance for contemporary Western women, who find that significant elements in their life-experiences are omitted from religious (and secular) rituals; and where this experience is present, it is often

> named or defined in ways that are alien to them. The process of creating rituals that fit more appropriately becomes an act of liberation, by which women name their experiences, choose their own symbols and tell their own stories, so defining their own identity in and over against a patriarchal worldview. (279)

Although female ritualising may not be a force for social solidity and control, it is a magical feminist tool and a strategy for women to challenge patriarchal constraints and thus to assert their agency and independence. It is thus this social and political power of the image of the magic and ritual-performing women, simply witches, which makes witchcraft/magic a strong instrument of magical feminism. Again, Holland-Toll notices a dual process where witches are erased and reconceived or reconceptualised at the same time. According to her, while the conviction of witches has been abandoned or relegated to the domain of fiction, the notion of a witch as an unsettling, transgressive force has been transferred to the bluestockings. By studying several stories written in the nineteenth century in the context of the Salem Witch Trial, she identifies the ways these stories redesign the role of witches from old women to include bluestockings. Holland-Toll opines that witchcraft has the tendency to align "itself with unwritten oral traditions, folk traditions, and wise women traditions as opposed to accepted written discourse" (44).

Witchcraft, female rituals, herbalism and medical knowledge, communion with spirits and female clairvoyance are a form of protest against patriarchy and thus a means of female empowerment. Women's (domestic) magic and spells are ways of responding to domestic abuse and, therefore, of overthrowing negative power structures which have controlled, oppressed, and harmed them. Contrary to common perceptions, domestic magic represents female strength, restructuring women's traditional (read feminine) understanding or knowledge through herbalism. Therefore, domesticity as the source and/or symbol of female empowerment emphasises the significance of the normality of feminine skills. By fusing a voice driven by women with common perception, magic normalises women's strength and freedom, showcasing to the reader women who possess a unique women's power and who can solve complex problems due to their special women-centred power.

Since the atrocities of various traumatic events or the stories of social, political, racial, cultural, and gendered subjugation cannot be represented in a realist narrative because of its inability to penetrate the outer shell of trauma, authors need some kinds of alternative narratives which resist representations.

Magical realism is the representation of what language cannot represent. Now, the question is how magical realism accesses and recreates the impenetrable and unreachable reality of various traumatic events from a more apprehensible point of view. Through multiple perspectives on reality and disruption of categories, magical realist writers create a fictional realm, and employ empathy and imagination in turning traumatic memory into a narrative. This narrative technique wraps stories of oppression and marginalisation under mist and magic and presents them to the reader in a graspable way so as not to disgust or repel them. Unlike traditional realism, magical realism can portray violent and traumatic events by mixing myth and magic with them, but at the same time, it succeeds in providing the reader with the intended message without distorting historical views. In this sense, magical realism should not, and must not, be considered an escape from violent or lethal situations, but rather a universal approach to representing social, cultural, and political reality and violent historical events. Writers who aim to depict stories of atrocious events, which official history and/or a dominant narrative have denied, are largely dependent on an alternative writing style. This alternative writing must not be one to merely imitate the traditional narrative, but rather one to challenge the hegemony of the dominant narrative so that it can bring inexpressible and silenced stories to light by giving voice to the oppressed. A magical realist text, dealing with marginalisation and trauma (personal and historical), provides characters with relief through the help of the supernatural, but it does not distort our or their sense of reality. It possesses the ability to depict what common perceptions and the realist narrative tend to ignore.

Chapter 3

Magical Feminism and Female Marginalisation in the Americas

The history of the countries in the Americas is full of violence, bloodshed, dominance and marginalisation. Starting from the colonisation from the fifteenth to the nineteenth century, which includes Spanish colonisation of the Americas (1492), the Portuguese colonisation of the Americas (1499-1822) and colonial Brazil (1500-1815), the geographical location suffered from various other historically violent events such as war, dictatorship and Civil War: American Independence War (1775-1783), Spanish American Independence Wars (1808-1833), US-Mexican War (1846-1848), American Civil War (1861-1865), Paraguayan War (1864-1870), War of the Pacific (1879-1883), Central American Reunification (1885), World War I (1914-1918), World War II (1939-1945), Civil Rights Movement in the US (1954-1968), Latin American and Central American Civil Wars (1960s to 1980s), Quiet Revolution in Quebec (1960s), Native American land crisis, and US Military invasion and ecological imperialism in Hawaii are some of them to mention. Among all the instances of violence, female marginalisation requires particular attention. Apart from being the victims of a patriarchal society, women in the Americas have also suffered racially, ethnically, politically, socially, culturally, financially and from what's not. They, thus, are the victims of multifarious means of marginalisation. For example, African American women have suffered because of their race; Native American women from political (colonial) turmoil; Chicana women from encroaching Western culture; Central American women from exclusion in political and nation-building spheres; Hawaiian American women from social, cultural and political identity crisis and the consequences of environmental destruction; Latin American women from dictatorial violence and political exclusion; Cuban women from forced relocation and the backlash of a socialist regime; and North American women from ideological constraints. It can, therefore, be asserted that the history of the Americas is very much about female marginalisation, a phenomenon which is clearly connected with colonialism or white invasion. This chapter will focus on female marginalisation across the Americas, literary features of the nations, various traditions of magical realism, and the way this genre or narrative technique is used by female authors from different American nations to challenge female marginalisation and to empower them.

Although American Indians were the original residents of the land, after American Independence, they were structurally demolished mainly in terms of culture and spirituality. In the newly independent America, the cultural and spiritual, if not the physical, death was ensured either by removing them from their land or by converting them into Christianity, thus changing their way of life and forcing them to adopt Western education. In the 1920s, an entire group of children was "encouraged to think that the wholesale abandonment of Indian ways would guarantee Indians' full incorporation into the mainstream of American society and the fulfillment of America's 'final promise' of compensation for the loss of Indian land" (Porter 53). Nonetheless, like many other promises, this one was also proved futile, relegating the Indians to the edge of American society. Just like their male counterparts, Native American women also found themselves oppressed and marginalised in front of white supremacy. According to the Native women's traditional roles and responsibilities, they possessed great spiritual and psychological strength, whereas their male counterparts were revered for their physical, spiritual, and social or political strength. It can be stated that a clear balance existed between Native male and female, making their coexistence harmonious. As Beverley Jacobs wrote,

> Women were respected for their spiritual and mental strength and men were respected for their spiritual and physical strength. Women were given the responsibility in bearing children and were given the strength and power to carry that responsibility through. Men had always respected that spiritual and mental strength and women respected the men's physical strength. There was always a balance between men and women as each had their own responsibilities as a man and as a woman. (35)

Apart from the fact that men and women played contradictory but corresponding roles, lots of the tribes were matrilineal, where women assumed powerful and leadership positions in their community, even played crucial roles in land holding and resources distribution. However, the White settlers forced their own beliefs and traditions on the Natives and thus destroyed their own way of life. The Indian Act, which was created in 1876, clearly conveyed the White concept of men as chiefs of families and women as subservient to their men. It also destroyed the traditional matrilineal relationship pattern and the post-marital residence system for women which had been in practice for generations.

Apart from suffering due to white supremacy, Indian women also started to be marginalised by their own people. Again, if a woman was not virtuous and chaste in terms of rigid Victorian standards, she was considered unworthy of respect. To rephrase, the Indian Act robbed women of their sexual freedom and relegated them to puppets to men of their own community. Finally, the colonial authority prohibited women from any kind of political involvement, giving them no chances to become chiefs or band councillors and entirely excluding them from making any decisions in their community. Women thus suffered at the hands of both the invaders and the males from their own community.

This structural way of depriving a group of people of their land, tradition, heritage, and language is the reason a number of Native American literary pieces anchor in the notion of identity. Louis Owens observes that "in Indian fiction, though, we are shown the possibility of recovering a centered sense of personal identity and significance" (19). In "History, Postmodernism, and Louise Erdrich's *Tracks*", Nancy J. Peterson emphasises the necessity to create a Native history (and perhaps also a Native identity) before Native American authors can start of deconstructing it. However, it is imperative for Native American Studies to show "indigenous intellectual sovereignty" (Cheyfitz 4) and "Native nationalism" (Womack 11) to show its difference from other postcolonial movements. It is in their protest against colonial power and attempt to find a native identity and to resist female victimisation, Native American authors, particularly female ones such as Louise Erdrich, Susan Power, Leslie Marmon Silko and Paula Gunn Allen, among others, have employed magical realism in their writing.

One of the striking features of Native American magical realism is that it draws a parallel between magic and Native American beliefs, values, and traditions. The magical or supernatural elements, oral traditions, and spiritual legacy are employed as a means of resisting colonial supremacy and outlook and of defending and mourning Native culture. This magical opposition gradually transforms into a new Native identity, having the ability to maintain a perception of magic in the postcolonial world. Magic is undoubtedly an inherent part of Native American spiritual reality, a means of going beyond the Western discourse of realist truth. In Native American reality, both earthly and spiritual worlds are intertwined, where their spiritual traditions—medicine men and women, vision quest, and non-human spirits—enable the narratives to go beyond realism and into spiritual realism or magical realism. The Native American authors are thus able to come up with an all-encompassing view of Native reality by juxtaposing the real and the magical. It is its subversive and transgressive features that relate magical realism with postcolonialism and feminism, and thus make it a suitable means of protest from a Native American perspective, in the forms of a challenge to colonial power and dominant worldview. Erdrich uses magic to subvert a realist worldview where the supernatural has its origin more in her skills as a writer and less in her tribal legacy. While Erdrich uses magic to destabilise the colonial worldview, she does not intend to reassert any spiritual traditions through magic. Interestingly, she employs magical elements not to advocate Native beliefs but rather to show a dissociation from them. She also equips her female characters with the power of magic to resist female marginalisation and to protest white supremacy. From this perspective, Erdrich's magical realism clearly serves a political purpose. It is this magical realism which provides some sort of hope in resisting colonial invasion of native culture and ideology. Her language itself dissolves the reader's understanding of the real and the magical where magical elements are introduced through the process of defamiliarisation. Tankersley opines,

> Erdrich's lyrical, metaphorical writing style—what Silko calls "poet's prose"—is its own form of subversion to realism. Despite the subtlety of the political messages in her novels, Erdrich's metaphorical prose undermines and casts off the confines of Western rationalism. In this sense, her work clearly belongs in the magical realist tradition alongside other influential texts that resist a colonial worldview. (25)

Silko, however, stresses on the significance of shaman and storytelling, witchery and native medicinal practices, which can quicken the healing process of an individual, help him/her to find the identity lost or distorted by white invasion, and thus function as a sort of resistance to white supremacy. Silko is thus more inclined to highlight the spiritual tradition of the Natives than Erdrich is. Susan Power, on the contrary, focuses on the personal experiences and values of the Native Americans within themselves while being able to avoid alienating non-native readers. She can be considered less political compared to Erdrich and Silko. Her magical realism includes ancestral forces, dream images and storytelling where there is no difference between past and present, and between the experiences of two people. Power considers the spirits of the ancestors as a driving force and guide. Again, the ancestors' appearance in the dream of the descendants provides them with a complete guideline to lead their lives. Since the Native American authors, particularly the three mentioned female ones, write from a Native perspective to uphold their culture and worldview and to provide an alternative version of history, they have employed one feature of magical realism—a repetitive non-linear narrative as well as the traditional mode of storytelling or orality. Since the Native Americans equate land with mother, the loss of land and culture is considered a direct attack on the Mother Spirit.

The history of Latin America is full of disastrous miscalculations, foreign exploitations, internal corruptions, and the repetitions of the same mistakes across generations. However, this disastrous history, which was "born in blood and fire" (Chasteen 15), developed distinguished cultures and a regional history which is unique and exotic to the rest of the world. After becoming independent from their European colonisers, mainly the Spanish and the Portuguese, the Latin American countries witnessed the rise of dictatorship and suffered from a cluster of Civil Wars. Political independence from European colonisers did not result in the abolition of black slavery but rather in political and economic instability, giving rise to a form of neocolonialism influenced by superpowers like the UK and the USA. Because of the significant political influence of the leftists by the 1970s, the right-wing authorities and the upper class of each individual country supported military coups to avoid a potential communist threat. According to Abdullah, Colombia, for example, suffered highly from "long-lasting Civil War such as the 'War of A Thousand Days' (1899-1902) and the oppression of government known as 'La Violencia' (1948-1958), [and possessed] a troubled historical past, featured by violence and exploitation, triggered by colonialism, cultural and political marginalisation, and the results of industrialisation and technological development" ("Rewriting Rural Community" 60). The Chilean history is notoriously marked by Pinochet Dictatorship (1973-1990), who rose to power backed up by the USA, overthrowing a legitimate government led by Salvador Allende. The hatred and brutality with which Pinochet regime pursued its ideological or political enemies shocked everyone. It used state terrorism to dominate and control the citizens. Chilean people were ruthlessly beaten, killed, or simply vanished. However, unlike the mass arrests and killing that took place following the coup in 1973, gradually the regime initiated an era of institutionalised state terrorism with prior planning and better coordination, attempting to change nation's mentality by eradicating Marxism and to terrorise people. Female exclusion from politics and their helpless victimisation in the form of gang-rape, poor living condition and forced exile with many other men form a significant feature of the time. However, women also showed great comradeship in overcoming the brutality of the regime.

It is the sense of anxiety caused by the dictatorial regime—families living through oppression, people living in exile, and physical and sexual torture of women—that occupies a major part in Latin American literature. Again, throughout Latin American society, women are shown as having no power of their own, particularly women from the lower strata of the society who are repeatedly raped by, or forced to have sex with, their landlords or people in power. Besides, the desire to reimagine a better, peaceful, or probably utopian Latin America highlights the notion of an alternative history or reality, which provides some sort of agency to the marginalised and shows their resistance to oppression. Gabriel García Márquez, for instance, raised his voice against Spanish invasion, North American neocolonialism, and the Civil War that ravaged the entire Latin America, particularly Colombia. Referring to the traumatic Latin American history, authors attempt to rewrite the past events to heal the grief and distress of their loss. Chilean writer Isabel Allende, for example, wrote to recall her past and to keep the memories of their family and nation from vanishing into the passage of time. Memory thus plays a significant role for authors to recall both their personal and collective past. Allende believes that memory recovers the individual past of a person and the collective past of Latin America. Referring to the female marginalisation in Latin America, authors like Allende talk about the spiritual power of women, which allowed them to form a new unity among themselves and, therefore, a new form of feminism, as a survival tactic in both colonial and patriarchal societies. To rewrite the nation's history, Allende includes female knowledge and experiences, and thus brings them to light. Many prominent Latin American literary figures such as Gabriel García Márquez, Carlos Fuentes, and Mario Vergas Llosa have been politically active in both their personal lives and literary productions. Partly due to the authors' involvement in politics, Latin American literature is concerned with the formation of a national identity and the reconstruction of reality itself.

Although the term magical realism was first applied to German post-expressionist painting, it was later popularised by Latin American authors. In distinguishing between European magical realist writing and Latin American magical realist writing, Cuban writer Alejo Carpentier claims that European magical realists produce 'artificial' forms of magical realism, which is unrelated to their ordinary reality, but Latin Americans write magical realism which emerges from their environment and understanding ("The Baroque and the Marvelous Real" 93). Márquez, who was the most famous exponent of Latin American Boom, has employed magical realism to rewrite and recreate the original history of Colombia, where he combines realistic and mundane details with fairy tales, folk legends, and story of magic. Bowers considers Márquez's "magical realist exuberance not only a celebration of the diversity of Latin America [...] but a way to express the excessive violence and confusion of Colombian, and Latin American, politics" (39). Abdullah says again, through the process of defamiliarisation, Márquez's clearly "demonstrates his technique of making the fantastic seem real and the real fantastic, thus removing the obstacle between objective and imaginary realities, and creating an entirely fictional world" ("Rewriting Rural Community" 58). Isabell Allende, on the contrary, highlights female experiences where magic enables them to fight both patriarchal and political oppression. Allende shows the way magical power or clairvoyance of women passes down from one generation to the other, where women resort to their magical past to survive both patriarchal and political torture. Allende thus shows magic as communal. Allende's magical realism inspires the female characters to write down their personal, family, and collective histories, providing an alternative to the masculine traditional history. Allende's female-centric magical realism allows them to establish a unique comradeship between women to survive in a man's world. Allende's employment of 'ghost' to emphasise the death of people during Pinochet regime clearly shows ghost as a politicised one—ghost and politics are intertwined. Allende's circular, fragmented way of writing undermines the traditional linear version of a masculine history. Her female narrative is a way of including female knowledge and experiences, while not entirely negating male understanding and their narratives. Just like Márquez, Allende also attempts to defamiliarise Chile to restructure it as a supernatural regime.

Mexican and American Southeast both share a colonial past, marginalisation and racial and cultural amalgamation. The political borders have produced a unique borderland culture. By residing on this borderland, the Chicanos have adopted the fundamental "cultural and identity conflict" of the region, and "they do not totally identify with the Anglo-American cultural values nor with the Mexican ones" (Sánchez 172). After the US-Mexican War (1846-1848), a Mexican American culture arose, which expressed the borderland people's bicultural and bilingual experiences under (North) American cultural, political, ideological, and economic domination. Because of the Chicano Movement of the 1960s, which included protest and resistance, Chicanos started claiming their own identity and language to depict their ethnic marginalisation in the US. Although Chicano women cannot consider to be minority, their social condition is mainly affected by a digressive picture of femininity and womanhood. Due to the social and economic structure of Mexican/Chicana society, the "desire for freedom by a woman [...] is on a collision course with the designated social responsibilities of a woman as wife and mother" (Valdés 11). Feminism in Mexico cannot be relegated to women's issues only but rather should be considered in terms of various ethnic backgrounds, class hierarchies, and political situations. The struggle between expected social rules and individual identity causes a crisis within an individual woman regarding her true status in the society but, at the same time, also offers the potential for the development of personal agency and independence.

Chicano literature has greatly been influenced by US and Latin American authors of the nineteenth and twentieth century. Chicano narratives of the twentieth century have mainly explored the elements of Mexican national identity caused by the conflict and combination of Western and Native cultures. Chicano authors also attempt to revise their own cultural metaphors. The works by Chicano female authors, which mainly appeared in the 1980s and 1990s, attempt to provide an alternative worldview through myth and narrative. Chicano female authors such as Sandra Cisneros's *The House on Mango Street* (1984), Denise Chávez's *The Last of the Menu Girls* (1986) and Ana Castillo's *So Far from God* (1993) have achieved critical recognition and opened a new cultural and literary space, and polyphony of voices and languages. Instead of providing experimental types of narratives preferred by contemporary male authors, female narratives of the period were mainly concerned with the social and political milieu of the era. Since these female authors write from, and about, the margins of the society, they can go beyond established literary boundaries and provide alternative aspects, thus gaining some sort of space within the dominant patriarchal discourse by rewriting and reinterpreting the male-centred organisation of the world. In expressing this (marginalised) female voice, these authors write in a language which goes with its perspectives, offers a sense of resistance against oppression, and addresses the plurality of languages.

Magical realism used in Chicana literature is of a unique type, having various significant aspects. Although Chicana authors use similar techniques like Latin American authors such as Gabriel García Márquez or Carlos Fuentes, they stand out because of their particular emphasis on women. In revising traditional female discourses and recovering a female voice, Chicana writers such as Ana Castillo use humour and hyperbole extensively. Their versions of magical realism are employed to study the female understanding of their borderland existence. Thus, Latin American magical realist strategies present a socially and culturally explained subversive form from a feminine perspective, which, according to Sánchez, "include a metafictional self-referentiality and parodic use of popular discourses [and] call attention to the fact that the division between 'real' and 'fantasy' may be dependent on how it is presented" (176-177). Chicana magical realist authors focus extensively on their tradition, rituals and ancient myths and attempt to put those in a contemporary context. In a way, they attempt to rewrite native myths. Their use of magical realism is a protest not only against patriarchal authority but also against religious institutions like the church since it is, by nature, patriarchal. Chicana authors attempt to revise the Latin American tradition of magical realism, which is thematically and formally preoccupied with the grotesque, deformity and exaggerations, and to incorporate a more metafictional and humorous mode and a stronger sense of absurdity. Therefore, Chicana magical realism can be characterised by the overlapping between metaphysical, ontological, and anthropological magical realism.

Because of the dominant white supremacy in the culture of the United States and its significant immigrant society, African Americans, like many other cross-cultural groups, consider that they are marginalised and un-represented in White American life, which is also true for African American women who face prejudice both as the members of a marginalised group and as women (Abdullah, "Speaking the Unspoken" 25). African American authors like Toni Morrison, Gloria Naylor and Alice Walker have attempted to give black people, particularly black women, a voice and to enable them to come out of exclusion and marginalisation. They have portrayed the dark, powerful, and dehumanising effects of slavery and attempted to recover a history that has been destroyed by forced silence and deliberate forgetfulness. Morrison says, "There is a necessity for remembering the horror, but [...] in a manner in which it can be digested, in a manner in which the memory is not destructive. The act of writing [books on slavery], in a way, is a way of confronting it and making it possible to remember" (qtd. in Matus 32). The concept of "double consciousness", which was formulated by Du Bois, represents the experiences of African Americans, a sort of double vision which arises from the historical conflict between black and white cultures. Authors like Morrison and Naylor attempt to use and restructure this doubly conscious black way of life in their writing, and to merge the spiritual and profane worlds. This double consciousness, which is very much associated with the African American trauma of displacement, became a survival tactic for those who were dislocated to the New World, struggling to adjust to the American culture and to retain their own African culture.

Authors like Morrison and Naylor draw their magical realist elements from cross-cultural context as African Americans and seem to base their magical realism on the belief system of the African American cultural group rather than that of a particular location. There is a strong influence of African American oral culture and mythology, adapted from West-African culture, on Morrison's *Sula* (1973) and *Beloved* (1987), and Naylor's *Mama Day* (1988). Since one important aspect of magical realism is the use of myth, fable, and folklore, they stress on African American oral culture to recuperate black historical experiences. They also feel a strong connection with the predecessors who were the holders of cultural essence, and they employ magical realism to be able to use black folklore instead of the authorised belief of the Western world. The female black authors employ magical realism "to talk about the cruelty of slavery, [to highlight female oppression,] to reinterpret the official history of white slave-owners and put an alternative history from the perspective of the slaves", particularly, female slaves (Abdullah, "Speaking the Unspoken" 25). The stories of their characters, particularly the female ones, challenge official history that has ignored and, more specifically, silenced horrifying personal stories of slaves in America. Sánchez argues that their writing "extends the political resonance of black writing in general in order to foreground a particularly gendered response to ethnic specificity" (30). In an interview with Taylor-Guthrie, Toni Morrison makes the distinction between African American folk culture and Latin-American magical realism where she says that the main difference between these two expressions is their different origin, and she identifies herself with the black people who had to invent their magic in the midst of a new American reality; she states that their magic was discredited because it was held by discredited people (243).

In North American countries such as the United States and Canada, female suffering is more due to ideological differences between men and women. Within the US context, literary criticism or activism is often based on the postcolonial roots of magical realism. Although magical realism has been employed in English within the US, according to Bowers, "[...] there has not been a long enough tradition in the English language to make it possible to trace influences from one English-language magical realist to another" (45). In the US, authors from marginalised backgrounds (racially, ethnically, culturally, and so on) are not only writing in magical realist style but also getting associated with other marginalised authors working on magical realism. Louise Erdrich, for example, highlighted the influences of authors like Toni Morrison, William Faulkner, and Italo Calvino on her work, saying, "Calvino is one of the most wonderful writers, and the magic in his work is something that has been an influence, as well as the South American, Latin American, writers" (Coltelli 49). The transnational influence of magical realism shows the flexibility of its political connotations, which becomes quite crucial during the post-Cold War United States.

The term magical realism has quite regularly been used by critics to many Canadian works since the mid-1970s, achieving a new emphasis through postcolonial and postmodern contexts in the late 1970s and 1980s. The mode gains a different dimension in the 1990s through its internationalisation and its association with Canadian social and literary landscapes. Unlike the US critical community, that showed no interest in applying the genre to mainstream American literature, Canadian critics showed a clear interest in the presence and development of a national magical realist version. Canadian magical realism can be characterised by its geographical location, its (post)colonial and postmodern status, and the presence of the gothic and the uncanny. Unlike in the US where magical realism might be labelled as 'ethnic', in Canada, it's more like geographical. The British Columbian version of magical realism represented by Jack Hodgins in *The Invention of the World* and Robert Kroetsch in *What the Crow Said* admits the significance of the international literary context, and probably therefore, many magical realist writings from the past and the present differ significantly from their standard. Because of the shifting of focus from geographical context to ethnic components, magical realism as a term in Canada is now more regularly opposed mainly by members from minority communities. As Agnieszka Rzepa writes, "[M]arginalities explored in magic realist texts in Canada are now more often related to gender and sexuality, frequently in their intersection with ethnicity [...] (30). Quite interestingly, although the critical debate over Canadian magical realism has established the mode as a sub-genre of Canadian literature, it is, at the same time, responsible for obscuring its varieties. Rzepa opines that "the focus on 'the works of well-known, white, male, Western or West-Coast-based authors' has resulted in the marginalization of East-Coast writers, ethnic minority and women writers in critical discussions on magic realism in Canada" (7). Canadian magical realists have shown the tendency to connect Canadian magical realism with Canadian geography—a distinct feature for which notable Canadian critic Jeanne Delbaere-Garant suggests the term "mythic realism" (253). These active landscapes possess an intimate connection with characters and constitute the origin of the magic as a characteristic of mythic realism: a number of magical realist features of post-settler colonies "from which indigenous cultures have largely vanished, even though they remain hauntingly present in the place itself" (Delbaere-Garant 253). Magical realism has the potential to emphasise the obscure (post)colonial condition of the country. Canadian magical realist novels often share a gothic location where the uncanny plays a vital role between the two. Novels such as Ann-Marie MacDonald's *Fall on Your Knees*, Gail Anderson-Dargatz's *The Cure for Death by Lightning*, Tomson Highway's *Kiss of the Fur Queen* and Eden Robinson's *Monkey Beach* are clear examples of the junction between magical realism and the gothic. Anderson-Dargatz's female-oriented magical realism is a means for women to fight patriarchal oppression, and, in the case of native women, both racial and patriarchal marginalisation. Connecting magical realism with postcolonialism, Stephen Slemon opines that Canadian magical realism would form a key example of postcolonial writing where Canadian magical realist texts would "recapitulate a postcolonial account of the social and historical relations of the culture in which they are set" (Slemon 409). Slemon thus highlights magical realism's potential to resist oppression and marginalisation.

The Cuban Revolution caused significant changes in the Cuban society, completely reforming the nation's economy, social codes, political domain, and literary and cultural contexts. By dismantling the bourgeois culture, Castillo formed a socialist culture, reestablishing the proletariat as a dedicated masculine hero working for the Revolution. Louis Pérez Jr. states,

> Cubans were exhorted to subscribe to a new code, nothing less than a new morality. Emphasis was given to *conciencia*, the creation of a new consciousness that would lead to a new revolutionary ethic. The goal was the making of a new man *(hombre nuevo)*, motivated not by expectation of personal gain but by the prospects of collective advancement. The *hombre nuevo* was disciplined, highly motivated, and hardworking. Work was an end to itself, the means by which to purge persisting bourgeois vices and complete the transformation into the *hombre nuevo*. (340)

The masculinisation of Cuban consciousness, and the militarisation of Cuban life showed the ideological shift which hastened the fundamental changes in the life on the island and thus created an environment which is hostile and oppressive towards the conformist. Under the circumstances, the oppressive regime aims to "attack the sense of history of those they wish to dominate by attempting to take over and control their relationships to their own past" (Morales 23). Oppressive regimes such as Castro's one marginalised people through destroying "records, oral traditions and cultural forms and through interfering with the education of the young" (23). The process marginalised many Cubans who were against the Revolution's restriction on personal and social ways of life, and religious and/or political ideology, systematically oppressed them, and ultimately forced them to leave the country. The Revolution tore down the fabric of many families, created an atmosphere of fear, and weaved a master narrative excluding the suffering of the oppressed and displaced. It is imperative to mention that Castro's obsession with the modernisation of Cuba resulted in him to "sanction discrimination against religious observers" and to destroy folk culture (Otero and O'Bryan 43).

Cuban exilic writing attempts to tackle the brutal response of Castro period and to repair the fracture, silences and alienation caused by the regime. They endeavour to recuperate the cultural traditions of the oppressed and to assuage individual and collective injuries after the Revolution. In the entire process, these writers allow the marginalised to remember and revive cultural and spiritual traditions, give them a voice to talk about their marginalisation and thus enable them to come up with their own, alternative version of history, challenging the official one. Soto opines that Cuban writers in exile have produced such narratives which "distrust 'official' [Cuban] history, for it is subject to the changing ideological constructions of whatever group finds itself in power" (145). In the autobiography, *Castro's Daughter: An Exile's Memoir of Cuba*, Alina Fernández talks about the way Castro's regime changed the official history, particularly changing the educational curriculum to mirror the significance of the Revolution. Female characters played a significant role in recovering healing traditions and spiritual experiences, and in producing a counter or alternative narrative on the Revolution. Authors like Flor Fernandez Barrios highlight the history of Cuban women for retaining cultural and spiritual knowledge practices which existed beyond the masculine identities of the state, and the ideologies and institutions it has sanctioned. As Corrigan wrote, "In recounting the narratives of women excluded from the 'official' history, Barrios is able to elevate these Cuban women to a position of knowledge, authority, and authenticity over the men who re-wrote Cuban history after Castro's elevation to power" (3). Therefore, several exilic writings are openly political, expressing the author's philosophical challenge or doubt about the Cuban Revolution. By showing mutual connection among Cuban women who survived the volatile Castro regime, writers like Alina Fernández, Flor Fernandez Barrios and Cristina García admit a history of trauma on the one hand and female resistance to the central politics in Cuba led by men on the other.

To provide a counter-narrative on the Revolution, Cuban writers, particularly the female ones, take the help of magical realist narrative, which includes the appearance of ghosts of dead relatives in reality, female magical healing power, the (re)writing of myth and the strong belief on the supernatural power of natural objects. Barrios was told by her grandmother, Patricia, that the "thunder and lightning were the powers of the Yoruba deity Changó, also known as Santa Barbara in the Catholic religion" (4). The use of magical realism in a Cuban female context enables women to challenge their social and political exclusion, and functions as some sort of defense mechanism for them. Cuban female magical realist authors highlight the folk medicinal practices of Cuban women, show its superiority over modern medical system introduced by Fidel Castro who dreamt of seeing Cuba as a medical superpower, and thus come up with an alternative version of the Revolution. In the entire process, memory and (oral) narratives function together to retain traditional Cuban way of life. By sharing their folk knowledge with the community members in difficult times, these female healers basically upgrade the entire community. Again, authors like Cristina García also investigate spiritual practices and knowledge spaces of Cuban women through examining 'santería', an ancient Afro-Cuban religion where Yoruba goddesses are worshipped. Both Barrios and García emphasise the significance of women in preserving conventional spiritual practices and, at the same time, shed light on the way spirituality can be subversive. The relationship between women and santería ritual is significant as it helps to reestablish the Afro-Cuban oral tradition in modern histories of Cuba, where Afro-Cubans are oppressed and excluded. Again, the spiritual connection between women and Yemayá—the goddess of water—destabilises the controlling Christian religious practices. The relation also emphasises the way female agency and empowerment come from goddess(es) and are transferred through the voice of women, showing solidarity with other women.

Although the white settlers (haole), who arrived in Hawaii in 1778 with James Cook's expeditions, were mesmerised by its mind-blowing natural beauty, their arrival irreparably altered the natural and political situations of the islands. The arrival of the white settlers forced the indigenous people of the islands to change their spiritual and social relationships. The white forces disregarded their customs, beliefs, spirituality and practices, turned them dispossessed and dislocated and caused the death of many natives through the diseases brought by them. Hawaii later becomes a heaven for tourism, prostitution, and excessive exoticism related to female bodies, which summarises the notion of otherness as something exotic for the staring visitors. Put another way, Hawaiian women were exoticised and objectified by the tourists. Apart from being beaten, oppressed and dislocated, female Hawaiians working in the sugarcane plantations were under constant threat of sexual violence and rape.

The Hawaiian ecological imperialism by white people can be emphasised by two main factors—establishing Hawaii as a vital trading centre in the Pacific Ocean, and prohibiting native traditions and rituals by Christian missionaries. Again, the Hawaiians were lured into leasing and selling their lands to the white settlers without realising the disadvantageous aspects of the terms of the contract. The strategically advantageous location of Hawaii gives rise to business mainly from trading and establishing sugar plantations, and ships involved in opium smuggling and human trafficking are seen anchored in Hawaii. Davenport writes, "In the early 1840's, [...] human cargo smuggled in from the Orient as cheap labour, opium packed in champagne bottles, rare jade and gold slipped past immigration authorities" (58). Because of a large influx and outflux of people and goods, diseases such as syphilis, measles, and smallpox spread, leading the Hawaiian government to put a ban on opium trading, which ultimately resulted in the rise of sugar plantations. It is the issuing of Great Mahele or land allotment which eradicated long-held feudalism, enabled the white settlers to buy land in bulk, and thus initiated ecological imperialism in Hawaii. The last phase of Hawaiian ecological imperialism can be considered the continuation of military domination started during WWII, which resulted in a large amount of toxic and pollution.

It is European and American colonisation, and its devastating consequences on the culture and environment of Hawaii that is mainly emphasised in Hawaiian literature. Authors like Kiana Davenport and Kristiana Kahakauwila assert the negative influence of American dominance on Hawaiian ecology and the marginalisation of the Native. They also show the clash between Western and Hawaiian points of view, and the irrecoverable transformation of Hawaiian landscapes because of American imperialism. In both her *Shark Dialogues* and *House of Many Gods*, Davenport discovers decayed Hawaiian landscapes with wretched lifestyle of the Natives who lost their inherited land to American Navy for their training. By focusing on the suffering of Native Hawaiian women at the hands of the white settlers, authors like Davenport have demonstrated the history of abuse through female voices and bodies. She knows the way the body of the Polynesian women is objectified, exoticised and eroticised, and she presumes that these women are not only objectified but also despised due to their dark colour. Davenport also finds a correlation between the resistance to environmental destruction and to social, political, cultural, and ethnic marginalisation. In order to explore marginalised voices, Davenport blends magical realism and history, links contemporary truth with ancient myths and dissolves the realistic concept of time and space. Davenport's magical realism is an instrument of judging an alternative history of Hawaii by women. Her magical elements are borrowed from the ancient Hawaiian myths, local rituals and traditions, female deities and the figure of healer or fortune teller, and are used as a protest against all sorts of marginalisation—social, political, cultural, ethnic and gendered—and an attempt to provide the deprived their history and culture.

The Central American country, Nicaragua, suffered from a volatile time in the 1960s and 1970s. The country was ruled by the Somoza dynasty, which came to power after the US occupation of Nicaragua in 1912, from 1937 to 1979. The Somoza rule was featured by a boom in the economy, although with increasing inequality and political corruption. However, the rise of the Sandinista National Liberation Front (FSLN), which was established in 1961, made it difficult for the Somoza dynasty to rule and ultimately caused the Nicaraguan Revolution. The Nicaraguan Revolution included the growing resistance to the Somoza government in the 1960s and 1970s, the FSLN Movement to overthrow despotism in 1978-1979, the attempt of the FSLN to rule Nicaragua from 1979 to 1990 and the Contra War between the FSLN government and the US–supported Counter Revolutionary Soldiers (Contras) from 1981 to 1990. The Sandinista government was charged with human rights violations, which included censorship of the press, surveillance on the potential dissenters, and the brutal killing of the country's Miskito (a Native people in Central America) and Jews. Women fought for both the Sandinistas, who made up of approximately 25-30 per cent of the FSLN, and the Contras, where they formed approximately seven per cent; women from both sides also worked together to restructure the nation (Cupples 85). Cupples also mentioned that during the Revolution, women provided help and shelter to female comrades, and persuaded their husbands to participate in the revolution (85). Santos and Engel wrote that the FSLN made it their prime target to establish gender equality and to help women achieve independence from Somoza dictatorship; that's why they were able to attract many women to their Movement. They were very strict against using women as sexual objects (43). Many Nicaraguan women also joined the FSLN to get rid of the sexual and political violence of Somoza dictatorship. Many women, however, joined the Contras mainly because of personal reasons; some of them were instructed by their men, who made political decisions on their behalf.

The writings of Female Nicaraguan authors like Gioconda Belli mirror their commitment to female empowerment, and their desire to inspire them in female liberation struggle. It is by invoking memories of strong women from the past that Belli attempts to empower women around her. Being herself an active member of FSLN and a feminist activist, Belli clearly understands the necessity of female agency and independence, and therefore wants to inspire her fictional character Lavinia, from *The Inhabited Woman,* who becomes a member of FSLN, by inserting into her the spirit of Itzá, a revolutionary woman who died almost five hundred years ago, representing pre-Hispanic myth, and Aunt Inés who has guided her and shaped her thoughts. In searching for female identity in a patriarchal society, Belli's novels blend elements of myth and politics. Being the witness of the political revolution in Nicaragua, Belli attempts to express women's voices, interweaves her/their personal experiences, writes alternative narratives which are mixed with the official story, and thus produces a new historical novel. She also shows the way women can achieve agency through collective memory, love, and spirituality. Female characters like Lavinia are empowered by collective memory in order to rediscover their female identity in a politically volatile time. Belli thus uses magical realism and collective memory in a female context, applies them in a time of political revolution, which has traditionally been a male sphere, and shows female agency and empowerment. The use of magical realism in Belli's novel connects national history and female experiences whose voice have long been silenced by both colonial and patriarchal society. Lavinia's active participation in the Movement has helped her (re)form her identity and to find her true self. The spiritual connection between Lavinia and Itzá stresses the bond between women through memories in general. The use of magical realism enables Belli to create this mythical native female soldier from the past that represents the significance of memory as an instrument of inspiration and liberation. Apart from including the spirit of a native warrior, Belli's magical realism also consists of local rituals and traditions, the influence of dead relatives on characters, oral tradition, and a skillful time shift.

Part I.
Attacking Dictatorship and Transforming Destructive Patriarchal System

Chapter 4

Resisting Patriarchy and Challenging Dictatorship in Isabel Allende's *The House of the Spirits*

In *The House of the Spirits,* Chilean author Isabel Allende employs magic to provide women the necessary power to change the disparaging patriarchal system. Instead of playing the traditional roles found in masculine writing, female characters in the novel form a female bond, thus a female force, which challenges patriarchal repression, social and sexual prejudices, tyranny, and political repression. In parallel to the political development in Chile, the novel traces the development of women of del Valle family in particular and Chilean women in general. The female characters in the novel fight for both female rights and fair treatment of the deprived and marginalised. Allende shows how the political upheaval is seen through female clairvoyance: Clara's power of prophecy constructs a lens through which to observe the nature of Chilean coup d'état. The move from spirits and predictions is a sensible feminist development. Allende's attempt to write in a circular style undermines the conventional, linear version of history, enabling women's history to overtake men's history: Esteban's rigid, linear account is contrasted by Alba's non-linear, circular narrative. By showing that magic is unachievable for men and is very much a female issue, Allende provides women with an alternative mode of communication and attempts to rewrite (male) history in order to include female knowledge and experience. Clara's clairvoyance allows her to predict the future, to interact with the deceased as a living person and to meet her granddaughter as a dead person and therefore enables her to transcend patriarchal constraints. The use of magic from a female context attempts to enhance women's perception or knowledge of the veiled human reality and to transform the vicious patriarchal system.

For Allende, writing *The House of the Spirits* was the means to keep the memories of her family, relatives, and nation alive and to remember her past: the novel thus functions as a bridge between her life in exile in Venezuela and her earlier life in Chile. While in exile, she realises that memory redeems the personal past of the individual and the collective past of Latin America. Put another way, personal memory signifies collective memory, suggesting the shared history of the nation as family. The novel is basically her collection of letters sent to her ninety-nine-year-old grandfather, living in Chile under the Pinochet regime, and moving towards death, in order to keep him alive. Allende believed, "[D]eath didn't really exist. Oblivion is what exists, and if one remembers those who die —remember them well — they'll always be with him and in some way will live on, at least" (qtd. in Earle 543). The novel is thus a memoir, a family saga and a political testimony infused with magical realist elements. The novel chronicles the lives of four generations of del Valle family, each fighting with the social and gendered (patriarchal) constraints of their own generations. Rachel Hubata-Ashton states that Allende attempts to "bear witness to socio-economic class lines, women's repression, and political violence —having been motivated by her traumatic experiences from the betrayal and resulting death of her uncle, President Salvador Allende, by right-wing conspirators and their U.S. counterparts and the brutal dictatorship that ensued" (Hubata-Ashton 3). One can also clearly see the military coup and violent regime that tends to suppress those who it considers dissenters. Women are given a voice through magic so that they can rewrite the official version of history from their own perspectives; linear and established version of time and space is destabilised and a non-linear and non-chronological one is advocated, which can be compared with the cyclical aspect of nature, in order to provide a more sacred space for women.

Destabilising Traditional History and Challenging Destructive Patriarchal System and Political Repression

From the very beginning of *The House of the Spirits,* Allende used feminised magical realism to draw the attention of the reader to a political-historical novel. The novel particularly focuses on the spiritual powers possessed by women to allow them to form unity among themselves as a survival tactic in men's world. We see the way Alba resorts to the magical past of her family to survive the torture in prison and the way she, inspired by the spirit of her grandmother Clara, records her family story, which can be considered an alternative to the traditional masculine history. Allende's story, which is based on the political account of Chile, is narrated from the viewpoint of Alba and her grandfather Esteban Trueba, in which their voices are incorporated to generate an alternative narrative, merging both male and female outlooks on the past historical events. Whereas Alba's voice represents the world of women depicting female emancipation, Esteban's voice emphasises the repressive male-controlled and aristocratic society which guides and controls the social norms for women and lower-class people. Alba's story, which includes the viewpoints of her female ancestors, directly challenges Esteban's egocentric, rigid and somewhat made-up version, and thus conveys the image of the victory of female expression. By employing her power of writing, Alba attempts to resist military power and so symbolises a more empathetic way of seeing history. Based on her grandmother Clara's fifty-year-old diary and many other family documents, Alba (re)writes her family story, joining all the events rather than just recording them, shows a more structured and convincing attitude to life and history and comes up with an alternative and/or marginalised (read feminised) version of reality and history. By claiming that Clara's narrative would help her reclaim her individual and family past and to overcome her sufferings of prison life, Alba focuses on the notion of female solidarity among Latin American women.

Alba's narrative is distinctively different from Esteban's in the sense that her story is the compilation of female experiences where she attempts to retell her family story to give her female ancestors and herself a legacy and to be empowered. She considers herself less of a participant in her family story and more of a significant part of Trueba women's legacy. Susan Frick states that by connecting "her female ancestors' experiences and her grandfather's male perspective, Alba is finally ready to admit to being the first-person narrator of *La casa de los espíritus*" (37). Alba's feminised version of narration or history allows her to find her own identity and to move on with her own life. Frick says again that in her narrative, Alba is "tapping into collective memory to evoke and interpret the stories and voices of the past and to learn how best to proceed with her own individual life experience" (29). However, the reader should not forget the spiritual presence and guidance of Clara behind Alba's attempt to write the history of del Valle family. Alba informs the reader that Clara's spectral presence helps her to write the family story and that in her presence, Esteban dies happily, calling her name. By allowing the del Valle women to create their own narrative and therefore to expose the suffering of Latin American women, which was unrepresented in the male narratives, and by equipping them with the power of communing with dead ancestors, Allende secures a place for women in the Latin American grand narrative, demonstrates their empowerment, and portrays a new form of feminism. The fact that Esteban contributes to women's stories and thus achieves redemption, albeit partially, for his past brutalities and mistakes, emphasises female counter-dominance or victory over males. Martinez argues that in order to reflect "[Esteban's] redemptive awareness, Allende makes him assist in the telling of the story, done by the main narrator, Alba" (290). Alba also shows the way women of del Valle family, in particular, and Latin America in general, have the power to reinvent themselves, and describes the constant presence of her female ancestors in the house in regard to the reappearance of the ghosts or spirits:

> "Si las empleadas oyen ruidos, creerán que han vuelto los fantasmas" dijo Alba y le contó del glorioso pasado de espíritus visitantes y mesas voladoras de la gran casa de la esquina. ... Los enamorados probaron uno por uno los cuartos abandonados y terminaron improvisando un nido para sus amores furtivos en las profundidades del sótano. Hacía varios años que Alba no entraba allí y llegó a olvidar su existencia, pero en el momento en que abrió la puerta y respiró el inconfundible olor, volvió a sentir la mágica atracción de antes.[1] (Allende, *La casa* 384)

However, the reader should not forget that apart from Esteban and Clara, her fellow female prisoners also play a great part in assisting Alba and carrying on female history. Although Alba desires death, it is Clara's spirit and the other female inmates who provide her renewed strength and inspire her to tell her individual and their collective stories, which otherwise would never have been told. Regarding the strength of female bonding, Carrie Sheffield argues that the "feminine collective [of the concentration camp] provides the support Alba needs to present the revision of history present in the novel; it is the chorus of women's voices following behind her that gives Alba the ability to write and preserve their (and her) testimonies" (37).

The House of the Spirits can well be considered evidence of the female version of history overtaking the traditional male version as Peter Earle argues that "the book is the struggle between Trueba and the forces he generates, on the one hand, and the female members of his family, on the other" (550). Earle opines, Esteban Trueba "is the blind force of history" together with "its aggressive, vigorous, physical manifestations" (Earle 550). Put another way, by creating

---

[1] "If the servants hear noise, they'll think the ghosts are back," Alba said, and she told him of the glorious past of visiting spirits and flying tables in the big house on the corner. ... One by one the lovers tried out all the abandoned rooms, and finally chose an improvised nest in the depths of the basement. It had been years since Alba had been there, and she had almost forgotten that it existed, but the minute she opened the door and inhaled its unmistakable odor, she felt again the old magical attraction. (Allende, *The House of the Spirits* 356)

alternative histories from their own perspectives, Alba and her female family members challenge the authoritarian history created by Esteban and her political party. Esteban strongly believes that he is powerful enough to control politics and people around him and that it is the aristocratic people who should write history, denying a voice to the marginalised. Concurring with Earle's idea of dual narration, it can be suggested that Esteban's account is a direct contrast to Alba's one. Sheffield opines that through a blending of Alba's liberal vision and Trueba's narrow-minded one, "we catch a glimpse of two distinct worlds, and through those worlds, we are offered a re-vision of history" (34). Esteban, who attempts to subjugate (both physically and psychologically) all the women he has come across in his life, can thus be associated with an oppressive regime that imprisons and tortures Alba. Although Alba watches the way the military regime deletes history and destroys the entire nation, she connects this power of writing to do something for women by recording their own stories. Alba thus comes up with a "more imaginative, more perceptive resistance" to the patriarchal and political domination of both Esteban and the government (Earle 551). Since Alba attempts to write her family history from a female standpoint, she inserts Nivea's empathy, Clara's clairvoyance, Blanca's passion, and her toughness. Ruth Jenkins argues that "[...] these narratives record stories of female experience neither sufficiently nor authentically articulated by histories constructed from patriarchal perspectives" (66-67). Jenkins also considers this novel an example of "the power to script history [because] Allende asserts the value of individual female experience while weaving it into generations of female history" (66). The novel thus highlights both individual and shared features of Alba's narrative, which distinguish it from Esteban's linear narrative. It is by focusing on her female ancestors and other surrounding female characters that Alba provides them and herself subversive and transgressive qualities. As Gabrielle Foreman claims that the novel "is a femino-centric novel in that the female characters here are not in the traditional roles found in masculine writing, rather they constitute [...] gynoforces that challenge patriarchal despotism, social-sexual prejudices, the dictatorship and political repression" (378). The novel thus poses a serious challenge to the male narrative, and patriarchal and political oppression.

Apart from having the intention of recording her own family history from a female perspective, Alba also writes to survive the torture she has received in the prison and to begin a new life. After being kidnapped, raped, and tortured by Colonel García and his men, Alba is thrown into a prison with other women who also have received the same experience of torture. Alba is visited and comforted by the ghost of Clara, who encourages her to establish a monument for those who have perished during the Pinochet regime. By emphasising the significance of women, the novel shows the way female agency or instinct is supported by both supernatural phenomena and political justice. The act of remembering thus functions as a reaction to trauma, retelling the past stories to structure the present and the future:

> Trató de no respirar, de no moverse, y se puso a esperar la muerte con impaciencia. Así estuvo por mucho tiempo. Cuando casi había conseguido su propósito, apareció su abuela Clara, a quien había invocado tantas veces para que la ayudara a morir, con la ocurrencia de que la gracia no era morirse, puesto que eso llegaba de todos modos, sino sobrevivir, que era un milagro. La vio tal como la había visto siempre en su infancia, con su bata blanca de lino [...] Clara trajo la idea salvadora de escribir con el pensamiento, sin lápiz ni papel, para mantener la mente ocupada, evadirse de la perrera y vivir. Le sugirió, además, que escribiera un testimonio [...] para que el mundo se enterara del horror [...].[2] (Allende, *La casa* 482)

It can be inferred from the above quotation that collective memory is included in the realm of spirits and ghosts, showing Clara as a force from the past, a guide, and a healer. Alba starts writing to survive; however, after getting released from prison, she keeps writing, inspired by her resolution of living with purpose. By connecting her individual and family motives, she is able to break the bloody and brutal chain/history of patriarchy and the political regime, creating an alternative, marginalised version of events. Alba's personal struggle symbolises the collective struggle of women in Latin America who attempt to rewrite their own history, including their alternative perspectives and incorporating a strong sense of hope. Alba's decision to give birth to the child she is carrying, not being sure if it is the result of her love with Miguel or the product of rape, symbolises the collapse of the recurrence of the oppressive

---

[2] She tried not to breathe or move, and began eagerly to await her death. She stayed like this for a long time. When she had nearly achieved her goal, her Grandmother Clara, whom she had invoked so many times to help her die, appeared with the novel idea that the point was not to die, since death came anyway, but to survive, which would be a miracle. With her white linen dress, [...] she looked exactly as she had when Alba was a child. Clara also brought the saving idea of writing in her mind, without paper or pencil, to keep her thoughts occupied and to escape from the doghouse and live. She suggested that she write a testimony [...], so that the world would know about this horror [...]. (ibid 447)

tradition. By showing that it is the collective memory of her female ancestors that guides Alba to (re)assert her identity, Allende turns the text into a self-discovery novel—a narrative in which the protagonist discovers her own self and worth by denying the male-imposed structure.

Collective Memory as a Source of Empowerment in Female Quest for Liberation

In *The House of the Spirits*, Allende employs magic to depict the spiritual power of Clara and the shared memory of women. Memory can be defined as "affective and magical" (Nora 8); Allende portrays Clara as magical and the harbinger of change, while Alba recalls the way the magical world of Clara remains alive even after her demise:

> Es una delicia, para mí, leer los cuadernos de esa época, donde se describe un mundo mágico que se acabó. Clara habitaba un universo inventado para ella, protegida de las inclemencias de la vida, donde se confundían la verdad prosaica de las cosas materiales con la verdad tumultosa de los sueños, donde no siempre funcionaban las leyes de la física o la lógica.[3] (Allende, *La casa* 97)

In the world of Clara, supernatural visions are intermingled with mundane objects of the physical worlds. The fact that Alba will be able to interact with Clara even after her death emphasises Clara's teaching that death does not separate us but rather unites us more strongly. It sheds light on the magical realist concept of post-mortem communication (between the mortal world and the spirit world). The combined or collective voice acquired in the spiritual world beyond the visible one, which Alba believes to be crucial for societal change, is the one which nonchalantly accepts the existence of the magical amid reality as something completely usual. When Alba mentions Clara's "mundo mágico", she depicts the intergenerational tie experienced by both grandparents and grandchildren which helps them form collective memory. In the narrative of Alba, the tumultuous history of 1970's Chile is intertwined with her memory of her grandmother, Clara, and her personal realm, where she is

---

[3] It is a delight for me to read her notebooks from those years, which describe a magic world that no longer exists. Clara lived in a universe of her own invention, protected from life's inclement weather, where the prosaic truth of material objects mingled with the tumultuous reality of dreams and the laws of physics and logic did not always apply. (ibid 92)

shown to represent change as she has the power to influence others with her magical world. Clara's magical world undoubtedly destabilises the rigid world of Esteban who is disturbed by the sensibility and irrationality of her feminine magical world. In fighting her oppressive husband, Clara seems to function beyond logic and rationality since she is led by female traditions passed down intergenerationally by body gesture, silence, and various other means of performance. Aligning with Pierre Nora's explanation of memory, Clara conveys "The warmth of the tradition, [...] the silence of the custom" (7), and memory in "gestures" (9). The significance of memory is emphasised by Clara as she contemplates on the worth of family memory extending over many generations:

> Blanca empezó a producir figuritas para el pesebre navideño [...] sin saber que estaba haciendo con barro lo mismo que su tía Rosa, a quien no conoció, hacía con hilos de bordar en su gigantesco mantel, mientras Clara especulaba que si las locuras se repiten en la familia, debe ser que existe una memoria genética que impide, que se pierdan en el olvido.[4] (Allende, *La casa* 202)

Although Blanca never met her Aunt Rosa, her embarking on creative and crazy activities, just like Rosa's passion for creating a gigantic tablecloth, emphasises the connection between women from two generations through the passing down of collective memory.

Concentrating on collective memory, it can be said that memory is as important as history, and it has the potential to stand on its own. Surmising from Pierre Nora, Gedi and Elam say that "Memory [...] is no longer a servant of history; it is, on the contrary, on a par with history" (33). Gedi and Elam infer the way Nora associates memory with magic as he strongly supports the notion that collective memory is associated with experience that is present in the tradition, in the voiceless customs that are passed down to other generations (33). Clara's magical influence on her children is connected to the experiences that are passed on to the next generations, where her two sons and only daughter receive the spirituality and the unspoken customs and traditions of their mother. However, Clara is also a changemaker in society. Her distinctive

---

[4] Blanca began to create tiny figures for the family's Christmas manger, [...] without realizing that she was doing in clay what her Aunt Rosa, whom she never knew, had done with thread on her enormous tablecloth. Clara decided that if craziness can repeat itself in a family, then there must be a genetic memory that prevents it from being swallowed by oblivion. (ibid 189)

relationship and instinctive union of solidarity with Pedro Segundo, the man who assists Esteban in his property, enables her to defy Esteban in his establishment. By struggling against the oppressive power with the help of Pedro, Clara once again proves herself as an agent of change as she dissolves the class barrier. Again, Clara's intimate relationship with Férula, Esteban's sister, also forms a solidarity where she defends Férula and brings happiness to her life. Férula, the unfortunate woman who was destined to take care of her parents, has a magical relationship with Clara, who senses Férula's death and declares it. The emotional relationship between Clara and Férula, which enrages Esteban who accuses Férula of witchcraft and Clara for forming a homosexual relationship, forms a defying alliance to Esteban's oppression. However, unlike Férula who silently accepts society's dominance, Clara defies the societal oppression, challenges the traditional role of women, and advocates female emancipation, fighting discrimination, living in the world of spirits and defying Esteban with silence.

In *The House of the Spirits,* Allende attempts to defamiliarise Chile to reconstruct it as a purely magical world where the supernatural is shown to triumph over the oppressive patriarchal and political system. Doris Meyer opines that the novel is a "direct refusal to accept the patriarchal oppression historically practised by the upper classes and the military in Latin America" (360). This rewriting and reconstruction of Chile is magical, and like other magical realist novels, Allende's text attempts to recover an authentic voice for those who have no options to express their specific experiences of reality in this case, Latin American women from an unprivileged part of society. Meyer opines that women preserve the notion of "hidden" realities, which "live in dreams, embodied but still deadly silent, in silences, in voiceless rebellions" (360). Alba recovers the experiences of her grandmother and other women she has come across by breaking this silence. In the novel, the magical realist language, reconciling both patriarchal and matriarchal ways of seeing reality, conveys some sort of hope for change in society in general.

In *The House of the Spirits,* Clara, who is the embodiment of the claim that magic is an entirely feminine realm, possesses clairvoyance to communicate with spirits and extrasensory power to move objects.

> Clara clarividente conocía el significado de los sueños. Esta habilidad era natural en ella y no requería los engorrosos estudios cabalísticos que usaba el tío Marcos con más esfuerzo y menos acierto. ... Los sueños no eran lo único que Clara adivinaba. También veía el futuro y conocía la

> intención de la gente, virtudes que mantuvo a lo largo de su vida y acrecentó con el tiempo. Anunció la muerte de su padrino, don Salomón Valdés [...].[5] (Allende, *La casa* 90-91)

As a child, Clara was preoccupied with her own world and often seemed to be distracted but happy and relaxed. However, her predictions were not given any importance, which confirms her suppression as a woman. Although Clara's nanny believes that her magical ability will decrease with time, it rather increases after becoming a woman with full family duties. Patricia Hart argues that Clara's magical ability fails to help her as she can only predict the future without being able to change it. However, magic might not be a practical strategy but it is undoubtedly one which helps the marginalised, here women, to survive. Contrary to Hart, Wendy B. Faris advocates the potential of magic, insisting that "magic is generally an empowering strategy if not a pragmatic one; thus, it diminishes in frequency as political activity increases, but it is also a precursor of that activity because it has helped Clara to survive and pass on her strength to her granddaughter" (*Ordinary Enhancements* 183).

Although Patricia Hart argues that since "clairvoyance is a metaphor for female passivity, then it is essential that this magic diminish gradually and finally be replaced by something better by Alba's generation [...] to accept the responsibility for the world in which they live" (59), magic does not really end with Clara. Put another way, Allende starts the story with magic and slowly moves to social and political spheres to establish the notion that magical realism is anchored in social and political realities. Thus, it is by grounding magic amidst social and political realities, Allende shows the way magic can give a voice to women and empower them. Alba who, unlike her grandmother, blends magic and political reality, is a political activist who, in order to retrieve the past uses Clara's manuscripts and thus joins the worlds of two different generations. As Devona Mallory writes, "Alba takes off where Clara and Don Esteban leave, connecting both worlds to move on, survive and endure, no matter what. Having collected everyone's stories by weaving a tapestry of the political and personal history of Chile, Alba and her country earn a much-

---

[5] Clara the Clairvoyant could interpret dreams. It was an inborn talent, requiring none of the trying cabalistic study to which her Uncle Marcos had applied himself with far more effort and far less effect. ... Dreams were not the only thing that Clara read. She could also predict the future and recognize people's intentions, abilities that she maintained throughout her life and that increased with time. She announced the death of her godfather, Don Salomón Valdes [...]. (ibid 85)

deserved hopeful future that becomes all-inclusive" (142). On the other hand, in *The House of the Spirits,* magic is unattainable for men, particularly for Esteban, who equates magic with other exclusively feminine affairs like cooking and religion. Being himself an epitome of patriarchy, Esteban seems unable to understand the magical abilities of women because he "with his elitist, colonialist, and fascist approach to life, signifies cold, harsh, unrelenting reality" (Mallory 125), and labels them hysterical—a label given to women who defy the mental health standards set by a patriarchal society or culture. Shoshana Felman considers hysteria "a manifestation both of cultural impotence and of political castration" (8). Although Esteban neglects magic, relegating it to purely feminine activities, magic has its effect on him—a phenomenon which shows the way women can challenge and, to some extent, defeat dominant authority or ideology with the help of magic. Although Esteban, who was six feet tall in his youth, tends to provide scientific logic behind his shrinking body, neglecting her sister Férula's curse that "[...] se te encogerá el alma y el cuerpo y te morirás como un perro!"[6] (Allende, *La casa* 155), Alba finds that Férula's curse works on him and his body shrivelled as much as his soul.

Allende's narrative structure undermines the governing system of her culture where magical realism as a narrative structure and philosophy provides an alternative conception of time and space deviated from linear ones. The Western notion of time, which is whimsically and tyrannically constructed, is divided into the domains of past, present and future, having a linear direction. According to the Western rationalist conception, the past takes place in a fixed, chronological pattern without having any other explanations for it. However, Clara knows that perceiving time as chronological hinders one from understanding the association between people and events. Interestingly, Clara mentions in her notebook that "creemos en la ficción del tiempo, en el presente, el pasado y el futuro, pero puede ser también que todo ocurre simultáneamente"[7] (Allende, *La casa* 503) and that "el pasado y el futuro eran parte de la misma cosa y la realidad del presente era un caleidoscopio de espejos desordenados donde todo podía ocurrir"[8] (Allende, *La casa* 97). Clara's

---

6 "[His] body and soul will shrivel up and [he'll] die like a dog!" (ibid 145)

7 "[W]e believe in the fiction of the past, present, and future, but it may also be true that everything happens simultaneously." (ibid 466-467)

8 "[T]he past and the future formed part of a single unit, and the reality of the present was a kaleidoscope of jumbled mirrors where everything and anything could happen." (ibid 92)

view on the simultaneous and non-linear conception of time refers to the cycle of nature, having the potential of birth, death, and rebirth. It is also a strong blow against the Western version of time. It is through recuperating the texts written by Clara and other women that Alba can connect time and realise that time is fluid and non-linear. She can also realise that the brutal shackle which has tied up her family and her fellow countrymen can be changed. In writing their narrative, both Esteban and Alba must revisit the past, having renewed the past and, in turn, renewing themselves. The fact that the text finishes where it starts emphasises the cyclical pattern of time. Again, the infinite, tortuous and simultaneous perception of time, which can be considered magical realist, can be compared to the female experiences of reality, particularly the nature of multi-faceted female sensuality, which contrasts the one-dimensional sensuality of men.

Another significant instance of defying the dominating ideology is seen in the association between Clara's worldviews and the magical beliefs and rituals of the native people—worldviews which are not based on Western empiricism but rather on the spiritual and natural world in which they live. Like the Native, Clara refuses to impose a non-natural schedule on Blanca and does not allow the male-designed or male-expected rules of female decorum to make her feel embarrassed about feeding her child publicly. It is through their common belief in the supernatural and the spiritual world that Clara is able to form an intimate link with the peasants. Although the old Pedro García has the ability to magically cure the ant plague, it is only Clara who finds the entire process totally normal. Instead of fighting Esteban directly, Clara silently defies him through her own activities, attempting to wipe out racial and gender discrimination. The huge modifications that Clara makes to her mansion symbolise her rebellion against artificial rules imposed by dominant ideology; it also enables her to achieve victory over Esteban without going into a direct fight with him. The reader should not forget that Clara's defiance also reaches her daughter Blanca, who learns to challenge the rules imposed on her by the patriarchal regime and to follow her own rules. Just like her mother, Blanca also possesses female spirituality which helps her to develop a magical system of communication with the child (Alba) growing inside her womb. Just like Clara, who defies the patriarchy through her writing, Blanca also challenges traditional perceptions of reality through her art, a skill possessed by other female members of the Trueba family, as art is considered a crucial means for women to highlight their alternative beliefs and ideologies. Blanca inherits the skill for conceiving and creating weird animals from Aunt Rosa, who embroiders magical animals and plants, defying any established laws of physics and biological sciences. This female art is a crucial passage for them to express their own philosophies and perceptions of the world silenced by dominant structures of society. By getting a voice through their artistic creations, these women find a platform to challenge dominant authorities—art is thus empowering for women.

It is through Alba that the voices of Clara, Blanca, and other oppressed Chilean women in general, the voices that would otherwise have been neglected and excluded, find an expression where Alba's created story covers the lives of her family and surroundings and brings their experiences to light. Through her magical realist text, Allende has attempted to create a new form of feminism, highlighting solidarity and interdependence among Latin American women, and a new hope for her country, which has suffered brutally due to military regime and patriarchal constraints. By providing a voice to women who have the potential to transform the devastated nation through their dynamic sense of human spirituality, Alba's powerful narrative is a model of the politicised women's literature discussed by Allende in her "Writing as an Act of Hope":

> Now, finally, women are breaking the rule of silence and raising a strong voice to question the world. This is a cataclysm. It is a new literature that dares to be optimistic–to speak of love in opposition to pornography, of compassion against cruelty [...] a literature that doesn't invent history or try to explain the world solely with reason, but also seeks knowledge through feelings and imagination. (54-55)

The main narrator of the novel Alba is undeniably the "strong voice" who will challenge the world by her unconventional, female narration. By subverting male-controlled writing and dominant history, Alba proves herself powerful individually and the women from different generations collectively. The political and gendered restrictions imposed on the three generations of Trueba family—Clara, Alba, and Blanca—are readdressed to produce a story for the women, by the women, and of the women, hoping for a better future where future generations will survive the psychological and intellectual destruction through love and human bonding.

Chapter 5

Reconstructing Personal Identity and Creating an Alternative National History: Magical Realism and the Marginalised Female Voice in Gioconda Belli's *The Inhabited Woman*

Nicaraguan author Gioconda Belli's 1988 novel *The Inhabited Woman* (*La Mujer Habitada*), which bears autobiographical elements, blends personal stories of Nicaraguan women over centuries with the social and political reality of Nicaragua in the 1970s. Belli's novel attacks both patriarchy and dictatorship, where she adopts a gendered standpoint, depicting the double victimisation of her protagonist Lavinia—a rebel and a woman. It is through the story of Lavinia that Belli reveals her own story of discrimination and marginalisation. By magically attaching Itzá—an indigenous female warrior who died centuries ago—to Lavinia's body and by giving her a voice, Belli breaks the silence of the marginalised native women in the history of the nation and allows her to create an alternative history capable of voicing the untold stories of female suffering. Belli's treatment (both fictional and non-fictional) of the role of women in Nicaraguan history, as well as her concern for more space for female participations in the revolution are significant parts of a social, cultural, and political trend. By magically connecting Itzá and Lavinia, Belli connects both past and present of Nicaragua, and shows how they end up being one and the same since both of them die for the sake of liberating their own people. Lavinia's magical association with Itzá and her memories of the past empower her on her way to being a new woman who seeks to be liberated from the patriarchal constraints of society. To rephrase it, magical realism enables Belli to bring back the magical Itzá from the past, symbolising the significance of the memory of other rebellious women, as a source of empowerment.

Belli attempts to rewrite the official version of the history of Nicaragua in the 1970s, placing the women at the centre of the story and reinventing their identity intertwined with the social and political condition of the nation. Lavinia's personal quest for self-discovery is directly associated with the social and political turbulence in her society as well as with the collective memories of the nation, functioning as a source of empowerment. By linking the worlds of Lavinia and Itzá, which are centuries apart, and the memories of her aunt and grandfather, Belli underscores the significance of the past and the ancestors in (re)shaping the present. To rephrase it, Belli represents the importance of the notion of collective memory. The memories of women empower other women to defy tradition and the patriarchal society and search for a new identity. By using magical occurrences, the presence of ghosts, the reincarnation of a woman in a tree and later her inhabitation of another woman, Belli connects both personal and collective memories of marginalised women with historical reality to show the inadequacy as well as the partiality of the official version of history.

The Inhabited Woman is a fictional representation of an event in Managua, Nicaragua, in 1974 when an FSLN (Sandinista National Liberation Front) guerrilla unit held a number of foreign diplomats and members of the Somoza regime hostage for many years. This incident forced the dictator to release the prisoners of the political group and to pay a large amount of money to the group. In Belli's fictionalisation of the 1974 event, one can find a mixture of facts concerning her own involvement in the preparation of the attack and with the original commando unit, which seized the home of Chema Castillo. The story, which is told by an omniscient narrator, depicts the protagonist Lavinia's awareness of love and patriarchal turmoil in the imaginary country of Fagus, fictionalising Nicaragua. However, interestingly, the novel begins and ends in a first-person narrative, which is at times intertwined into Lavinia's story. This is the voice of an indigenous warrior Itzá, who followed her lover Yarince in the battle against the Spaniards. Although she died in the battle, she is later reincarnated in an orange tree in the garden of Lavinia. Lavinia drinks orange juice from the tree and ultimately starts talking with it. As Itzá enters Lavinia's blood, her spirit of resistance seems to guide Lavinia's social and political awareness.

Just like Belli, the protagonist, Lavinia, goes through a process of self-awareness and self-development. By deciding not to stay with her parents and to become a member of the Revolution, she no longer adheres to the conventional role of a woman. Although in the beginning, Lavinia seems to be more worried about her own subjectivity and independence, being disconnected from people around her, her introduction to the Movement and later active participation there brings her into close fellowship with other women. It is only through her association with other women in the novel that she moves towards self-awareness and self-realisation female solidarity is thus enriching and empowering for women. Her magical association with the spirit of Itzá—an indigenous woman who died defending her people against the Spanish conquest—provides her some sort of agency and initiates her process of social awareness. Both Itzá and Lavinia represent women at different phases in the history of Nicaragua who strive to assert their identity and freedom in a volatile time. By providing Itzá and Lavinia a voice, Belli paves the way for female voices to be included in the history of the Americas.

Reconstructing Social and Political History and Re-connecting the Past and the Present

In *The Inhabited Woman,* we see an amalgamation of culture, history, memories, and myths which function to convey alternative visions of the history of the Americas. As a brilliant storyteller, Belli blends subjective stories with historical truth so that she can take history down to the reader's individual level. In *The Inhabited Woman,* Belli works on Central and Latin American conventional historical novel, focusing on a realistic re-creation of a historical setting, which excludes women's experiences. It, on the contrary, uses magical realism to generate spaces, giving scope for the expression of women's alternative views. Here, magical realism also bridges history and communal memory to provide women a voice, enabling them to assert their identity and a discrete position in the struggle towards independence. Thus, by revealing the lack of inclusiveness of official history and the potential of collective memory to provide multiple versions of reality, magical realism links both history and memory, and offers an alternative record from a marginalised viewpoint—in this case, a gendered one.

Belli's association with magical realism clearly helps her include a female discussion, reflecting a more reliable female experience. According to Wendy B Faris, although feminist thought strives to unshackle itself from patriarchal society, it also develops in relationship with it (*Ordinary Enchantments* 171). Faris again states, Julia Kristeva relates the female discourse with a "hidden and unconscious form of discourse that relates back to a connection to the maternal and the spiritual more than to a symbolic or (realistic) kind of speech which is aligned with the patriarchal society" (*Ordinary Enchantments* 171). In

The Inhabited Woman, magical realism and the inclusion of ghosts and female memories function together with the patriarchal rational discourse, linking Belli's narrative to a more divine level. Belli portrays the role of women in the Americas from the standpoint of strong women who are empowered by memories and spirituality. These delicate ways of confronting the dominant and oppressive social and political systems can pave the way for the understanding of the role of women in the Americas as harbingers of social changes who are no longer confined to their traditional space, rather are working along with men to influence their society. Both Itzá and Lavinia experience a total change in their identity and challenge their gender roles imposed by society by attempting to free their people. Both women are connected through magic to highlight the influence of women in each other's lives. So magic reveals, gives immaterial form to what has long been suppressed—the 'longue durée' of colonisation.

Roland Walter considers magical realism a literary mode, having the potential to represent social, cultural, and political practices that articulate the history of colonisation and decolonisation in the Americas. Walter argues that the author listed in his research work uses magical realism as a technique to recreate cultural practices based on native beliefs, rituals and traditions—a world supported by myths, magic and legend. Apart from working as a magical woman from the past, as Lavinia's source of empowerment, Itzá also stands for the memory of the past—a past which is restructured to create a meaningful present. Itzá's magical association with Lavinia empowers her to be a new woman in her attempt to find a position in a society which is changing during the social and political revolution. However, although Itzá possesses Lavinia's body, spiritually influences her, and helps her assert her identity and build awareness, she does not possess the power to change her. Itzá thus represents a feminist potential which has long been repressed but has always been in her, waiting to be magically discovered and embraced by the present.

According to Halbwachs, one significant feature of history is the fact that it restores the continuity between the past and the present (80). By allowing Itzá to occupy the body of Lavinia, Belli re-establishes the continuity of the past and the present, as well as shows the power of communal memory in the lives of individuals, particularly in the life of Lavinia. Halbwachs also focuses on the significance of past on individual groups when creating their collective memory and underpins the significance of the individuality of each group when remembering the past, which stops time to unite the groups by their collective memory. In *The Inhabited Woman*, Belli, with the help of magical realism, goes five hundred years back in history to underscore the importance of women in the past as the source of empowerment for women like Lavinia who belong to the twentieth century. By providing Itzá a voice in the story, Belli breaks the silence and passivity of marginalised native women in the history of the struggle. Belli also describes the disastrous consequence of the conquest of the Americas in the name of civilisation:

> Los españoles decían que debían 'civilizarnos', hacernos abandonar la 'barbarie'. Pero ellos, con barbarie nos dominaron, nos despoblaron. En pocos años hicieron más sacrificios humanos de los que jamás hiciéramos nosotros en la historia de nuestras festividades. Este país era el más poblado. Y, sin embargo, en los veinte y cinco años que viví, se fue quedando sin hombres los mandaron en grandes barcos a construir una lejana ciudad que llamaban Lima, los mataron [...] les cortaron la cabeza, los fusilaron [...] ¿Y de todo eso qué de bueno quedó?, me preguntó. [...] Nuestra herencia de tambores batientes ha de continuar latiendo en la sangre de estas generaciones. Es lo único de nosotros, Yarince, que permaneció: la resistencia.[1] (Belli, *La Mujer Habitada* 97-98)

The above quotation clearly depicts the brutality of the Spanish conquest of the Americas. By giving a voice to Itzá and recognising the importance of collective memory, Belli gives a voice to the marginalised and is able to rewrite history from their own point of view. Itzá believes that collective memory binds them together in fighting oppression.

Magical realism enables Belli to unite different perspectives of the history of Central America and create an alternative history from the perspectives of marginalised women by including their experiences. Both Itzá and Lavinia represent the female experiences in search of their liberation from tradition and patriarchy in different volatile periods in the history of Central America. Collective memory, magical realism, and the inclusion of women's experiences

---

[1] The Spaniards said they had to make us 'civilized', make us give up our 'barbarism'. Yet they defeated us, they decimated us barbarously. In Just a few years they made more human sacrifices than we had ever made in all the history of our festivals. This country was the most populated. And yet [...] it lost so many men. They sent them in great ships to build a distant city they called Lima. They killed them [...] cut off their heads, shot them. ... And what good remains of all this? I wonder. [...] Our legacy of beating drums is still pulsing in the blood of these generations. It's the only thing left of us, Yarince: resistance. (Belli, *The Inhabited Woman* 106-107)

in Belli's novel function together to underline the role of women in various phases in the history of the Americas, including both individual and communal perspectives of history. In *The Inhabited Woman*, individual experiences of women and their role in the history of Nicaragua add a different meaning to the official history. Magical realism as a mode of writing enables Belli to recover or discover the magical and mythical indigenous woman Itzá from the oblivion of history, symbolising the importance of the memory of other women as a source of empowerment. Being immersed in the reality of the social and political turmoil of her society, Lavinia seeks to change her life—a search which is guided by her collective memory.

Belli's employment of magical realism allows her creative freedom to deal with the notion of dispossession, particularly premature death. Itzá's magical and eternal existence stands for dispossession on multiple levels. Judith Butler and Athena Athanasiou's formulation of the term is apposite here:

> [B]eing dispossessed refers to processes and ideologies by which persons are disowned and abjected by normative and normalizing powers that define cultural intelligibility and that regulate the distribution of vulnerability: loss of land and community; ownership of one's living body by another person, as in histories of slavery; subjection to military, imperial, and economic violence; poverty, securitarian regimes, biopolitical subjectivation, liberal possessive individualism, neoliberal governmentality, and precaritization. (2)

Itzá's dispossessed condition, which was reinvented by magical realism, transforms understanding of the past through the trope of reincarnation. Focusing on time itself, Itzá states, "Porque no es tiempo de floraciones; es tiempo de frutos. Pero el árbol ha tomado mi propio calendario, mi propia vida; el ciclo de otros atardeceres. Ha vuelto a nacer, habitado con sangre de mujer"[2] (Belli, *La Mujer Habitada* 7-8). However, cycles of nature symbolise not only the passage of time but also female reproductive bodies. Elizabeth Grosz says, "[C]yclically regulated flows [...] emanate from women's bodies" (198). Grosz thus discusses the enigma of female bodies. By magically attaching the spirit of a female warrior, died some five hundred years ago, into the body of a present-

---

[2] "Because it is not flowering time, it is time to bear fruit, yet this tree has taken on my seasons, my very life, the cycle of other twilights. It has been born again, Inhabited by the blood of a woman." (ibid 8)

day female revolutionary, Belli shows the ways magic becomes flesh. This act of becoming flesh flows through female bodies from generation to generation, creating the possibility of a feminist present and future.

In *The Inhabited Woman*, Belli discovers the boundary between corporeality and temporality, where it is evident how time is divided: the body functions as the converging point between past and present. We are introduced with magical realist elements at the very beginning of the novel:

> Al amanecer emergí. Extraño es todo lo que ha acontecido desde aquel día en el agua, al última vez que vi a Yarince. Los ancianos decían en la ceremonia que viajaría hacia el Tlalocan, los jardines tibios de oriente – país del verdor y de las flores acariciadas por la lluvia tenue – pero me encontré sola por siglos en una morada de tierra y raíes, observadora asombrada de mi cuerpo deshaciéndose en humus y vegetación. Tanto tiempo sosteniendo recuerdoes, viviendo de la memoria de maracas, estruendos de caballos, los motines, las lanzas, la angustia de la pérdida.[3] (Belli, *La Mujer Habitada* 7)

The above-mentioned quotation clearly shows Itzá's long, lonely journey where her body dissolves and turns into plants. She, however, can remember her violent past and is ready to ignite the fire of resistance and revolution in women like Lavinia. In the novel, Belli eroticises traumatic experiences—body signifies both oppression and liberation. In "Uses of the Erotic", Audre Lorde considers the erotic a personification of "creative energy empowered" (55). To Belli, erotic energy has a remedial function: "reclaim[ing] the wounded erotic" (Morales 118) and engaging in a "decolonizing act of healing" (Lara 114). For Belli, the body is the storehouse of oppression, power and ecstasy.

Both Itzá and Lavinia represent women at different phases in the history of Nicaragua, who, by asserting their female identity and seeking freedom from oppression, search for their place in the official history. In the novel, the active

---

[3] I emerged at dawn. What has happened since that day in the water when I last saw Yarince is all so strange. The elders announced in the ceremony that I would travel to Tlalocan, the balmy gardens to the East—verdant country, land of flowers caressed by gentle rains—but instead I found myself alone for centuries, enclosed by earth and roots, watching in astonishment while my body dissolved into humus and vegetation. I had been holding onto my memories for so long: the sound of the maracas, the thundering of horses, rebellion, spears, the anguish of defeat. (ibid 7)

role of women in the liberation struggle arises when Felipe dies. Felipe has always attempted to dissuade Lavinia from taking an active part in the armed struggle against dictatorship in Fagus (symbolising the attempt of the Sandinista guerrillas to liberate Nicaragua from the Somoza dictatorship in the 1970s). He rather wants her to play the role of a passive supporter of the struggle. Felipe thus inherits the traditional perception about the role of women in war or revolution. His reluctance to give Lavinia the opportunity to take an active part in the war symbolises the desire of patriarchal society to deny women the entrance into history. Felipe's act of denying Lavinia access to the war alludes to women being dispossessed by patriarchal power. However, when he is deadly injured, he asks her to take his place. The reality of the war, which demands the inclusion of women, ultimately changes her perception about the role of women in war. Lavinia's narrative is thus a narrative of remembering. It tries to narrate not what history has included but what history has excluded: an attempt to fill in the gaps of women's absence in history. Later, Lavinia also dies during a sudden attack at General Vela's house. Lavinia's death symbolises what Judith Butler and Athena Athanasiou would regard as the final dispossession, that is, the "varied concepts and practices of resistance which involve dispossessing oneself as a way to dispossess coercive powers" (146). Put another way, it is only through sacrificing oneself that one can topple the oppressive power.

By rewriting Itzá'a narrative and by bringing her stories to light, Belli deals with the issue of female absence from official history. Itzá's spiritual crisis symbolises her desire and attempt for material presence, and signifies a history of colonial violence against women. However, ultimately, Itzá envisages an act of decolonisation. Itzá foretells, "Serán nuestros el oro y las plumas / el cacao y el mango / la esencia de los sacuanjoches / Nadie que ama muere jamás"[4] (Belli, *La Mujer Habitada* 342). In Itzá's prophetic vision, both utopia and dystopia merge, and land and natural objects go back to their glorious state. We see the physical death of the heroic Lavinia; however, we, the reader, hope for a society free from violence and oppression where justice will be restored. Itzá' statement thus focuses on the worthy sacrifice of her people.

Lavinia's desire to enter the men's revolution, staying outside their controlling power, comes from the magical presence of Itzá. She, therefore, wants to make the revolution her own. To save her people from the brutality of Spanish

---

[4] "The gold and the plumes will be ours / The cacao and the mango / the essence of the sacuanjoches / No one who loves will ever die." (ibid 412)

conquest by joining men on the battlefield, Itzá must struggle against her parents, her lover Yarince, and her social norms and traditions, which dub her a 'witch'. Her mother clearly warns her that the battlefield is not an appropriate place for women. However, a stronger force—a fusion of her love for her lover and for the people of her race, encouraging her to sacrifice her life for greater interest—helps Itzá break the societal barrier. She, however, is killed by the Spaniards. Through Lavinia, Itzá embodies the core concept of the novel that female agency sometimes proves itself stronger than male agency.

The spirit of Itzá, which was alive centuries ago, is a guide and counsellor for Lavinia. Roland Walter points out that Itzá is an archetypal "woman spirit [who] guides the destiny of those living in the present" (66). Itzá dies fighting the Spanish invaders, but she does not leave the mortal world. She starts living in nature and among her people. In order to fulfil her unfulfilled dream of achieving freedom and asserting identity, she tries to convince her descendants to fight oppression. We find a similar scene in Maryse Condé's *I, Tituba, Black Witch of Salem*, where the protagonist Tituba launches a war against Caribbean slave-owners as well as the patriarchal society but fails and is hanged. However, even after her death, she keeps residing in her native island, where she convinces her descendants to keep the fire of freedom alive. In both scenes, the ancestor's spirits function as guide, counsellor, and healer. It also shows the transmission of power from one woman to another and therefore advocates female solidarity and a new form of feminism.

The novel seems to consider both Itzá and Lavinia's death an exemplary sacrifice. The question may arise of what has been gained in exchange for their life. Their sacrifice clearly demonstrates the necessity of the victimised to engage in violence and to be ready to sacrifice their life to get rid of their sense of inferiority. Lavinia realises that what the revolutionaries want is to switch on the lights to put an end to the tyranny as if it was a bad film. Itzá, whose voice mingles with the voice of Lavinia, asserts, "La luz está encendida. Nadie podrá apagarla"[5] (Belli, *La Mujer Habitada* 340). Lavinia's statement shows her determination to put an end to dictatorship. The end of the novel also hints at a collective voice, which includes not only the voices of Itzá and Lavinia but also of those who have achieved a sort of eternal life (who have conquered death) by sacrificing their life for their people, for their nation. Lavinia has fused into a force and a history way loftier than herself.

---

[5] "The light has been turned on. No one will be able to put it out." (ibid 409)

Belli attacks both male bigotry and dictatorship and concludes the novel with Lavinia as a female revolutionary. In "Re-membering the Dead: Latin American Women's Testimonial Discourse", Nancy S. Sternbach states that although dictatorship and political unrest are nothing new "to the Latin American political scene, [...] women's open and direct opposition to and participation in them is" (91). Sternbach's statement, therefore, highlights women's active participation in the Movement against dictatorship. Tracing Chilean women's resistance, Annie G. Dandavati says,

> Women struggled to become independent agents involved in determining the direction in which their country would move. They not only protested the political, economic, and socio-cultural domination of the military regime, but also sought to transform the existing situation and offered an alternative vision of society based on democracy, equity and horizontal social relations. (6)

The above-mentioned quotation clearly suggests Latin American Women's desire to protest political and social violence as well as to come up with an alternative history based on democracy and equal opportunity. According to Dandavati, the movements of Latin American women are "more than a reaction to the cultural model of domination and authoritarianism envisaged by the regime [involving] a process of creation as well" (8). Margarite Fernández Olmos argues that recently, there has been a surge of "female 'voice' in literature that distinguishes itself from the Latin American patriarchal tradition" (139). Concerning women's desire to be heard, written and read, Sternbach notes, "Women's participation in revolutionary struggles witnessing murders of loved ones, suffering disappearances, rapes, tortures, and perhaps most poignantly, women's specific resistance to military rule, all attest to their own condition [...] which propels them to ensure that their story is heard, written, and read" (96). Belli keeps protesting all sorts of atrocities against women through her writing, provided that her tales are listened to and read. In *The Inhabited Woman*, Belli attacks the patriarchal constraints as well as the Somoza dictatorship. Taking a gendered standpoint in her novel, Belli describes the double marginalisation (gendered and ideological) of the protagonist, Lavinia. Through the stories of marginalised women, Belli offers an alternative and feminine version of Nicaraguan history.

The inclusion of Itzá as a character of the invasion of the Americas by the Spanish symbolises a philosophical standpoint, questioning the function of violence in various wars across time. The protagonist, Lavinia herself, is doubtful about the use of violence in the liberation struggle when a rebel named Sebastian is injured and brought to her home by her boyfriend Felipe. Witnessing the high extent of violence associated with the freedom struggle, Lavinia gets confused whether to take part in the Movement. Itzá witnessed the same violence some five hundred years ago when people of her tribe had to fight the Spanish invaders. As a magical and mythical character, Itzá is also a way to connect both Lavinia's and her world divided by time, enabling Belli to show the continuity of violence. Although time has changed, violence and oppression still exist in Nicaragua and, to a greater extent, in the Americas. There is a lack of female participation in decision-making or in other important issues, and some sort of gender inequality, although female desire to take part in the Movement is accepted by fellow male warriors. Magic enables women to have their own voice and, thus, alternative expression. So, it is something which has the potential to create a space where alternative views may emerge and sustain.

Lavinia's Process of Self-discovery and Re-defining her Identity

At the beginning of the story, Lavinia seems to be disconnected from the oppression around her and more worried about the assertion of her own identity, subjectivity and independence. Paradoxically and interestingly, Lavinia's desire for independence alienates her from other women as they prefer not to come out of their comfort zone and assert identity, and places her in the hand of male dominance. Throughout the text, Belli highlights the fact that it is Lavinia's involvement in the Movement and "the vicissitudes of class struggle [which] bring her into fellowship with other women" (Reid 63). At the beginning of their relationship, Lavinia magically arouses memories of gender repression in Itzá's mind. However, gradually Itzá is able to convince Lavinia and provides her with the courage to be involved in the Movement against dictatorship. Both Itzá and Lavinia end up at the same point: dying for their people. By remembering many women of her time who failed to gather the courage to protest oppression and thus lived and died like slaves of the Spanish invaders, Itzá allows Belli to place the anti-dictatorship movement by her people in the tradition of previous struggles for liberation from a cruel oppressor. Narrating the battle where Itzá's people sacrificed their elders and wore their skins to terrify the Spaniards, shows the way(s) Belli's narrative attempts to present the guerrillas' death as courageous, and the armed struggle as the only choice against tyranny.

Being magically inhabited and thus motivated by Itzá, Lavinia initiates her process of growing social awareness. However, she does not turn to her boyfriend, and rebel, Felipe, for any answers, as he never encourages her to take an active part in the Movement. She later turns to Flor, the female nurse who helped to cure Sebastian's wound in Lavinia's house. Although Flor is a die-hard revolutionary, in questioning the attitudes of self-announced male revolutionaries like Felipe and Sebastian, she sides with Lavinia. Flor's action sheds light on the fact that even in war, women feel more comfortable with other female comrades than with male ones. There is a clearly gendered standpoint in the way Flor narrates Lavinia her own involvement in the Movement, whereas Lavinia is encouraged by her aunt Inés in her childhood to be an independent woman. Flor was adopted by her uncle in her childhood and by the time she reached her teen, she became his mistress. Being introduced to the Movement by Sebastian, Flor finally realises by herself that she cannot find in the Movement the only way to achieve her and her people's freedom. Here, Belli is gendering the communal responsibility of revolutionary ideology. In her novel, women enter the war with the help of other women to change the situation of other marginalised women. Itzá's act of inhabiting Lavinia's body and mind clearly shows her desire to fulfil her abortive attempt to fight oppression and to find a place in history.

Although Lavinia is involved in the Movement by her boyfriend Felipe, she has always been inspired by her aunt Inés and later by the magical warrior from the past, Itzá, to assert her independence and thus to defy patriarchal constraints. The magical presence of Itzá ignites some sort of fire in Lavinia to change her marginalised status and slowly but steadily assert her identity. The employment of magical realist narrative, possessing subversive and transgressive ability and the ability to provide an alternative history, also symbolises a postmodern standpoint of doubting a singular version of truth or history and of changing the realist narrative technique to be able to provide a voice to the marginalised women and thus to secure their inclusion in the official history. Lavinia's journey can be considered a self-discovery narrative as it deals with her search for identity and assertion of freedom amid violence and oppression. The memories of Aunt Inés and the presence of the magical female warrior Itzá, who also attempts to persuade Lavinia to continue the legacy of the Revolution, inspire her to initiate the slow process of self-discovery and to assert her identity and independence.

Lavinia's spiritual connection with Itzá represents the connection of women through memories in general. Being connected with Lavinia, Itzá symbolises collective memory, allowing history and collective memory to be interpreted in order to recreate the past, to understand the present and to build a better future. Lavinia's desire to create her own private space and to have an independent life defies the norms of the patriarchal society of Fagus where women are supposed to marry and have families. However, this desire is also followed by her doubt and tension to break away from tradition. Characters in the novel, representing both past and present, help Lavinia redefine her female identity and reassert her independence, challenged by the social and political turmoil in Fagus. To rephrase it, it is Lavinia's situation in the present and memories of the past which merge together to empower her in search of her true identity. Understanding Lavinia's doubt and fear, Itzá takes care of her and provides her with mental strength: "[...] puedo comprender su temor, teñirlo de fuerza"[6] (Belli, *La Mujer Habitada* 79). This statement thus strengthens my view that magical realism in the form of ancestors' spirits provides characters with guidance in difficult times so that they remain courageous and on track.

By showing mutual respect and solidarity, female characters in the novel play an important role in the development of the new history in Central America. Apart from Itzá, the memory of Aunt Inés also motivates Lavinia in her search for change. The orange tree, which is the reincarnation of Itzá grows in the garden Lavinia inherited from Inés, who has encouraged her in a number of ways. Belli provides Lavinia with an entire house, which inspires her and gives her the opportunity to be alone and on her own. Put another way, the house with the orange tree, which Lavinia has received from Inés, symbolises the space which allows Lavinia to initiate her independent life. In the warmth of her house, Lavinia received affection from Aunt Inés, which she missed from her parents, and thus developed a life-long relationship with her. Inspired by Inés, Lavinia initiates a lonely search for change as well as engages herself in a collective social and political change to uproot oppression from society. During her strenuous training in the guerrilla recruitment camp, she remembers Inés, which gives her physical and mental comfort:

> [Lavinia] Tenía frío. Al poco tiempo le castañeteaban los dientes y los escalofríos le recorrían el cuerpo. Pensó en Flor para darse ánimos, en Lucrecia, en Sebastián. Recurría de vez en cuando al recuerdo del general Vela para que la rabia y la repulsión la sostuvieren. Finalmente pensó en su tía Inés [...].[7] (Belli, *La Mujer Habitada* 244)

---

[6] "I can understand her fear and imbue it with strength." (ibid 85)

[7] [Lavinia] was cold. Soon her teeth were chattering, and she felt chills through her whole

Lavinia, through her memories, retains Inés' experiences so that she can assert her identity in volatile times. The memory of revolutionary like Inés conveys their craving for a change in the role of women in a male-dominated society.

The Inhabited Woman is a wonderful display of female agency and female contribution to Nicaraguan history, which has been largely ignored in the official history. By magically associating Itzá with Lavinia's body, Belli enables Itzá to fulfil her unattained desire for freedom and assertion of identity. By employing magical realist elements in the form of Itzá, Belli has not only established a connection between the past and the present but also showed the significance of communal memory on individuals in fighting oppression. By breaking the silence of marginalised women in the history of Nicaragua, Belli has created an alternative history from the perspectives of women, capable of voicing the unspeakable stories of female sufferings during the Spanish invasion and the Somoza dictatorship. Although Lavinia is not encouraged by her lover Felipe to take an active part in the Movement against the dictatorial government, it is the spirit of Itzá that ignites in her the fire of resistance against, and freedom from, a patriarchal society. Belli has employed the magical realist figure Itzá also as the source of comfort and guidance for women like Lavinia in fighting oppression. By giving voice to the marginalised women through spirits and memories of strong women in various phases of history, magical realism has provided a crucial platform to women and thus created a certain consciousness about the radical potential of gender. Even today in the twenty-first century, magical realism keeps proving its worth by giving the oppressed a voice and identity and providing an alternative history from their own perspective.

---

body. She thought of Flor, Lucrecia and Sebastian to keep her courage up. Once in a while she thought of General Vela so that rage and revulsion would keep her going. Finally, she thought of her Aunt Inés [...]. (ibid 281)

Part II.
Resisting Colonial Constraints and Asserting Female Identity

Chapter 6

Relating Women with Cultural and Socio-Political Framework and Highlighting the Issues of Marginality in Kiana Davenport's *Shark Dialogues*

Kiana Davenport's 1994 novel *Shark Dialogues* emphasises the role of memory in creating alternative realities, restoring the process of cultural memory, and thus reconstructing social identity distorted by colonial rule. By including Hawaiian women with complex identities as having a strong role in the history of the nation and describing their participation for the wellbeing of the descendants, Davenport attempts to investigate the colonial and neocolonial (postcolonial) history of Hawaii. She also shows female resistance against both patriarchal and colonial systems, thus confirming cultural and environmental unity. By linking bodies, lands, and languages, she attempts to establish a relationship of women with social, cultural, and political frameworks, and resistance against environmental destruction with a battle against socio-political marginalisation. Davenport takes a brave and ambitious attempt to redefine Hawaiian history from a Hawaiian, particularly female Hawaiian, perspective; it is, therefore, through female voices and bodies that the history of violence on, and abuse of, women is described. The brutality against Hawaiian women and the destruction of environment, both of which are interrelated, opens the multiple history of a huge cultural dispossession suffered by Hawaiian people, particularly women. This novel is thus about the feminisation of Hawaii in the backdrop of native cultural recuperation and identity formation. By blending magical realism and proven facts (history), linking present realities with ancient myth, and disrupting traditional concepts of time and space, Davenport allows the multiple perspectives of the marginalised voices to surface. When the narrative depicts Pono's journeys and the entire family history, and ultimately focuses on female bodies and their memories, it creates a web of polyphonic narratives, which echoes through the narrative and adds potency to it and the history of Hawaii.

In *Shark Dialogues*, Davenport tells the story of six generations of a Hawaiian family which starts with a runway Tahitian princess named Kelonikoa and a white seaman called Mathys. Sensing her death, the matriarch Pono, who rejected her own daughters due to their marrying non-Hawaiians, summons her four granddaughters to pass on pieces of their heritage to them and to create within them a sort of commitment to the Hawaiian soil. The granddaughters, who have mixed identities and fragmented personal histories, follow Pono's order to learn their past, as Lyons considers "the granddaughters [...] a spectrum of Hawaiian hybridity and history" (265). There is Rachel, a *hapa*-Japanese who never met her father and has been eroticised and objectified by her Yakuza husband; Vanya, a *hapa*-Filipino advocate of native rights; Ming, a *hapa*-Chinese who is often under drugs to get rid of the pain of *lupus*; and Jess, a *hapa-haole* veterinarian in New York. The various backgrounds and elements of the four granddaughters of Pono weave a tapestry of history, creating a sense of hybridity and fragmentation of female selves. Lyons argues that Pono's acceptance of her granddaughters' hybridity "is a way of coming to terms with the complexions of modern Hawai'i and perpetuating her own connection with the land" (265). The story, which develops through the narratives of Pono, Run Run (Pono's friend), Duke (Pono's lover), and Pono's four granddaughters, tends to emphasise the strong bond between women and their families and the political subjects they encounter as individuals where their existence is moulded by colonial and postcolonial establishments.

Under the layer of magical realist narrative, Davenport investigates controversial issues of tourism, prostitution and sexual desire, and regional subjugation of native women by male colonisers. Rotating around the lives of the members of a Hawaiian family and entailing their personal history within the public sphere, Davenport enables the native women to reinterpret history from their native perspectives. It is through Pono and her magical gift as a *kahuna* to remember her forefathers, Davenport attempts to record the initiation of colonisation in Hawaii until the way it is described in the present day by including more recent issues where the vast wealth of Hawaii was considered a mere commodity for the colonisers to be exploited to benefit the metropolitan areas. The US ecological imperialism has widespread consequences on the Hawaiians, displacing them from their ancestral living environment. Indriyanto opines that "though the land itself are returned through the abolishment of Great Mahele, reconciliation with the past living of indigenous Hawai'ians prove to be impossible (131)." Honolulu, the capital of Hawaii, turns into a luxurious western city and becomes a representation of American colonisation in Hawaii. The ecological colonisation becomes severe through the military domination in Hawaii, which started during WWII and continued through the Cold War period, causing the amalgamation of nuclear weapons in Pearl Harbour and increasing the threat of the accumulation of pollution and nuclear radiation.

Using Cultural Memory to Reconstruct (Social) Identity and to Create an Alternative Reality

Shark Dialogues can quite easily be called a narrative of, and about, memory from Davenport's dedicating the novel to "the memory of [her] mother [and] the memory of [her] aunty" (Davenport 1) to Jess's expectation about the family past which will be "more beautiful in remembering" (481). The novel can be an outstanding piece of literature to understand the ways postcolonial subjects employ cultural memory to reconstruct social and political identity, to challenge the consequences of colonialism and to create an alternative reality from a marginalised standpoint. To Hawaiians, the power of cultural memory has long been significant in constructing identity. Cultural memory is almost always subjective, manifold, and fissured; however, it is a strong force in constructing identities—both individual and collective. As Mieke Bal writes, cultural memory has "displaced and subsumed the discourses of individual (psychological) memory and of social memory" (vii). In *Shark Dialogues*, characters experience a shift from a colonial to a postcolonial identity, try to negotiate with both identities, and ultimately attempt to describe a new and alternative identity which is combined and emancipated.

The novel severely criticises the negative effect of colonialism and postcolonialism on the Native—the destructive outcomes of the Pearl Harbour attack, the forced recruitment of the Hawaiians in the Vietnam War, and the risky decision to tackle the US hegemony through terrorist activities. The story moves back and forth from the historical to a fictional level, creating some sort of fissured narrative which supports the formation of characters in their personal domain. Official history thus becomes personal and subjective, giving a chance to characters to place them in a historical timeline and to reinterpret history itself. In the novel, family history thus parallels the history of Hawaiian colonialism. From the moment of the first meeting between Kelonikoa and Mathys, which occurs in the moment of history when Hawaii gets colonised by the whites, Davenport records all the historical moments—the loss of land, wiping out of Hawaiian population due to the spread of western diseases, the US annexation of Hawaii, the removal of Queen Lili'uokalani, the consequence of Pearl Harbour attack and the Second World War, ecological imperialism, nuclear pollution and so on—from the viewpoint of the colonial victims. Coming to visit the islands, US President Franklin Roosevelt wished to see a sample of the "islands' majestic 'aborigines', a stately reminder of what Hawaiians had once been" (Davenport 153). Fully realising the outcomes of colonial history, Pono says, '"That's how they see us,' [...]. 'Porters, servants. Hula dancers, clowns. They never see us as we are, complex, ambiguous, inspired humans"' (341). Dominant colonial culture portrayed the Hawaiians as a romantic, disappearing race to be extinct by modern development, and their culture has been stereotyped for tourist enjoyment. Rimstead argues that the state and the dominant group or culture have the ability to manipulate the past to utilise the present for their benefits, and it is thus the responsibility of the marginalised "groups or individuals to construct counter-memory to oppose state control" (2) which will definitely challenge colonial authority. Davenport's treatment of historical treatment of Hawaii forces the reader to face the colonial history not from the standpoint of the victimisers but from the victims.

In the beginning of the novel, all four granddaughters of Pono are shown in a stage in moving to postcolonial identity where their identities are determined in a colonial milieu, in terms of colonial cultural memory where each character feels physically and psychologically displaced due to their separation from families, cultural heritage and communities. The granddaughters' confusion regarding their identity is the outcome of a colonial discourse which considers them as incomplete, as mixed-bred. Being the descendants of the Tahitian princess, Kelonikoa, and the white sailor, Mathys, the granddaughters have been in-between two cultures and have never been able to fully accept either side of their heritage. They also feel torn between two contrasting cultures or worlds: that of the colonisers and the natives. As Davenport writes, "Half-caste children were considered blessed with the superiority of white blood, cursed with the native half" (57). However, to be able to initiate the process of restructuring their pasts and of establishing new identities, they have to recognise the operations of colonial history. They must understand that their sense of isolation and displacement is the outcome of such colonial history. Chanady talks about the way(s) cultural memory is created and substituted for official colonial version of the past. She writes that cultural memory "always involves a complex process of selection and transformation that raises problems of representation, access to privileged channels of expression and competing constructions of the imaginary community" (Chanady, "Cultural Memory" 183). Cultural memory thus requires the intervention of many individuals and groups. After achieving an understanding of history and the manner it is depicted by colonial authority, characters have the ability to initiate the process of constructing alternative realities.

Regarding the four granddaughters' identity crisis, it is Pono who needs to provide the ultimate pieces, the "unraveled narrative they needed to solve" (Davenport 14). Although initially, Pono is against her granddaughters, considering them as "half of something else" (Davenport 233) due to their containing white blood, it is her lover Duke who assures her about the significance of memory by saying, '"I CONFESS to remembering"' (326). Duke says, '"You're hybrids, all of you. You're what the future is'" (374). Although Pono retells Duke about their oath not to remember the past in order to '"not mourn what could have been"', he replies, '"[...] what is the difference? Memory. Dreams. At this age, it's much the same"' (278). Pono realises that if she and Duke fail to provide her granddaughters with the much-needed cultural memory, they are simply to be '"women without history"' (282). As Stephen Spencer says, "Pono comes to understand the power the telling of memory holds—that it can open to them new, previously hidden vistas of experience" (16). She tells her granddaughters, "Now. I am going to tell you a story. When I finish ... you will know who you are" (Davenport 328). After starting to narrate the past, she gets "access to a world that had remained invisible, therefore not real, until the telling" (330). It is thus Pono's telling stories from memories which turns the invisible visible, negates colonial history and refines their (her and the granddaughters') identities. After Pono's death, it is her granddaughter Jess who assumes the role of carrying on the family history, including all family members whose lives are "still attached and flowing, in myths, dreams, imaginings. Lives permanently because someone, Jess, was there to pass them on" (481). As a present-day female Hawaiian, Jess will, therefore, rebuild a postcolonial reality, combining personal, collective, and cultural histories. Besides, as male and female Hawaiians vehemently protested cultural integration, indigenous culture did not go extinct in spite of being dominated by colonial rules. Run Run thus stress on the significance of conveying family history to connect the granddaughters with the land and to recuperate ancient knowledge practices: '"You do it for *kahe koko*, flow of blood, for *kahe 'aumakua*, flow of ancestors. Dese girls been livin' empty-handed in da world. Now you gonna' give dem dere destiny'" (Davenport 324).

Linking Bodies, Lands, and Languages to Critique Phallocentric Discourse

The arrival of the first group of colonisers in Hawaii and later the Christian missionaries brought a devastating cluster of events, forcing the native people to drastically change their social and spiritual relationship patterns and thus almost destroying Hawaiian culture. Apart from the dislocation and cultural degradation of Hawaiians, the arrival of the sailors also brought various diseases to the island, which removed a large portion of the population: "their bodies carried 'sailor's pox', always fatal to natives, [...] they were spreading it island to island as a way of conquering the Pacific" (Davenport 44). Apart from placing history within the historical context of Hawaii and highlighting the significance of reevaluating the position of the native in postcolonial discourse, Davenport quite visibly explores the essential connection between women and nature, giving women a voice and consciousness which has the ability to knock down male authority and to foresee a world devoid of female oppression. It is obvious that through the confrontation between male colonisers and native females, there arises some sort of sexual desire and territorial subjugation. Leela Gandhi writes, "[M]asculinity of empire was articulated, in the first instance, through the symbolic feminisation of conquered geographies, and in the erotic economy of colonial 'discovery' narratives" (98-99). As Rocha says, "Indeed female characters in *Shark Dialogues* encapsulate a multiplicity of cultural histories in their agency and they are portrayed as metaphors of a colonized country dealing with the fragmentation of identities" (86). The novel demonstrates the way its characters identify and manipulate history. Thus, the history depicted from the viewpoints of Hawaiian women is an alternative and hotchpotch one which interweaves the past, present and future and where their identities are constantly shifting.

By linking magical realism with historical realities and disrupting the traditional notion of time and space, Davenport gives the marginalised a voice and allows them to create multiple or alternative versions of history, challenging the official one. By placing magical realism underneath a family chronicle, she enables its female characters to include their own version of history. The protagonist Pono—a *kahuna*, meaning someone with healing and supernatural powers—has the psychic power and the ability to magically transform herself into a shark deity. Nevertheless, Davenport exposes the obscurity of the transformation in a magical realist manner where the reader is free to decide if it was an illusory or a real transformation: "Then she remembered she was asleep, that her shark form was imagined. ... In her mouth there was blood and the taste of raw fish. ... And though she was in the world of humans, she was no longer wholly of that world" (Davenport 106). Instead of mythologising the events, Pono's magical power, and her transformation into a shark are treated very much like any other ordinary occurrences of her life. The narrative combines opposing realms or realities where magical or improbable events take place frequently and are treated as probable. Although the doubt or confusion found in magical realist narratives are probably a means to "reconcile two contradictory understanding of events" (Faris, *Ordinary Enchantments* 17), Davenport's novel quite clearly accepts the simultaneous existence of two different, and possibly contradictory, realms. Thus, Pono's spiritual interaction with nature, her transformation into a shark, the *kahuna* power and her granddaughter Jess's ability to predict the future are all placed within a real(istic) setting and are considered mundane.

The introducing of magical (realist) elements in the story emphasises the notion of marginality, the best example of which will be Pono's ability as a soothsayer. Since she was left by a parent and is a woman without identity or community, she is ultimately a symbol of marginality, and is therefore dreaded, othered and antagonised by those who come to her to get advice on personal issues. However, although as a *kahuna* Pono possesses shamanistic power and has access to ancient native knowledge, she is incapable of foreseeing her own future. Faris elucidates,

> Beyond the connection to primitive cultures or mythologies, magical realism is a narrative in which, as in a shamanic performance, the viewing or reading community experiences a discourse that suggests the existence of a different kind of reality contiguous to or within their ordinary one. This form of discourse with its magical images of uncertain origin can also be seen to continue the tradition of a shamanistic visionary or vatic stances. (*Ordinary Enchantments* 75)

Quite apparently, the two opposing realms—everyday and magical—are overlapped and intertwined to assert the peculiarities and uncertainties of Hawaiian identities. By focusing on Hawaiian culture, tradition and folklore, Davenport exposes a "submerged politics of cultural appropriation and dissemination, and an unconcealed politics of personal solidarity and resistance" (Rocha 94). Nonetheless, magical realism does not show any lack of interest to social disorder, and social and gender issues, but rather provides the space to shed light and question those issues as well as to doubt a singular conception of reality or history as Faris asserts, "[I]t seems as though the magic frees the discourse, the history grounds the story, and the vitality of the text depends on keeping the lines open between them" (*Ordinary Enchantments* 165). Connecting magical realism with its postmodern approach to historiography, Anne Hegerfeldt opines,

> [A] considerable number of magic realist works may also be categorized as "historiographic metafiction" or "fantastic histories". These works undertake rewritings of official versions of history, playfully offering alternative accounts. By telling the story from a different, usually oppressed perspective, they reveal the extent to which history never consists of purely factual and impartial accounts, but serves the interests of those who write it. Historiography's claim to objectivity again is critically examined in texts that probe the possibilities of accurately knowing the past in the first place, drawing attention to gaps in historical knowledge and the way these are filled through interpretation and reconstruction. ("Contentious Contributions" 63)

Concurring with Hegerfeldt, I can assert that magical realist authors attempt to rewrite the past from a marginalised perspective—in *Shark Dialogues*, from a female and (post)colonial perspective—to include the excluded stories of the unprivileged due to ideological differences. In the novel, women, mainly Pono, and the postcolonial characters come up with their own versions of history to let the world know the abuses inflicted on them and to find a place in history.

Davenport constantly points to the gap between the way non-Hawaiians see Hawaii and Hawaiians, and Hawaiians (both insiders and outsiders) see Hawaii from the shore. Davenport writes about Jess: "Living here now, she saw in the papers and on TV tragedies that never reached mainland America" (Davenport 371), and "She felt herself slipping into Pidgin, which always made talk more intimate and real" (245). However, it is obvious that it is not only about a simple difference in perspectives. There are significant differences between Hawaiian and coloniser cultures. For Hawaiians, one's shark deity is sacred, a concept which is undoubtedly bizarre to Western empiricist culture. Pono's sprouting fins and becoming a shark is the most magical realistic event of the novel, and the cultural clashes between two spiritual systems become obvious when a shark kills a swimmer, and the hunters attempt to kill the shark. Pono, meaning good or righteous in Hawaiian, is a woman of "epic height" (377), "mythic proportion" (241) and "dark fairy tale" (14). She is a *kahuna*, a shaman and healer possessing a magical connection with nature, who holds out her arms, reciting, and "wild boar in the jungle went down on their knees. When she sang, flowers changed color, spotted deer dissolved into the bark of trees as hunters passed with bow and arrow" (Davenport 29). As a shaman, Pono is able to "peer into the life of her ancestors, a *haole* (white person) named Matthys Conradson as her great-great-grandfather, Pono's grandmother Emma and her maternal lineage from Lili" (Indriyanto 128). Pono's communion with her dead ancestors is her source of delight and guidance, which underlines my proposition that in a magical realist novel, dead ancestors play a significant role in the lives of characters if a meaningful relationship with them can be established. Since Pono possesses a spiritual connection with nature and the landscape of Hawaii, she is tremendously afflicted by its destruction. Sometimes she hears the land screams in horror: '"Ainaaaa ... Ainaaa ...' The land. The land" (Davenport 191). As Pono considers it her own responsibility to save her land and culture, she vehemently protests the disrespect of American government in their plan to establish power plants just above the ancient graveyards of local Hawaiian ancestors. Pono explains that the government has the plan to '"raze this rain forest of old *koa* trees, build five power plants [...] over ancient, burial shrines'" (191), have the holy trees '"splintered into wood chips, burned to generate further electricity"' (191), build a "'huge spaceport [...] on the [...] grounds of our ancestors'" (192), and establish "'a nine-hundred-million-dollar Riviera Resort'" that "'will [...] kill off everything this side of the island'" (192). All these initiatives clearly show the US authority's lack of respect towards nature and indigenous culture and rituals and highlight the tendency towards materialistic achievement.

Female discourse in magical realist tales is contradictory, containing both the dominant mode and the silenced or marginalised group. Feminist narratives can well be associated with ethnic literatures on the ground that both can encourage decolonising practice and provide the space to imagine alternative possibilities. Many female writers find magical realism as the way to question, protest and decolonize, and consider it as a potential narrative style to voice their (hi)stories, unsettling the dominance of realism as a narrative mode. The supernaturally real bodies of Davenport's female characters are inscribed in their social, political, cultural, and geographical location, providing them with a sort of subjective and corporeal aspect; therefore, "the stories and the bodily events combine into their joint lived experience" (Faris, *Ordinary Enchantments* 191). It is with the magical realist technique/narrative that Davenport links bodies, lands, and languages to enable her female characters to negotiate different domains, and to critique phallocentric discourse.

Regarding Native American women and gynarchy—women-run societies highlighting matrilineality, female goddess and female control on domesticity—Paula Gunn Allen states, "the colonizer saw (and rightly) that as long as women held unquestioned power of such magnitude, attempts at local conquest of the continents were bounded to fail" (3). Several authors have talked about the issue of women as significant and influential in Native cultures and emphasised the necessity of outwitting them in order to dominate the native males by the colonisers or conquerors. The capacity of female bodies to give birth to children confirms women's essentiality in preserving purity and solidarity within a race or community. Therefore, rape and other sorts of sexual violence on women sticker them as 'taken' by the opposition, and make them, as well as their community, impure and polluted. Women being raped by the opposition and getting pregnant brings shame to their male counterparts and weakens their confidence, as the newborn babies will not carry on the native legacy but rather that of the conquerors. Women are thus used as commodities or means through which the invaders can destroy native culture and tradition.

Same notion can be applied to the portrayal of women regarding their sexuality, as women's sexuality and the capacity to give birth to children are quite significant in preserving the purity and honour of a community and in escaping from dominant authorities or structures. However, due to their differing sexual and maternal experiences, women view maternity or childbirth differently, where it can bring the greatest joy and the worst nightmare for them as well as subjugation to men. Pono's personal account of her story clearly sheds light on the brutal side of motherhood and childbirth. After being raped by the white landlord of the sugar plantation, Pono conceived, and none of her desperate attempts to abort the child helped her. In an attempt to take revenge of her rape and at the same time of colonial violence and racial subjugation of the natives, she killed her own newborn child without any hesitation: "An infant bleat. And then a smaller strip of sheet into its tiny mouth, round its tiny neck" (Davenport 134-135). Davenport graphically describes Pono's cry as the representative cry of people who are tortured, victimised, and murdered, women who have been sexually assaulted and/or raped, and people who got infected with fatal diseases brought by the colonisers:

> She screamed for the indignities, the years she died innumerably. She screamed for her grandmother, Emma, dead of plague, her grandfather, murdered in cold blood. She screamed for strikers murdered in their sleep, and women forced to lie with syphilitic strangers. ... She screamed, mourning slaughtered innocence, the part of her forever dead. (Davenport 134)

Pono's cry represents those marginalised dehistoricised people—women, natives, colonised—who are deprived of their history and are not given any voice to speak about their suffering. Although Pono has been dependent on her lover, Duke, concerning her private matters, she proves herself self-determining and transgressive when it is all about public issues, therefore putting a challenge to patriarchal dominance on the public level.

Shark Dialogues is both a postmodern and magical realist novel as it does not offer any solutions or answers to any raised questions; it rather depicts multiple, even contrasting, versions of history and discloses power discourse. Davenport's narrative can be termed 'herstory' due to its emphasis on issues related to women; however, here, men are not discarded from female genealogies. Since Davenport challenges narrative singularity to achieve plurality and variety, she depicts "fictive corporeality which tends to fragment or render uneven the traditional coalesced identity or subjectivity of characters" (Rocha 100). As Linda Hutcheon writes, "[T]here is a view of the past, both recent and remote, that takes the present powers and limitations of the writing of that past into account. And the result is often a certain avowed provisionality and irony" (90). Davenport's novel emphasises the excluded past of the marginalised, where history is told from the unexpressed tales of women intertwined with the creation of a hybrid and/or postcolonial identity. Women working together to oppose postcolonialism or neocolonialism assert their own feministic views gathered or constructed from their cultural struggle. Concerning female unity as strength and a means of creating alternative history or narrative, Haunani-Kay Trask argues that women should assist and guide each other to "create alternatives [and] to fashion new ways of resisting" (108) since "to be doubly colonized–as a woman and as an indigenous nationalist–means to struggle twice as hard, twice as long [...]" (15). Pono's act of calling back her granddaughters and informing them everything about their cultural heritage is a way of women supporting other women to avoid cultural and gender subjugation and to fight patriarchy.

Davenport's analysis of social and political issues in her novel is continuously arbitrated through the human body as metaphor, and therefore there is an employment of corporeal symbolism. According to Rocha, Davenport offers "an extended interrogation of Western constructions of the female exotic body [and] uses the human body as a vehicle for presenting new conceptualizations of the position of women in a contemporary Hawaiian society" (101). Bhabha explains, in colonial discourse "the body is always simultaneously (if conflictually) inscribed in both the economy of pleasure and desire and the economy of discourse, domination and power" (*The Location of Culture* 96). Bhabha identifies the bodily standard on which the formation of differences relies inside the colonial backdrop; again, it connects sexual cravings with desire for dominance. Julia Kristeva's notions of "clean and proper body"

(Kristeva 72), and the contrast between impure bodies and socially appropriate bodies can be a suitable means to explore the response to decay or corruption in Hawaii. Although in most of the cases, it is women who are depicted as abject or impure, in *Shark Dialogues,* it is Duke's body which has been discussed. Davenport symbolically extends the issue that leprosy describes the humiliation of the nation, the destruction of law and order induced by contamination, and corruption accompanied with colonialism. The fact that Pono tries hard to contract the illness so that he can be transported to the island where leprosy patients are objects of medical research but is proved immune to it, turns the gender hierarchy upside down, placing women in a more privileged position than men.

Kiana Davenport relates female victimisation as well as their empowerment with their cultural and political, more specifically (post/neo)colonial, contexts through magical realism in *Shark Dialogues* where she resorts to their local belief and myth. Quite interestingly, Davenport equates geographical land with a female body, and colonial invasion of the land with physical and sexual oppression of women and, therefore severely criticises a colonial and phallocentric discourse. Besides demonstrating the disastrous consequences of cultural and environmental destruction on women, Davenport also highlights their resistance to both colonial and patriarchal constraints. By describing colonial invasion, and socio-political history of Hawaii from a female perspective, Davenport gives the marginalised women a voice and creates an alternative and, more specifically, feminised version of Hawaiian history. It is by incorporating magical elements in the story, she comes up with the notion of marginality, represented by the character of Pono, who possesses ancient native knowledge. Pono's anguish represents the collective suffering of her own people at the destruction of native culture. Her shamanistic healing and supernatural power, and her communication with her dead ancestors enable her to fight both patriarchal and colonial oppression. When the narrative depicts Pono's journey towards a remote land, far away from civilisation, and into entire family (hi)stories and ultimately focuses on female bodies and their memories, it creates a web of polyphonic narratives, which adds potency to Pono's narrative and to her version of the history of Hawaii.

Chapter 7

Resisting White Supremacy and Constructing Ethnic and Female Identity: Magical Resistance in Louise Erdrich's *Tracks*

Native American author Louise Erdrich's 1988 novel *Tracks* highlights conflict between the Native and US government regarding land and territory, and the internal struggles of the members of the tribe. By incorporating myth and magic, the novel focuses on the Native in a Chippewa reservation between the winter of 1912 and the summer of 1924, depicting white invasion and the subsequent loss of native lives and lands. The narration of the entire story mixes both oral and written style and alternates between Nanapush, a tribal leader, and Paulne, a mix-blooded girl who, over the course of the novel, shows her inclination to white culture, ultimately showing the novel's potential to be analysed from both postcolonial and postmodern viewpoints. The plot of the novel is circular, moving back and forth in space and time, blurring the borders between the mortal and the intangible/immortal world, and creating coherence. By giving Native American women a voice by the means of magic, the novel centres on alternative version(s) of history or reality, and the postmodern notion of comprehending the past and memory. Through the dominance of encroaching white supremacy over Native culture, Erdrich attempts to show the way the male natives start practicing the gendering of social roles, ignoring the fact that Native American societies have always demonstrated gendered equality. However, by giving women magical power, Erdrich enables them to free themselves from both patriarchal and colonial constraints and to assert their gender identity. However, the reader will find fewer number of magical elements in her writing than in other authors' writing included in this book. Instead of painting narratives through magic, Erdrich has employed the supernatural as a means of resistance to colonial supremacy and to protect and mourn her native culture as Caleb Tankersley asserts that "this magical resistance morphs into a future-focused vision of tribal rebirth and a new Native identity that can retain a sense of the supernatural in the post-colonial world" (Tankersley 21).

Tracks depicts the time when being deprived of their rights on their lands and resources, Native Americans were forced to live in the wretched conditions of the reservation and to face cultural extinction at the hands of white invaders where their descendants were forgetting their glorious past, traditions and rituals. Because of the arrival of white colonisers and, the violence they inflict on the Natives, and the diseases they bring with them, the number of native people in the US went down from "between four and five million at the time of the Columbian invasion" to "250,000 to 300,000 Indians by the end of the nineteenth century" (Cheyfitz, "Introduction" viii). This violence towards native people is the setting of the novel that can be perceived from the very first chapter where Nanapush tells Lulu:

> We started dying before the snow, and like the snow, we continued to fall. It was surprising there were so many of us left to die. For those who survived the spotted sickness from the south, our long fight west to Nadouissioux land where we signed the treaty, and then a wind from the east, bringing exile in a storm of government papers, what descended from the north in 1912 seemed impossible. (Erdrich 1)

Joy Porter notes that after the American Revolution, Native Indians were methodically devastated when "Americans created a national mythology that consigned Indians to a 'savage' past" (Porter 50). For the success of the changed America, "Indian absence, through death or the cultural death of complete assimilation, was deemed necessary" (50). This absence was done through various techniques, ranging from removing people from their land to converting them into Christianity or Western mood of education. Porter again says that targeting Indian children "was part of a pattern of erosion of Indian family life, augmented by child placement and adoption within non-Indian families that was not formally or comprehensively halted until the passage in 1978 of the Child Welfare Act" (52). Through Nanapush's tale, the novel explores the events that took place in the ultimate years of the extermination of the Natives and their systematic displacement from their own land. It also emphasises the heroic struggle of the Natives against both natural calamities and colonial forces, bravely attempting to protect their own culture from the clutches of dominant authorities. As Ahmad and Fatima assert, "They are resisting the invasion of the foreign culture by practicing their traditional ways and inculcating in the minds of their younger generations the love and significance of having to remain attached with the original culture" (112).

Erdrich's work can be considered magical realist due to her employing supernatural phenomena in her writing and creating a notion or atmosphere of the imaginary through language, as Faris states, magical realism blends "realism and the fantastic in such a way that magical elements grow organically out of the reality portrayed" ("Scheherazade's Children" 163). Many critics have interpreted Erdrich's work as the assertion of native beliefs, thinking that the magical elements and figurative language lends an indigenous feature to her work. Although magic is employed to challenge the colonial outlook, there is no assertion of spiritual traditions through magic. Giving more importance on Erdrich's writing techniques and styles over her tribal heritage, Tankersley argues, "Erdrich achieves this organic quality not by proliferating her works with magical events but by instilling the language itself throughout her novels with a sense of the fantastic. The supernatural, therefore, emerges from Erdrich's techniques and skills as a writer rather than from her Ojibwe heritage" (21). Although Erdrich's novels might include a smaller number of magical actions compared to other magical realist works, and even those events can be doubted or questioned, it is other elements of her writing which basically cement her position as a magical realist. Erdrich's distinctive writing style and narration have a strong ability to create a magical effect, undermining the real as Stirrup considers the "fluidity of Erdrich's lyrical prose" a way of refusing "critical determinism" (Stirrup 91). Before introducing any magical scene, Erdrich employs her flowing sentences, which are laden with metaphors, to surprise or confuse the reader. She allures the reader by forming a realistic world before breaking it into pieces, creating a scene where both the magical and the real are intertwined. Using dream motifs, the reader is defamiliarised, and the magical elements are incorporated; it is also used to undermine the colonial depiction of her native culture, and to advocate an alternative and/or marginalised version of reality. The political message in Erdrich's work might not be as strong as that of many other writers, but her metaphorical writing style itself is a way of undermining realism and Western rationalism. From this context, her work can be placed side by side with other magical realist novels which challenge a colonial world view.

Magical Realism as Means of Resisting Colonialism

It has been mentioned that the novel *Tracks* has two narrators—Nanapush and Pauline—who provide a non-linear and fragmented narrative. The struggle and different, sometimes opposing, narration of the two homodiegetic narrators centre on Fleur Pillager, the protagonist of the novel. Susan Friedman considers both narrators physically opposite, where Nanapush "represents resistance to Euro-American culture" and Pauline "represents the colonized subject" (112). The tension between the two narrators also reflects the struggle between a decaying tribal tradition and culture and an invasive Western religious system. Both Nanapush and Fleur are associated with 'Anishinabe' practice and, therefore, with magic. In the novel, it is Fleur who is the main source of the magical, and a metaphor for the dying indigenous culture. She has a strong association with nature, particularly with water and the lake monster, Misshepeshu, which is narrated as "love hungry with desire and maddened for the touch of young girls, the strong and daring especially, the ones like Fleur" (Erdrich 11). Fleur also possesses the formidable power of metamorphosis, which is believed by the entire community without any doubt: "[T]he next morning [...] we followed the tracks of her bare feet and saw where they changed, where the claws sprang out, the pad broadened and pressed into the dirt. By night we heard a chuffing cough, the bear cough" (Erdrich 12). This magical event takes place in the middle of reality and is considered an ordinary occurrence by the community people. Again, Fleur being respected and feared by her community as she possesses healing power, clearly shows the way magic and healing abilities are empowering for women. Her return to the reservation causes many strange events to take place: "The dust on the reservation stiffed. Things hidden were free to walk. The surprised young ghost of Jean Hat limped out of the bushes. ... A black dog, the form of the devil, stalked the turnoff to Matchimanito" (Erdrich 34-35). Fleur also takes revenge on Boy Lazarre, who kidnaps Margaret and shaves her hair, by killing him by a mere bite of Margaret. In the novel, Fleur has employed her magical power against Pauline and other characters who have developed a stronger tie with colonial culture.

Fleur's revenge against her three coworkers who have raped her in Argus also highlights the way she uses magic against men to defy patriarchy and to assert her agency: magic is thus empowering for women and a resistance to patriarchy. By magically transforming herself into a tornado, Fleur ensures the rapists' death after they took refuge in the meat lockers and freeze. The most crucial aspect of the tornado is that it is very selective in causing destruction since no one else is injured or died and no property is destroyed. The freezer is found locked from outside and the event is considered "a tornado's freak whim" (Erdrich 30). Although the inhabitants of Argus do not hold Fleur responsible for the tornado, it is through Pauline's narration the reader is able to establish a connection between the tornado's weird characteristics and Fleur's magical ability.

Tracks begins with Nanapush's description of the death of a significant number of his family members and tribal people in the winter of 1912 due to an illness brought by white people. The realistic depiction of the infection and its consequences are mingled with magical beliefs and the presence of ghosts who patrol the forest of the tribe. The tribal police have strictly been instructed by the white government to burn down the houses of people who died by consumption with their dead bodies inside, denying them a proper burial and thus insulting their tribal culture. Although Pukwan, a member of the tribal police, travels to the Pillagers' residence to accomplish government order, which clashes with a proper traditional burial, the house magically remains intact. It also seems to him that it is the angry and dissatisfied spirits of the Pillagers that saved their residence from burning down. Erdrich writes,

> He carefully nailed up the official quarantine sign, and then, without removing the bodies, he tried to burn down the house. But though he threw kerosene repeatedly against the logs and even started a blaze with birchbark and chips of wood, the flames narrowed and shrank, went out in puffs of smoke. Pukwan cursed and looked desperate, caught between his official duties and his fear of Pillagers. (Erdrich 3)

There is no logical explanation for why the Pillagers' residence cannot be burnt, but the event is crucial for many reasons. It helps us have an idea about the magical powers of the Pillagers, who "knew the secret ways to cure and kill" (2). It also shows the inability of Pakwan and the colonisers to demolish Pillagers' residence along with their dead bodies and his realisation that the Pillagers' more powerful magical scheme is at work to challenge his constant attempt to make and maintain power. Despite being dead, it is the Pillagers' magical power that challenges and wins, albeit temporarily, over the colonisers. It also shows Pakwan being torn between two ideological conflicts in him: his official duties and his respect for tribal culture. Finally, it is his tribal identity that wins the battle since "[h]e finally dropped the tinders and helped [Nanapush] drag Fleur along the trail" (3). If readers look at the event more closely, they can realise that Pakwan's conflicting behaviour is part of a much larger problem. If the US government had not forcefully imposed any law on the tribal people or if the European colonisers had not brought any fatal disease to the Natives, Pakwan would not have been forced to burn dead bodies instead of giving them a traditional Indian burial. This scene also shows the way evil colonial venture destroys the cultural integrity of a tribe and turns the tribal people against one another. Right after the abortive attempt to burn the Pillagers' residence, the death of Pakwan is narrated in such a matter-of-fact manner that it is considered a straight result of the curse of the Pillagers': "[He] came home, crawled into bed, and took no food from that moment until his last breath passed" (4).

Fleur's resistance to colonial authority through magic is also evident in the scene in which the tribal agent who visits her to collect the fee of the allocations of the land given to her by the government loses his mental sanity and is heard to be living in the forest:

> He [the agent] went out there, got lost, spent a whole night following moving lights and lamps of people who would not answer him, but talked and laughed among themselves. They only let him go at dawn because he was so stupid. Yet he asked Fleur again for money, and the next thing we heard he was living in the woods and eating roots, gambling with ghosts. (Erdrich 9)

Although the reader gets a story based on reality—collecting fee on land allocation and a real treaty, the 'Dawes Act'—the passage highlights supernatural issues or events such as ghosts or spirits of dead tribal ancestors. The act of driving away the colonial agent and later slowly driving him mad, clearly demonstrates the magical power of the Pillagers, having the ability to secure the future of their family and the tribe, and to resist colonial power. By continuing shamanistic traditions and keeping the tribal rituals alive, Fleur becomes an advocate of the faith, antiquity, and heritage of her tribe.

In *Tracks*, the blending of the supernatural and the real gradually becomes problematic in Pauline's narration because of her constant untrustworthiness as a narrator. As a multifaceted and ambivalent character, Pauline transgresses different borders: between indigenous and colonisers, supernatural and ordinary, regeneration and decay, and between stability and madness. Pauline is someone who never fits in her own tribal community, and is more interested in Western civilisation, and by being converted to Christianity, she frees herself from her traditional beliefs. In the course of the novel, Pauline starts losing her mental sanity, which begins with her magical interaction with the deceased. At the death of the girl she has been taking care of, Pauline feels excited, elevated, and emancipated, and considers it the future responsibility to support people to reach the world after death. Her meeting is depicted in a magical realist manner, and her freedom is represented by her thrilling journey:

> If I took off my shoes I would rise into the air. If I took my hands away from my face I would smile. A cool blackness lifted me, out the room and through the door. I leapt, spun, landed along the edge of the clearing. My body rippled. ... The sky hardened to light. And that is when, twirling dizzily, my wings raked the air, and I rose in three powerful beats and saw what lay below. They were stupid and small. (Erdrich 68)

The question or doubt that the event can be hallucinatory is strongly dismissed by the sheer height and smooth body of the tree, making it almost impossible for any human being to reach there. Although people are shocked to find her in such a high tree, she is not at all astonished as she can clearly remember the way she has reached the top of the tree: "I knew that after I circled, studied, saw all, I touched down on my favourite branch and tucked my head beneath the shelter of my wing" (68-69). However, since Pauline is considered an unreliable narrator and the entire scene is described through her words, it might also be possible that the incident is a part of her hallucination. Concerning Pauline's close association with death, Sánchez opines, "In a sense, Pauline precipitates the young girl's death and, consequently, the whole episode signifies her awareness of death as a form of grace and the discovery of her place in community, passing death on" (120). She becomes "the crow of the reservation" (Erdrich 54), "death's bony whore" (86).

The hunting scene where Nanapush spiritually guides Eli to accomplish his task is a remarkable instance of Erdrich's magical realist technique to blur the borders between two opposing realms, and to magically connect two men over a great distance. This scene also clearly shows the communal aspect of magic: the way magic can guide and assist community people in danger and unite them. In the rough winter of 1917, Eli's journey to the North with his gun to get some food parallels Nanapush's act of performing rites in his cabin to help Eli in his hunt. Nanapush's shamanistic rituals, where he calls his magical helpers through chanting, empower Eli and enable him to come back with sufficient amount of meat:

> In my fist I had a lump of charcoal, with which I blackened my face. I placed my otter bag upon my chest, my rattle near. I began to sing slowly, calling on my helpers, until the words came from my mouth but were not mine, until the rattle started, the song sang itself, and there, in

> the deep bright drifts, I saw the tracks of Eli's snowshoes clearly. (Erdrich 101)

By the assistance of his magical helpers, Nanapush gains the power to observe Eli's activities, to read his mind, and thus to pass instructions: "I exerted myself. Eli's arms and legs were heavy, and without food he could not think. His mind was empty and I so feared that he would make a mistake. ... *Do not sour the meat, I reminded him now, a strong heart moves slowly*" (102). It is Nanapush's mysteriously conveyed directions which help Eli kill the animal, and it is his drum beats which enable the exhausted Eli to return home. In this outstanding occurrence, the spiritual and the mundane world fuse, and the spatial distance and the borders between human beings become blurred and ultimately disappear. The spiritual assistance enables the tribal people like Eli to survive the hardship, and thus poses a threat to the colonial authorities.

One of the main characteristics of magical realism is that it challenges or doubts the traditional notions of time and space. By writing from within two literary traditions—the Western and the Indian—Erdrich merges two different, and confronting, concepts of time: the Western linear concept of time and the Indian cyclical and fragmentary concept of time. In discussing Native sense of time over Western sense, Paula Gunn Allen opines that the conventional native notion of time is timeless and ritualistic: "The achronological time sense of tribal people results from tribal beliefs about the nature of reality, beliefs based on ceremonial understandings rather than on industrial, theological, or agricultural orderings. ... The basis of Indian time is ceremonial while the basis of time in the industrialized West is mechanical" (150). The chronological and linear organisation of Western time supports the separation of individuals from the environment and God. Such understanding opposes the ritualistic conventions of time, which "considers the individual as a moving event within a moving universe" (Sánchez 128). In Erdrich's *Tracks*, the inclusion of flashbacks, digression and intertwined dream imagery defies the conventional chronological notion of time and challenges Western colonial authority. The chronological event depicted between 1912 and 1924 later turns into a mythical notion of time. The non-linear notion of time is created by giving titles to the chapters and years regarding natural seasons and elements both in the European and native languages. The supernatural scenes like Eli's moose hunt, Fleur's conjuring a tornado in Argus, and Pakwan's inability to burn the Pillagers' house and his strange death are all temporarily taken out of time and placed in a mythical sphere. Just like time, space is also placed in a mythical dimension. The dark, holy space of the forests, which is patrolled and controlled by ancestors' ghosts, is starkly contrasted with the Western modes of sophisticated spaces like schools, churches and offices where Western identity is prioritised, and native identity is subjugated and ultimately made extinct. Erdrich's novel basically chronicles the final resistance against the conquering of the Native lands by the government and lumber company. The novel is thus not wholly a triumphant portrayal of the tribal people but rather the description of their decaying final days, which is hinted by Nanapush's account of the wasting away of the tribal land, life, and culture.

Magical realism has often been associated with Bakhtin's concept of the grotesque and the carnivalesque. In his research on Rabelai's work, Bakhtin places grotesque realism, which is featured by exaggeration and humiliation, at a significant point of time when traditional culture, humour and oral custom begin to wane (Bakhtin 18). Associating Bakhtin's carnivalesque with Native American culture in Erdrich's novel, Robert Morace says,

> [Erdrich's] use of carnivalizing techniques supports the communal, egalitarian values that [...] characterize traditional Native American culture and thereby offer an alternative to, a decrowning double of, the nominally democratic but in fact deeply hierarchical and, by comparison, monologic Euro-American culture to which the contemporary Native American writer is inextricably and unavoidably connected. (36-37)

Since the carnivalesque attempts to dissolve hierarchies and prohibitions of an official system, it also has the potential to represent the struggle between colonised traditions and colonising supremacy. Like magical realism, and at the same time as an instrument of magical realism, the carnivalesque is also inspired by our necessity to transgress borders and to turn the world or established notions upside down. In *Tracks*, Lily, who is Fleur's colleague in the butcher shop, gets involved in a fierce fight with a snoozing sow, which is depicted in grotesque terms:

> They leaned into each other and posed in a standing embrace. They bowed jerkily, as if to begin. Then his arms swung and flailed. She sank her black fangs into his shoulder, clasping him, dancing him forward and backward through the pen. Their steps picked up pace, went wild. The two dipped as one, box-stepped, tripped one another. She ran her split foot through his hair. He grabbed her kinked tail. They went down and came up, the same shape and then the same color until the men couldn't tell one from the other. (Erdrich 25)

In this terrible fight, the boundaries between men and animals dissolve, and they become one. Although this comic scene contrasts the next scene of Fleur's brutal rape, to some extent, the inflicted violence on the animal body (the sow) substitutes the sexual violence of Fleur.

The association between the carnivalesque and Native American literature can particularly be drawn through laughter and trickster figures. In Native American culture, trickster figures are characterised by the ability to change physical form and to use bawdy humour. Alan Velie analyses contemporary Indian American novels which include trickster figures where he describes them "Footloose, amoral drifters with strong appetites for women and wine, they play tricks, are the victim of tricks, are callous and irresponsible, but essentially sympathetic to the reader" (122). Nanapush who is a legendary trickster figure in *Tracks* and whose name has been taken from Anishinabe trickster, "*nanapush or nanibozhu*" (Owens 212), is told by his father "'Nanapush. That's what you'll be called. Because it's got to do with trickery and living in the bush. ... The first Nanapush stole fire. You will steal hearts'" (33). Along with his trickster skills such as irony, laughter, and humour, Nanapush also possesses supernatural and healing abilities, the healing scene of Fleur after her miscarriage being one of the greatest examples of it. Although Nanapush's act of putting his hands in boiling water without getting burnt is later explained by the fact that he has used ingredients made of herbs in his hands, the magic lies in his coming across this healing method in his dreams:

> I mixed and crushed the ingredients. The paste must be rubbed on the hands a certain way, then up to the elbows, with exact words said. ... But the person who visited my dream told me what plants to spread so that I could plunge my arms into a boiling stew kettle, pull meat from the bottom, or reach into the body itself and remove [...] the name that burned, the sickness. (Erdrich 188)

By stressing on Pauline's effort to execute the identical trick, chanting in Latin (the language of the Catholic) and getting severely burnt, Erdrich shows the conflict between both Native and colonial practices, and by highlighting the Native superiority, she thus poses a challenge to colonial authority and their practices. Here, magic is shown to be empowering for the Native.

Through a mocking and disparaging treatment of Paulne, Erdrich links the trickster activities with the grotesque as Bakhtin considers humiliation to be typical of the grotesque: "To degrade also means to concern oneself with the lower stratum of the body, the life of the belly and the reproductive organs; it, therefore, relates to acts of defecation and copulation, conception, pregnancy, and birth" (Bakhtin 21). Through the humiliation process, everything that is high and spiritual is lowered down and is linked to the material level, exactly what Nanapush has done to expose Pauline's double standards. By offering Pauline a different type of tea and cutting several obscene jokes, Nanapush performs a brutal joke in the trickster fashion and makes her feel embarrassed. Bakhtin says again, "laughter degrades and materializes" (Bakhtin 20), and carnival laughter is distinctive because of its "indissoluble and essential relation to freedom" (89). The collective laughter caused by Nanapush's treatment of Pauline can thus be considered a resistance against the invading Catholic belief of the colonisers: (crude) humour is a survival technique for Native Americans. Highlighting the role of humour in the life and literature of the Native, Erdrich says in an interview that "it's a different way of looking at the world, very different from the stereotype, the stoic, unflinching Indian standing, looking at the sunset" (Coltelli 46). It can be surmised from this statement that Erdrich is emphasising on an alternative worldview and reality, highlighting the significance of Native belief and culture.

Rewriting History and Reclaiming the Past

Nancy J. Peterson emphasises the parallel progression of history and the narrative(s) in *Tracks* where she discusses the colonial invasion, diseases, treaties between the government and the tribes and many other documents to verify various occurrences in the novel. She considers Nanapush's tale "revisionist because it defamiliarizes the popular narrative of American history as progress by showing the costs of that 'progress' to native peoples" (Peterson 985). She believes that it is crucial for Erdrich, particularly for Nanapush, to give history a tribal identity and to rewrite history from the viewpoints of the tribe by renaming various historical events and accounts. Nanapush seems to be aware of the significance of naming and renaming in the case of ownership and identity, which is evident from his act of passing down his alternative (hi)story to his granddaughter, Lulu. His statement to Lulu—"'Nanapush is a name that loses power every time that it is written and stored in a government file'" (Erdrich 32)—suggests that the tribal people's authority over their land decreases with every time their lands and people are documented by the government. In the same essay, Peterson also highlights the significance of the use of oral storytelling and the way the novel "establishes two competing and contradictory frames of reference: one associated with orality, a seasonal or cyclic approach to history, a precontact culture; the other linked with textuality, a linear or progressive approach to history, a postcontact culture" (986). However, Erdrich neither prefers one over the other nor does the novel begin with an oral depiction of actions and ends with a direct, textual one. The novel rather moves through these two representations just the same way characters float between acculturation into white culture and preservation of tribal culture, simultaneously belonging to both and neither.

In magical realist narrative, magical events take place in a realistic framework. Although the realistic description of man and society in *Tracks* emphasises its socio-political dimension, the employment of magical realist technique challenges traditional orders and notions and proves prolifically effective. Erdrich's depiction of 'Turcot Company' and the destruction of an entire forest to be economically benefitted brings back to our mind the 'Banana Company Massacre' in Gabriel García Márquez's *One Hundred Years of Solitude* and the Jallianwala Bagh Massacre in Salman Rushdie's *Midnight's Children* where in order to create a sense of collective amnesia, neither of the brutal events is included in official history. Just like Márquez and Rushdie, Erdrich also wants to let the whole world know of the destruction of tribal heritage and the way of life by the white colonisers, and thus comes up with a marginalised version of history. The destruction of the ancient forest, a place where the Natives bury their dead ancestors on tall trees and which is patrolled by the ancestors' ghosts, stands for the disappearance of the entire tribe. Fleur, who is the last resident of these ancient forests, finally leaves her area in the midst of magical changes in nature: "[N]othing about this weather seemed proper. Morning began with a greenish light. There was thunder in the distance, the smell of a storm drove me among the twisted stumps of trees and scrub" (Erdrich 219). Nanapush's magical communication with his departed family members helps him enter the kingdom of the dead and absorb in the past:

> I saw my wives. Oniiimii, the Dove, her little cries and her small unlucky face. Zezikaaikwe, the Unexpected. I touched the hands of White Beads, Wapepenasik, whom I'd loved painfully. I held our small daughter, Moskatikinaugun, Red Cradle, whom I'd called Lulu. ... I was with my father for a moment, Kanatowakechin, Mirage, as thick snow came down all around us, obscuring our trail, confusing the soldiers and covering the body of my mother and sister. I closed my eyes. I felt the snow of that winter and then the warmth of my first woman, Sanawashonekek, the Lying down Grass. I smelled the crushed fragrance of her hair. (220)

The mentioning of the magical snow and the name of Nanapush's relatives in Chippewa language situates the novel "in a past of suffering, war and dispossession, and establishes a strong contrast with the materialistic present of predatory lumber companies" (Sánchez 136).

In a final powerful act of resistance against colonial power, Fleur summons a magical whirlwind which uproots the trees and thus frightens timber company people: "Around me, a forest was suspended, [...]. The fingered lobes of leaves floated on nothing. The powerful throats, the columns of trunks and splayed twigs, all substance was illusion. Nothing was solid" (Erdrich 223). The ultimate magical wind, which knocks down trees on the company people and takes revenge for Fleur's death, can easily be related to the scene in *One Hundred Years of Solitude* where the tornado destroys Macondo. The final cyclone is foreshadowed in Nanapush's narrative, which becomes real at the end, announcing the death of both the forest and the tribe: "Suddenly a loud report, thunder, and they toppled down like matchsticks, all flattened around me in an instant. I was the only one left standing" (127). Fleur offers the last resistance to the invading foreign ideas, and although, in the end, she has to leave the Pillagers' territory, she walks away victorious against colonial forces. Nanapush, the only survivor, opposes the coloniser's legal method as a means to reclaim, revise, and rewrite his tribal history.

Tracks ends with an optimistic tone in the Native's struggle against white invasion on land and culture. Instead of entirely depending on a simplified account of her nativity to attain this optimistic resistance, Erdrich employs her fluid language and magical realist technique to make sure that "her readers are always aware, not of pristine culture, but of the strategies of survivance that have seen a people endure, adapt, and persist against stark odds" (Stirrup 204). *Tracks*, which is rooted in Native American cultural context, expresses the 'other' or alternative version(s) of events and attempts to fill in fissures or silence of official history from the contexts of the followers of particular social, cultural, and religious practices of reality: this reality is as much real and plausible to the Native as it is supernatural and improbable to the Westerner. Many critics have interpreted Erdrich's work as the assertion of Native beliefs, thinking that the magical elements and figurative language lend an indigenous feature to her work. Although magical realism is used as a form of resistance to colonial invasion, it would be too much to say that Erdrich considers these magical elements as a substitution for colonialism. By intertwining the magical and the real, Erdrich attempts to resolve differences between two conflicting worldviews or patterns, Western and Native American, so that people from both cultures can live together by showing mutual respect and cultural harmony without one group trying to suppress the other in terms of different prejudices.

Part III.
Protesting Cultural Domination and Challenging Nationalist Male Politics

Chapter 8

Linking Magical Realism and Transnational Feminism: Developing Female Identity in Cristina García's *Dreaming in Cuban*

In her debut novel, *Dreaming in Cuban*, Cuban American author Cristina García investigates the complex social, cultural, political and psychological impact of postcolonialism on identity formation through the journey of Cuban women. Through the remembrance and reimagination of three generations of del Pino women, which is made possible by the help of myth, magical occurrences and traditional healing practices, García attempts to recover, to reconceive and to create and develop awareness of Cuban women and cultural heritage that might have been erased. By highlighting the heritage of Cuban women who strongly survived the volatile time during the Revolution, García admits a history of trauma and female opposition to central male politics. In the novel, the del Pino female characters—Celia, Felicia, Lourdes and Pilar—are shown as strong and empowered through their mystic and spiritual experiences, and their alternative narrative(s) of the Revolution. By allowing these women to have a voice, García provides them with some sort of agency and authority over men who basically manipulated Cuban history after Fidel Castro assuming the power. Again, the recurring experiences of these women from three consecutive generations expose García's employment of a major metaphor based on the 'phoenix' myth. The female characters go through cycles of cultural and sexual changes where García rewrites the myth with the cycles of death and resurrection. Magical realism in the novel combines multiple voices and alternative viewpoints on past and present, making it an apposite vehicle for examining global spaces and issues, and attempts to render marginal voices and realities and to subvert and deconstruct Eurocentric notions of identity, reality, and truth. Again, through the use of myth and magical events such as post-mortem visit of family members and telepathic communication between female family members, García attempts to remove physical distance among women who are torn between cultural differences between Cuba and America, and provides them with the sense of togetherness and empowerment.

In *Dreaming in Cuban*, the relationships among del Pino women reflect the broader political rivalry between Cuba and the USA in the aftermath of the Socialist Revolution that occurred between 1953 and 1959. The fragmented multi-vocal narrative tells the story of a modern Cuban family without providing any unified and verifiable truth where Celia, the matriarch, was attempting to preserve her family story. Since immigrants normally lose touch with their homeland, often family histories are lost. Celia wants to make it sure that there is something that can connect her granddaughter Pilar with her motherland, Cuba and Cuban identity. Celia finds the intergenerational transformation of family histories crucial as a transformation of information makes it possible for the tie between homelands and adopted lands to be created where the immigrants find them in a hyphenated space. According to Anja Mrak, "[...] narrative fragments, flashbacks, glimpses of the future, and non-chronological events which nonetheless manage to reveal a curious interconnectedness manifest that unified and linear narratives are no longer viable in a transnational context" (Mrak 184). Chapter arrangements of the novel also disrupt the traditional notion of the logical course where one event leads to another. Whereas some chapters expose past events through flashback, others narrate the same event but from another narrative point of view. The labelling of chapters with the name of focalisers, significant years or titles of prose or poem makes it utterly difficult for the reader to form a consistent narrative. It thus criticises the Eurocentric conception of reality as something linear, progressing from a beginning to an ending, and advocates the existence of multiple versions of reality. A fragmented narrative emphasises the fact that time and space are relative constructs and encourages us to have subjective versions of history or reality. The narrative structures of the novel and the magical realist narrative used there create a space where conventional ideas of time, space and identity are taken apart. By using multiple focalisers and narrators, different time and space dimensions and a narrative that moves back and forth, García questions the notion of a unified and consistent narrative and individual identity, paving the way for a flexible and hybrid culture.

Subverting and Deconstructing Eurocentric Notions of Identity, Reality and Truth

Nira Yuval-Davis states, "Identities are narrative stories people tell themselves and others about who they are" and thus comprise the "constructions of belonging" (Yuval-Davis 202). García's writing investigates cultural hybridity and the way maintaining a hyphenated existence confuses one's identity. Alvarez-Borland opines, "Cuban-American writers face two challenges: how to reconcile their past experiences in their country of birth with present experiences in their adopted country [and] how to navigate between bicultural and monocultural readers" (43). The novel explains the construction of identity through three different levels of relocation of Cuban people—the story of those who remained in Cuba (Grandmother Celia), the first generation of immigrants to America (Celia's eldest daughter Lourdes), and those who came to the US as children (Lourdes's daughter Pilar). In the whole story, each woman's account is a crucial variable in the creation of a communal culture and hybrid identity. Born in Cuba but brought up in America, Pilar is conflicted between the opposing perceptions of her identity and heritage, where her displaced mother and physically distant grandmother form two crucial aspects of her identity. Pilar is the only protagonist in the novel who provides a first-person account of her story and performs as some sort of agent or subject in forming her account, whereas both Celia and Lourdes's narratives are told by a third-person omniscient narrator, which places them in the position of victim or object of their own prejudiced ideas.

The narrative of Pilar symbolises an intersecting point between Cuban and American cultures. Although she reached America at the age of some two years without having any ideas about Cuban culture, in the beginning, she finds more proximity to her Cuban identity. In spite of defining herself as a Cuban, she has never experienced Cuban life. Therefore, Pilar is unable to fully understand the political discourses between her mother and grandmother. She thus adds some sort of fresh perspective or an outsider perspective on the issues of dislocation and identity. Although Pilar attempts to build a connection with Cuba, it becomes difficult for her due to Lourdes's silence on, and denunciation of, the topic. Interestingly, both issues intensify her isolation from Cuban culture or tradition, and her desire to (re)connect with it. It ultimately creates distance with Lourdes, and Pilar finds consolation in communicating with Celia through the magical process of mind reading, making communication possible regardless of geographical distance: "[…] I hear her speaking to me at night just before I fall asleep. She tells me stories about her life and what the sea was like that day. She seems to know everything that's happened to me" (García 22). Therefore, the magical realist means of communication between women enables them to get in touch with each other in spite of their physical distance, to share their stories and to be empowered. Oscillating between her known surroundings of New York and her imagined, and probably fantasised, Cuba,

Pilar seeks belongingness, which brings her closer to her grandmother and pushes her to visit Cuba. As Elena Sáez says, "Pilar's negotiation of her identity is nevertheless overshadowed and overdetermined by this nostalgia and its own confused origins" (Sáez 131). Pilar admits, "I feel much more connected to Abuela Celia than to Mom, even though I haven't seen my grandmother in seventeen years. [...] she's left me her legacy nonetheless-a love for the sea and the smoothness of pearls, an appreciation of music and words, sympathy for the underdog, and a disregard for boundaries" (García 139). Both Celia and Lourdes had the option to embrace either Cuba or America, where they went for opposite paths. However, as Pilar personifies the meeting between two cultures, languages, and heritages, she chooses both and is, therefore, able to create a new identity for her.

However, Pilar, who entertains various facets of her identity, is demotivated by Lourdes, who advocates a linear and closed version of history: "This is a constant struggle around my mother, who systematically rewrites history to suit her views of the world. ... It makes her see only what she wants to see instead of what's really there" (García 139). Whereas Pilar represents a more flexible approach to the construction and negotiation of one's identity, both Lourdes and Celia uphold a rigid construction of identity based on dominant political ideologies. Anja Mrak rightly says that both Celia and Lourdes's "slavish adherence to hegemonic ideologies and their identity politics, in fact, originate in a traumatic experience, which forecloses simplistic judgment of their actions and interactions with others" (185). Lourdes's violent rape and later leaving Cuba for the USA makes her see migration as an opportunity to reinvent herself and to restart her life. However, she is haunted by her brutal past memories in Cuba. She finds it essential to regain control over her body which bears the mark of sexual violence and rape. She tries to do so first by an irresistible appetite and sexuality and then by obsessive dieting. Here, the reader can see the way magical realism disrupts traditional temporality, giving the opportunity to the past to invade the present as the manifestation of her memory of the rape, and memory in general: Lourdes "smells the brilliantined hair, feels the scraping blade, the web of scars it left on her stomach" (García 154). Lourdes's trauma is emphasised by a magical realist metaphor, enabling a "movement from the abstract to the concrete, from the figurative to the literal, from the word to the thing" in order for nonrepresentational words or voices to "acquire a distinctly material presence" (Hegerfeldt, "Contentious Contributions" 68-69). Hegerfeldt says again that by "rendering the metaphor 'real' the text emphasises the power such constructions have over human thought and human action, and the very real suffering they can inflict" ("Contentious Contributions" 69).

If Lourdes considers migration a fresh start for her, she should reexamine her past and memories and employ them as a tool for her new identity. Although Lourdes wishes to erase Cuba and everything Cuban from her mind, including her mother, she was quite attached to her father before his death. However, they keep interacting with each other even after his death, a phenomenon which is clearly magical realist. Through supernatural events like telepathic communication and post-death appearance, the ontological and spatial boundaries between reality and fantasy are resolved. Lourdes is afraid of crossing the geographical boundary between Cuba and America, fearing that old trauma might return. The initiation of Lourdes's conversations with her dead father and borderless communication between female characters provides the characters the strength to come to terms with their traumatic past, and to (re)build relationships. When Lourdes receives the death news of her father, she asks Sister Federica at Charity Hospital: "Did he say where he was going?" (García 15), a question which highlights Lourdes's dismissal of borders between the living and the dead and introduces the possibility of her future meetings with her dead father. She will be involved in conversations with her father partly due to the fact that there is no one else to talk to; however, going deep into the issue, the reader can understand that her communication with her dead father is a way of coming in terms with her trauma of being raped as trauma victims need a listener to share their traumatic stories and to turn them into narratives. In other words, Lourdes's communication with her dead father offers her a safe resort.

Although Lourdes and Pilar's trip to Cuba is a significant one, Pilar immediately realises that the passing of geographic border does not have to involve the passing of ideological border: "Cuba is a peculiar exile, I think, an island-colony. We can reach it by a thirty-minute charter flight from Miami, yet never reach it all" (García 170). Pilar's statement refers to both physical accessibility and cultural inaccessibility between Cuba and America. Pilar's trip to Cuba provides her with the chance to reconnect with her grandmother, where the re-establishment of the bond between them is presented with a touch of magic or supernaturalism: "[...] I feel my grandmother's life passing to me through her hands. It's a steady electricity, humming and true" (172). This statement highlights the magical realist way of passing information, (hi)stories and culture from one generation to another. Through Celia's confession of the atrocities of the Revolution—"I know what my grandmother dreams. Of massacres in distant countries, pregnant women dismembered in the squares" (169)—Pilar's fantasised version of Cuba is replaced by a more impartial interpretation, containing both positive and negative aspects. Ultimately, she becomes able to establish a connection with her lost tradition and culture and to reconcile between two cultures. In order to comprehend her mother and grandmother without being judgmental, Pilar is the embodiment of transnational feminism and a model of identity politics that "deconstruct prevalent concepts of selfhood and thus open up new channels of cross-cultural conversations" (Schultermandl and Toplu 23).

Lourdes's father Jorges visits her for the first time forty days after his burial in the US, thanking her for the royal burial he was given. On their first meeting on the street, Lourdes fails to see him but can only smell his cigar, and she reaches home after a very short conversation accompanied by a feeling of disaster:

> "Where are you, Papi?"
>
> ...
>
> "Nearby," her father says, serious now.
>
> "Can you return?"
>
> "From time to time."
>
> "How will I know?"
>
> "Listen for me at twilight." (García 51)

She shares this story with her husband and surmises that things are "very wrong" and later considers the entire events as her mere imagination (52). The reader can easily understand that Lourdes is a bit sceptical about the idea of talking with her dead father, unlike Celia, who accepts Jorge's words as if it was normal and expected. Lourdes's scepticism is quite explicit during Jorge's second visit after seven days:

> "You didn't expect to hear from me again?"
>
> "I wasn't even sure I heard you the first time," Lourdes says tentatively.
>
> "You thought you'd imagined it?"
>
> "I thought I heard your voice because I wanted to, because I missed you. When I was little I used to think I heard you opening the front door late at night. I'd run out but you were never there."
>
> "I'm here now, Lourdes." (García 58)

Since Lourdes sincerely loves her father and is reluctant to let him go, her conversation with her dead father is her only possible way of working through her trauma. By forcing her repressed memories from the past to the present through the interactions with her dead father, Lourdes initiates the process of reconnecting to herself and the world around her and breaks the isolation resulting from traumatic experiences. As Pettersson says, "Despite the pain that re-emerges with her dead father's appearance in her life, it becomes clear that Jorge has returned to help his daughter remember and to give her hope" (52). This clearly shows the flimsy border between those who are dead and those alive, and the way dead relatives can be our guides and healers. Lourdes's being in constant communication with her dead father for long seven years is the time for her to be under healing treatment. When their communication starts declining after that, it seems to Lourdes that her father is "dying all over again, and her grief is worse than the first time" (García 151)—a clear indication of her reaching the final period of grief and getting ready to accept his death. Realising that she does not have much time before her father leaves her eternally, Lourdes asks the most difficult of all questions:

> "Did you love Mama?" Lourdes asks tentatively.
>
> "Yes, *mi hija,* I loved her."
>
> "And did she love you?"
>
> "I believe she did, in her way." (García 152)

Being convinced by his father's assurance, Lourdes decides to go to Cuba and be (re)united with Celia. The fact that it is his father's spirit that convinces Lourdes to be reconnected with her family and past shows the significance of spectral guidance on the characters.

In Cuba, Pilar also mentions her possessing clairvoyance, a magical realist phenomenon which seems to have been initiated when she was molested by some young men in America: "Since that day in Morningside Park, I can hear fragments of people's thoughts, glimpse scraps of the future. … The perceptions come without warnings or explanations, erratic as lightning" (García 167). Pilar's magical power of sensing people's thoughts and of smelling the future can clearly be linked to the responsibilities her grandmother has given her—to record both family and collective history and to cover the void of official history. In other words, Pilar's magical ability enables her to rewrite the official history from a marginalised perspective and to provide a voice to the oppressed. Her story will thus be all-encompassing, as her grandmother comments, "She will remember everything" (191). Again, Pilar's magical connection with her grandmother, regardless of her physical distance, provides her guidance and helps her reconcile her hyphenated identity. It also shows the way magical realism keeps all the three del Pino women closer, regardless of their different political ideologies, and functions as a valuable device behind their empowerment.

Overcoming Physical Boundaries and Gaining Agency/Authority through Myth and Magic

In *Dreaming in Cuban*, magical realism enables all three del Pino women, who are not staying in the same location, to cross geographical boundaries, to communicate with each other, and thus to draw them closer to each other and to get a sense of unity and empowerment. Again, Cristina García works within the phoenix myth and associates it with the figurative sequence of death and rebirth. She also uses metaphors connected with different 'orishas' or Santeria goddesses from classical mythology to feature her women characters. Although Celia and Pilar have no meeting between them since the latter's family settled in America, they keep in touch and stay closer to each other through magical means of telepathy as Pilar testifies she "hear[s] her speaking to [her] at night just before [she] fall[s] asleep" (García 22). Their telepathic connection draws the women so close that Celia wants to see Pilar: "[...] Celia says she wants to see me again. She tells me she loves me (22).

Apart from having meaningful verbal conversations, there are instances in the novel where characters are able to see dead family members, as in the case of Celia, who sees her dead husband Jorge "emerges from the light and comes toward her, taller than the palms, walking on water in his white summer suit and Panama hat" (4) but fails to communicate with him as she can only see the movements of his face but "cannot read his immense lips" (4). Here, Jorge's presence as a gigantic person, his ability to walk on water and, most importantly, his reappearance from a post-death world, which is taken quite normally by Celia, who is even expecting gifts from him just like in their early days of marriage—all these phenomena disrupt the logical aspect(s) of reality and advocate the employment of magical realism in the novel. Again, the broken communication between Celia and Jorge might symbolise their opposing political views. In other words, due to their having differences in political ideologies, their communication hampers even during Jorge's post-death visit. Nevertheless, Maria Rice Bellamy identifies, as "García uses alternative forms of connection, specifically total recall and dreams, to create relational bridges between characters even when they do not consciously seek them" (80), they are unconsciously interacting with each other although they think they cannot understand each other. Pilar also describes a similar scene where she has an image of Celia calling her, but she cannot hear: "I have this image of Abuela Celia underwater, standing on a reef [...]. She calls to me but I can't hear her. Is she talking to me from her dreams?" (García 170). Pilar's vision can be connected to Celia's movement on the ocean: a vision which enables Celia and Pilar to communicate although the pronounced words are not understood.

In *Dreaming in Cuban*, García creates characters who are embodiments of 'orishas' or Santeria goddess, having the ability to recreate themselves just like phoenixes. Carine Mardorossian draws an association between Santeria and the notion of 'postcolonial third phase'. Like the "relation identity [that] challenges the separatism of identity politics, cultural purism, and ethnic absolutism in favor of mappings of identity that emphasize the deep interconnectedness of our lives across the globe", Santeria merges various cultures—mainly Yoruba of Africa and Catholicism of Europe—in order to create some sort of pluralistic identities for its gods, goddesses, and followers (Mardorossian 3). *Dreaming in Cuban* has phoenix pattern, appearance of ghosts, Santeria rituals and goddess figure—all these characteristics help the novel to be categorised as a magical realist one. Celia's extreme suffering after her lover Gustavo has left her is lifted to a supernatural level: "Celia took to her bed by early summer and stayed there for the next eight months. ... Celia had been a tall woman, a head taller than most men, with a full bosom and slender, muscled legs. Soon she was a fragile pile of opaque bones, with yellowed nails and no monthly blood" (29). Celia's transformation reflects that of an ageing phoenix, and her upcoming infertility symbolises death. When, in order to tempt her to take food, a well-wisher of Celia attempts to make a baked Alaska and sets the entire kitchen on fire, a neighbour takes the fire as the sign of her "determin[ation] to die" just like the way the phoenix decides when to die (García 29). In the process of Celia's recovery, a *santera*'s prophecy—'"Miss Celia, I see a wet landscape in your palm. [You] will survive the hard flames'" (37)—summarises two parts of a quintessential argument: García's employment of a phoenix design and Celia's rebirth as an embodiment of Santeria sea goddess—Yemayá.

Gradually, Celia transforms into an avatar of Yemayá— "the model of the universal mother and queen of the sea and of salt water" (Barnet 92). However, she does not either realise or acknowledge her association with goddess until

Jorge dies. Although Jorge's ghost utters unintelligible words in its first appearance, Celia's attempt to establish a meaningful communication with her husband goes in vain. Although Celia "tempted to relax and drop", thereby having a permanent association with Yemayá, she rather remembers her dedication for the Cuban Revolution (García 7). Celia's act of drowning herself in the ocean after Lourdes and Pilar have left Cuba for America can be the symbol of another rebirth: "The water rises quickly around her. It submerges her throat and her nose, her open eyes that do not perceive salt. ... She breathes through her skin, she breathes through her wounds" (189-190). Celia's ability to breathe via her skin—a magical realist phenomenon, defying the law of nature—symbolises her development of grills and coming back to her nature as the sea goddess. Celia releases her pearl earrings, which she has used for more than forty years, one by one to the sea as pearls are product of the sea, thus the proper possession of Yemayá: "Celia closes her eyes and imagines [the pearl] drifting as a firefly through the darkened seas, imagines its slow extinguishing" (190). Celia is reborn, achieving immortality.

Celia's second daughter Felicia's cyclicality is exposed to the reader after her father's demise. She asks the assistance of a *santera* to remove the distance between herself and her father which suggests the way magical realism possesses healing or soothing abilities. It seems that her phoenix cycles are based mainly on her association with men, particularly in relation with her marriage. Her first husband, Hugo, regularly beats her and transmits syphilis to her. In order to protest her husband's brutality and to gain agency or, to some extent, emancipation, Felicia reincarnates herself like a phoenix with fire:

> Felicia carefully brought the blue flame to the tip of the rag. ... She watched until the delicate flames consumed the rag, watched until the blaze was hot and floating in the air. Hugo awoke and saw his wife standing over him like a goddess with a fiery ball in her hand.
>
> "You will never return here," Felicia said and released the flames into his face. (García 66)

The extraordinary description of fire, an ordinary thing, gives the entire scene a magical aura; again, comparing Celia with a goddess, holding a burning ball in her hands, also provides the scene a mystic touch, suggesting the significance of myth and magic in empowering women.

Before marrying for the second time, Felicia seeks the advice of a *santera* who informs her of her two more short-lasting and unsuccessful cases of marriage:

"Four days later, [...] Ernesto dies tragically in a grease fire at a seaside hotel" (García 118). Smelling a conspiracy behind her husband's death, Felicia suspects Garciela, a troublemaking client at the saloon where she works, and decides to avenge her husband's death: "She mixes lye with her own menstrual blood into a caustic brown paste, then thickly coats Graciela's head. Over it, she fastens a clear plastic bag with six evenly spaced hairpins, and waits. ... That is the last thing Felicia remembers for many months" (119-120). Once again, Felicia burns a person, but this time with a paste of caustic soda and menstrual blood, a phenomenon that defies the law of nature but provides her with the required strength to take revenge for any wrong committed against her, thus empowering her. The fire imagery is used again when she attempts to get away from her manifestation as the wife of Otto, her third husband; fire thus provides agency to Felicia and assists her in accomplishing her tasks. When she invites her husband for a roller coaster ride, he gets ready to perform oral sex by unzipping his pant, an essentially dangerous task which proves to be his last. Although Felicia testifies it was a mere accident, later, the reader gets a crueller version of the accident from Herminia, who holds Felicia responsible for her husband's murder. Associating the event of Otto's (Felicia's husband) ashes to be blown by the wind to the north with his choice of leaving Cuba for Minnesota, USA (America is situated to the north of Cuba)—"Felicia said his body turned to gray ash, and then the wind blew him north, just as he'd wished" (146)—can be considered a fantastic idea. Otto fails to physically migrate to the USA in his lifetime but is able to do so after his death in the form of ashes. Felicia again takes responsibility for her own metamorphosis and achieves agency through fire. She initiates the ultimate manifestation as a *santera* and the votary of Obatalá where after losing consciousness for the last time, she is "possessed by Obatalá" (147). Her deteriorating health can easily be compared with the demise of an ancient phoenix: "[H]er fingers curled like claws [...]. Even her hair, which had been as black as a crow's, grew colorless in scruffy patches on her skull. Whenever she spoke, her lips blurred to a dull line in her face" as if she has the beak of a bird instead of mouth (149). She ultimately finds peace in her death.

Celia and Jorge's eldest Child Lourdes's cycles, which include uncontrolled consumption, extreme dieting and obsessive sexual urge, are related to posttraumatic stress, and express themselves through both fast weight gain and loss. Due to her monstrous appetite, Lourdes turns into a lump of flash, which ultimately provides a sense of grotesque, and her hyper-appetite is paralleled with hyper-sexuality. Lourdes actually goes through a long period of powerlessness due to the impending death of her father, which also invokes her powerlessness she experiences during and after her rape. As Rufino is unable to give her the feeling of control, she would like to regain control over her own sexualised body by herself. In the same manner, Lourdes takes control over her body through excessive dieting after her father's death and the post-death return. She considers both weight loss and weight gain as the representation of her control over her body. Her loss of food appetite is also followed by her loss of sexual appetite: "It's as if another woman has possessed her in those days, a whore, a life-craving whore who fed on her husband's nauseating clots of Yellowish milk" (García 133). Her another phoenix-like cycle of monstrous weight gain and seeming hyper-sexuality begins when she again decides to eat everything within her reach. Jorge's return as a ghost explicitly helps Lourdes to come out of her powerlessness and the trauma of being raped, and thus functions as a source of empowerment. It also offers the cultural picture of a Latin world where the boundary between the dead and the living is fragile and where the dead appears as a normal and integral part of reality.

The reader witnesses a magical realist scene where Lourdes's dead father meets her forty days after his death. Although initially she is horrified by her experience, the meeting with her father later proves beneficial for her. The interactions with her deceased father reveal hidden truths to Lourdes, which are imperative to her identity (re)construction and her empowerment. It is her father's ghost that convinces Lourdes to visit Celia in Cuba, thus attempting to reduce the distance between mother and daughter who express opposing political ideologies. In other words, the magical realist communication between Jorge and Lourdes helps the latter to reunite with her physically separated family in Cuba, and to meet her ideologically estranged mother. Bellamy opines that magical realism "facilitate[s] the interaction of people distanced by ideology, geography and even death" (79). Celia, who is an ardent supporter of the Revolution, terms Lourdes as "a traitor to the Revolution" (García 20) when she shows her disgust for Cuba and everything Cuban and decides to settle in the USA, an event that marks their ideological estrangement. Lourdes seems to have been haunted by Jorge's ghost, so that she learns the secret of her family, gets reunited with her family and her past memories, and comes to terms with her traumatic past. Here, haunting serves a positive purpose, as Justine Edwards mentions Toni Morrison, who "asserts that the literary use of haunting offers the possibility of representing 'unspeakable things unspoken'" (119). In García's novel, Jorge explains Lourdes all crucial events between Celia and him—Jorge's act of resurrecting Celia by loving and marrying her after her lover Gustavo leaves her; his leaving Celia with his mother and sister while taking extended business trips, knowing that they will abuse her; and his role behind Celia's subsequent mental instability when Celia, after the birth of Lourdes, announces, "I will not remember her name" (García 34)—which point out a haunting scene of Jorge's ghost bringing to light what remained unspoken in his life as a human being. By allowing a ghost to reveal his story, García is able to unearth the buried stories of Lourdes's childhood, to alleviate the gap between the mother and the daughter, and to help Lourdes assert her identity.

Among all the female protagonists in the novel, Pilar showcases the most magical ability. She can remember, or at least believes to remember, everything which has taken place around her since her birth, and even goes on narrating a repetitive childhood event: "[B]ack in Cuba the nannies used to think I was possessed. ... They called me *brujita*, little witch. ... I remember thinking, Okay, I'll start with their hair, make it fall out strand by strand. They always left wearing kerchiefs to cover their bald patches" (García 22). In the novel, Pilar's cyclicality is the most difficult to perceive probably because García uses the first-person narrative in writing Pilar's section. Her cycles include her engagement with diverse cultures and actions like dancing, painting, enjoying protest music and playing the bass guitar. The turmoil in her sexual and emotional life caused by her college boyfriend Rubén with whom she seems to have an assured sexual relationship but whom she later catches cheating on her launches a ruthlessly depicted phoenix cycle, which she realises when she "feels [her] life begin[s]" (143).

Picking up the worship of the 'orisha' Changó, the god of fire and lightning, in order to visit Cuba to meet her grandmother Celia, Pilar enters a 'botanica', a market for Santeria suppliers where she is recognised by the shopkeeper as "a daughter of Changó", telling her to "finish what [she] began" and providing her herbal medicine to use in bath "for nine consecutive nights" (157). In order to regain her power lost in her near-rape incident in the park, she initiates the bathing ceremonies to invite Changó, who has the power to throw flames from his mouth in a phoenix relation. Here, García uses the phoenix cycles to give Pilar some sort of proximity not only to Celia but also to cultural memories of Cuba and to enable her to (re)assert her control over her body and mind after the incident of sexual harassment in the park; myth is thus shown to possess an empowering aspect. The use of myth and magic also helps Pilar to come up with a different or subjective version of Cuban history from her own imagination, a history which starkly contrasts the male-oriented official history. She laments, "Every day Cuba fades a little more inside me, my grandmother fades a little more inside me. And there's only my imagination where our history should be" (García 109). After bathing for nine consecutive nights, Pilar realises that she, along with Lourdes, should go back to Cuba to complete the cycle of imagination and to regain the fading memory of Cuba. The connection between Pilar and Celia epitomises the phoenix myth—Celia has the rebirth in the memory of Pilar as she writes in the final unsent letter to her Spanish lover, Gustavo, "My granddaughter, Pilar Puente del Pino, was born today. … She will remember everything" (191).

In many cases in the novel, different magical events help the female characters to network with each other and to give them a sense of togetherness and belongingness by allowing them to overcome geographical and ideological borders, providing them with some sort of agency and empowerment. Although *Dreaming in Cuban*, may not be considered a quintessential magical realist novel, García has employed magical realist ties to remind us about her characters and, probably, her Latin origin. Again, by using multiple languages and, therefore, multiple expressions, various stylistic devices, different viewpoints and thus multiple versions of reality or history, García attempts to create a cross-culture. The female characters' association with ghostly figures helps Pilar to (re)connect with her ancestry and initiates Lourdes's healing stages, relinking her with her family and culture. By allowing her female characters to tell their stories, García attempts to liberate the conventional narrative and/or history from the grasp of dominant discourse, and thus opens up an alternative (read female) space, standpoint and history.

Chapter 9

Political and Gendered Magical Realism in Ana Castillo's *So Far from God*

In *So Far from God*, Chicana author Ana Castillo writes against marginalisation of non-Western cultures and against the exclusion of women in male-dominated narratives. The novel depicts damaging American influences on the lives of Chicanos who are marginalised and are forced to integrate into American culture to be successful. In the novel, she creates a new *mestiza* myth to show the negative treatment of Chicana women in the US society and to show female empowerment by refusing to follow the patriarchal rules imposed on women. Castillo also criticises the brutal patriarchal forces that attacked Caridad through the Mexican folk healing process and a magical healing which comes from the love and prayer of her female family members and women around her, starkly contrasting Western medicinal views of healing. By emphasising Caridad's magical and harmonious connection with nature, which provides her with the necessary but magical strength to fight patriarchy, Castillo shows the way both female body and natural backdrops are abused by dominant power structures such as patriarchy and capitalism. Although the story considers Fe's mysterious disappearance as magical, it also places the incident within a patriarchal and racist society. Castillo's act of rewriting pre-Columbian and post-Conquest myth and legend is a way of resisting or challenging hegemonic forces and/or ideas, of giving a voice to the ones historically silenced (read women) and of attaining self-agency.

In the novel, Castillo employs magical realism to shed light on social, cultural, or political injustice and, at the same time, engenders the mode by using it from a female context. As Aldama writes, "[...] Castillo's novel self-reflexively engenders her magicorealism to write within and against its primitivist and masculinist identifications. She uses the mode to write within and against ideologies that primitivize non-Western cultures [...]" (76-77). Castillo also employs the narrative technique to write against the tradition, although being within it, that excludes women from male-dominated stories. She also rectifies a magical realist tradition which typecasts female characters by employing a Chicana-identified third-person magical realist narrator and by emphasising the experiences of Chicana characters but in a contemporary American setting. Castillo's characters, particularly the female ones, both resist and conform to patriarchal philosophies in the mainstream US culture. Although her Chicana characters Sofia and her four daughters—Fe (Faith), Esperanza (Hope), Caridad (Charity) and La Loca (The Crazy One)—all live in New Mexico, interacting with Mexican mythic characters such as La Llorona[1] and causing tumultuous cries from the indigenous god Tsichtinako, they are culturally, socially and historically very much involved in mainstream America. Aldama says again, "Castillo's narrator presents these characters within a seamless mixture of Mexican, Amerindian, and United States mainstream cultures" (79).

Chicana literature has been enriched by both Anglo and Hispanic conventions, receiving influences from renowned nineteenth and twentieth-century US and Latin American authors. Since both Mexican and Chicana literature hold a junctional position, mirroring a borderland culture, magical realism becomes a suitable literary mode for them; especially, for Chicana authors, the particular mode of writing offers a more meaningful and insightful way of depicting life. Chicana fiction has been marked for the attempt to provide an alternative version of the universe by the use of myth, magic and narrative, thus providing a renewed view of individual and society. The borderland—a space with contradictory domains and multiple expressions and languages—has motivated Chicana authors to explore different survival tactics.

Writing against Marginalisation of Non-Western Cultures

In *So Far from God,* Castillo sheds light on the oppressive structures or ideologies which work to repress or silence her characters, similar to the way dominant power structures silence cultures which do not fall within these structures. Castillo's main characters Sofia and her four daughters travel the worlds which are inclined to repress Chicana narrative or history. Due to this history of exclusion or repression, Alvina Quintana considers Chicana literature a resisting force: "[...] Chicana literature crosses disciplinary boundaries because it unifies the cultural, historical, and literary in a way that

[1] La Llorona, which is a mythical figure in Mexican or Chicana culture, is summarised by Domino Perez as "a woman abandoned by the man she loved and left alone to raise their children. Grief or desire for revenge compels La Llorona to murder her children and throw their bodies into a river. Despair ultimately contributes to La Llorona's death, and in the afterlife, she is condemned to wander for all of eternity until the bodies of her children are recovered". (2)

forces scholars to confront the limitations of artificial barriers" (13). Castillo talks about the way these boundaries trouble and, more particularly, repress them. In telling the story of the Santos family and generations of Chicanos with no identity, Castillo uses magical realism as a key means for resistance. As Zamora and Faris say, "Magical realist texts are subversive: their in-betweenness, their all-at-onceness encourages resistance to monologic political and cultural structures, a feature that has made the mode particularly useful to writers in postcolonial cultures and, increasingly, to women" ("Introduction" 6). Castillo's narrative sheds light on and criticises notions of rationalism, realism and capitalism as they are the structures which have isolated the Chicanas generations after generations. She also highlights the role of myth, magic and supernatural elements as a survival technique for the women characters against patriarchal oppression and capitalist dominance.

Sofia's third, and the most beautiful, daughter Caridad's promiscuous sexual activities and lifestyles put her outside of society's accepted norms, and she pays the price for it by being punished in the form of sexual violence: "[Her] nipples had been bitten off. She had also been scourged with something, branded like a cattle. Worst of all, a tracheotomy was performed because she had also been stabbed in the throat" (Castillo 20). Caridad's experiences visualise the gendered and racial violence which a consumerist society tries to normalise. However, the reader finds out that she was not attacked by a person but rather a mysterious force:

> And they three knew that it wasn't a man with a face and a name who had attacked and left Caridad mangled like a rundown rabbit. ... It was not a stray and desperate coyote either, but a thing, both tangible and amorphous. A thing that might be described as made of sharp metal and splintered wood, of limestone, gold, and brittle parchment. It held the weight of a continent and was indelible as ink, centuries old and yet as strong as a young wolf. It had no shape and was darker than the dark night, and mostly, as Caridad would never ever forget, it was pure force. (Castillo 58)

Caridad's physical mutilation represents the mutilation of cultures and individual identity as Holtzman opines that this particular force, which is named as *malogra*[2], "and its physical mutilation of Caridad represents the way

---

[2] The ruthless attacking force *malogra* [also known as *la malora*] which appears in Chicana

oppression mutilates, or damages, minority cultures and individual identities. Specifically, *malogra* can be read as a symbol of the patriarchy in the way it exploits Caridad's body and silences her after the attack" (7). Concurring with Holtzman, Theresa Delgadillo also says, "By envisioning the violence against herself as one caused by the *malogra,* Caridad allows us to see it in all its systemic force—it represents the overarching hegemonic discourse of patriarchy" (906). The policemen's reluctance to investigate the brutal attack on Caridad shows the way the law enforcement authority, which is also patriarchal, considers her sexual promiscuity— better say, her enjoyment of life— some sort of criminal offence, and thus justifies the attack on her by not initiating any search for the suspect. Caridad's attacker can be considered a folk figure, coming out of two patriarchal cultures: American and Mexican. Caridad being brutally attacked by a folkloric figure and refusing to be helped by the police symbolises her double marginalisation—her sexuality or sexual promiscuity is condemned not by one culture but by two. Aldama considers Caridad's assailant the agent of "a sexist and racist hegemony [where] Caridad's society of the spectacle brands, maims, and disfigures gendered bodily sites—and it silences" (80). In depicting *malogra,* Castillo shows the way this powerful force brutally affects the individual. However, Caridad's magical recovery from the wounds of the attack, which attributes to La Loca's prayers and Mexican folk healing process, underscores the resistance of the *mestiza,* who, in spite of being victimised by the patriarchy of two cultures, is able to heal herself.

Sofia's second daughter, Fe, who spends her entire life in the US, leaves behind her Mexican roots and desires for American consumerist values and dreams that eventually lead to her death. Fe totally conforms to American notions of hard work and material success and fails to see the richness of her own home and culture. She is getting estranged from her own culture both physically—by taking a good care of her body and skin—and socially—by constantly maintaining a distance with her family members and friends. Anzaldúa opines that it is Fe's fear which is the main reason for her rejection of home—some sort of "homophobia" (20). Fe considers marriage the first step to embark on her 'American Dreams' and after her failure to get married, she lost her own voice. However, after her magical recovery of her voice, she got married

---

folklore is "an evil spirit which wanders about in the darkness of the night at the cross-roads and other places. It terrorizes the unfortunate ones who wander alone at night, and has usually the form of a large lock of wool [...]. It is also generally believed that a person who sees *la malora,* like one who sees a ghost [...], forever remains senseless". (Espinosa 400-401)

and "got the long-dreamed-of automatic dishwasher, microwave, Cuisinart, and the VCR" (Castillo 135), and she and Casey "settled into a three-bedroom, two-car-garage tract home in Rio Ranch with option to buy. They furnished it all new, sold Fe's car and bought a brand-new sedan model" (140) and was about to fulfil her dream when her voice, which is a marker of her personal trauma, becomes a marginalising factor and an obstacle towards fulfilling her dream. Unable to continue his job at the bank, Fe decides to take a job in a Factory and thus moves closer to her destruction. Through the Acme International, which mainly employs uneducated Chicana, Mexican and indigenous women and forces them to work long hours, Castillo emphasises the misuse and brutal treatment of these marginalised women who are considered readily obtainable to large companies like Acme. Although Fe thought that her job with Acme will provide her financial agency, it, ultimately, proves illusory as Marta Caminero-Santangelo says, "Consumer society offers the illusion of choice to disguise the absence of real agency to change one's life" (95). Fe's inability to reappear to her family and friends after her death explains her systematic and violent erasure from this world, which is clearly patriarchal, extremely racist, and notoriously capitalist. Although Fe dies as a result of her desperate attempt to reach 'American Dream', she is able to gather the necessary strength to protest the toxic environmental state, which is an outcome of the ideology behind that dream. Castillo thus emphasises the necessity of waging a collective protest against the violence inflicted on ethnic labourers such as Chicanas. However, instead of relying on a masculinist attitude, she does so from a female perspective. Fe's act of resistance reflects Castillo's desire to rewrite the interaction between minority groups like Chicanas and the dominant power structure.

Through the story of Sofia's eldest daughter Esperanza, Castillo also highlights the marginalisation of the Chicanas by white culture. A television journalist, Esperanza goes missing while covering news in Saudi Arabia during the Gulf War. Ironically and interestingly, it is through her physical disappearance that she gets recognised. Put another way, no one notices her when she was alive; however, through her absence, she becomes significant for them. By implying that American media care for a captured and dead Chicana journalist and not for a living one, Castillo underscores the marginalised condition of the minorities such as Chicana in the US culture. As Castillo writes, she becomes "a famous prisoner of war [and] instead of giving the news live in person like she did in the old days, her picture was flashed" on the screen (46). Even after death Esperanza's body remains absent as the US Army were unable to find her body despite claiming her dead. While talking about the absence of minorities in US television or media, Phil Chidester explains that whiteness on the television asserts its dominance over other ethnic groups through the absence of these groups from the screen, while the presence of whiteness fades from mind in its presumed neutrality (159). Castillo shows the way Esperanza's presence in the dangerous condition of the Gulf War makes it possible for white reporters like Diana Sawyer to continue her job from the safety of the newsroom and thus to exert white dominance.

Rewriting Myth/Creating a New *Mestiza* Myth to Show Female Empowerment

Contemporary Chicana authors attempt to rewrite the pre-Columbian and post-Conquest myths and legends as rewriting mythology is an effective means of questioning or challenging oppressive power structures and correcting negative mythological representation of women. Barbara Cook opines that the act of rewriting myth gives a voice and agency to those who have been silenced historically, politically, and culturally:

> Rewriting of traditional communal stories are acts of cultural resistance. ... Through the revision of their own traditional narratives, Chicana writers [...] challenge prevailing ideas that see storytelling as just serving a creative end. ... The revision of these traditional stories, rooted in cultural tradition, create both identity and community in a marginalized group, and act as a site of resistance to change language and concepts of dominant history. (125)

Although this rewriting of myth is subversive and disruptive, it has the power to induce communal healing within the Chicana community, where it is crucial to identify the contemporary reverberation of folkloric characters. In *So Far from God*, Castillo rewrites myths like La Llorona and La Malogra from traditional Mexican American mythology in order to question the narrow, patriarchal understandings of Chicana discourse. She rewrites La Llorona to depict a strong female identity and to investigate the issues associated with class, gender, and spirituality within a hybrid context. La Llorona plays a great role in the lives of Sofia's daughters—in the case of Fe, it's about her environmental concerns, and For La Loca, it's the denial of western logocentrism. According to Martínez, "Castillo draws on myth to underscore the psychic and physical consequences that can result from internalizing oppressive dominant ideologies (as is the case with Fe), and from challenging them (as La Loca demonstrates)" (220). Sofia's youngest daughter La Loca's constant communication with La Llorona makes it possible for her to predict the death of other people. La Llorona's act of giving La Loca the death news of Esperanza establishes her as a feminist force. The subversive act of rewriting the myth of La Llorona, which includes many magical events surrounding La Loca's life, shifts the power from the dominant to the dominated, readdressing the concept of reality from a marginalised (read Chicana) perspective. Again, La Loca's magical resurrections after her mysterious death but before her burial is considered by the white-male-dominated Catholic Church as the work of the devil. La Loca's entering the church after her resurrection with the people following her invokes a Christ-like image and produces an alternative history or myth. Although Castillo recreates the story of Catholicism, she places a young female Chicana at the centre instead of a white male and, therefore, attempts to alter the established power structure. Following the way Anzaldúa opines the connection between *mestizas* and new myths, Castillo places Christianity around the *mestiza* women and highlights the way Roman Catholic Church contributed to reinforcing the dominance of white males.

After becoming the first mayor of the city Tome, Sofia starts a new model of social development, enabling the community people to live in the land of their ancestors, and becomes the president of "M.O.M.A.S., Mothers of Martyrs and Saints" (Castillo 199), an association of mothers who rejoice the sainthood of their daughters. Sofia's belief that the association is a means to remember her daughters and, at the same time, to resist patriarchy provides the novel with a positive vision of breaking down dominant discourse. M.O.M.A.S. subverts the authority of the Catholic Church, which refuses to see the values of her daughters and people like them by pronouncing La Loca and other victimised girls as saints without any interference of the church. Sofia's initiating a co-op helps the community to be self-sufficient and provides local products to its inhabitants at a cheaper rate. Sofia becomes successful in establishing a common space for women in Tome with the help of the spirits of La Loca and Esperanza. The M.O.M.A.S. conference shows a close association between both mortal and spirit worlds, where both saints and spirits mingle with the living and face the difficulty of the contemporary materialistic world. Castillo writes,

> Wandering among the living would be their all-too-glorious (if hard to pin down) santito and martyred 'jitos. They came to converse with their moms, as well as with each other. … But what a beautiful sight it all became at those reunions: 'jitos from all over the world, some transparent, some looking incarnated but you knew they weren't if you tested them in some way, like getting them to take a bite out of a taquito

> or something when, of course, after going through all the motions like he was eating it, the taco would still be there. (203)

The description of saints and spirits conversing with their mothers in a matter-of-fact manner and the supernatural beings performing mundane tasks such as eating tacos dissolves the border between the real and the magical and highlights the use of magical realism in the text, connecting magic with political issues.

While Chicanas are socially and culturally marginalised, within the community, women are seen inferior to men. The negative effect of the male-centred society upon women is shown through the myth of *malogra*, meaning 'the evil hour'. The violent and inhuman attack on Caridad shows the way women are the helpless victims of a patriarchal society, presenting *malogra* as some sort of agent of patriarchy. However, Castillo also produces a *mestiza* myth to demonstrate female assertion of their agency by challenging patriarchal constraints. The news of the magical incident where three men try unsuccessfully to pull Caridad, who is not heavy at all, spreads like wildfire and turns her into some sort of saint with people paying a visit to her cave—a new *mestiza* legend—and makes her more powerful than the men both physically and spiritually. It can be claimed that it is Caridad's reluctance to men and her homosexual desire that empowers her as Collette Morrow terms it a "feminist-lesbian miracle" (75) and depicts the way *malogra* legend is replaced by "the vision of a woman defying traditional heterosexual constructions of gender" (76). Caridad's homosexual tendency, her indifference towards men, and their expectations of women all distinguish her and liberate her from the patriarchal society which once victimised her. Caridad's death, along with Esmeralda where both women jumped off a high mesa is considered supernatural as their bodies, whether whole or splintered, were not found:

> [Francisco] went to the edge of the mesa along with the other tourists in Sky City [...]. There was nothing. Just the spirit deity Tsichtinako calling loudly with a voice like wind, guiding the two women back, not out toward the sun's rays or up to the clouds but down, deep within the soft, moist dark earth where Esmeralda and Caridad would be safe and live forever. (Castillo 170)

Caridad's death is a mythical return to her native origin and is considered by Ralph Rodriguez "a romantic connection to the earth and a rebirth. ... They have returned to what the Acoma myth of creation refers to as the earth's womb" (Rodriguez 90). The spirit deity Tsichtinako, who guides both women, stands for the omnipresent female spirit, simply the Mother Earth. Through the *mestiza* myth, Castillo wants to show that although women fail to free themselves from the patriarchal oppression during their lives on the earth, they will certainly be free in the world of spirits provided that they are connected with the *mestiza* spiritually. Caridad'a death becomes an expression of a deep and intense feeling of spirituality, which she has been looking for since her meeting with *malogra.*

Castillo employs magical realism to show the way women are marginalised and brutalised by reanalysing the legend of La Llorona or 'The Weeping Woman'. It is through connecting Esperanza with La Llorona that her story is redefined. Instead of the traditional portrayal of an evil spirit, La Llorona is redefined as a loving but desperate mother or a "mother [who] was only human and anyone is capable at some point when pushed into a corner like a rat to devour her babies in order to save them, so to speak" (Castillo 128). Although Esperanza receives cultural and gendered marginalisation in both personal and professional levels, she overcomes all sorts of victimisation through her death and becomes free as Lanza claims, "Once Esperanza becomes a spirit, she is no longer a victim or an object of the white world. She belongs to [...] a spiritual world that 'the whites are so adamant in denying"' (69). Esperanza's act of sending La Llorona as a messenger to let her family members know of her own death and later herself visiting the world from the afterlife clearly shows that La Llorona is not wicked the way society has pictured her. Through rewriting the story of La Llorona, Castillo seems to be saying that women commit misconducts because they are victimised by the external factors. Through the use of myth and magic, Castillo criticises the negative depiction of women, challenging the way society attempts to cover up men's wrongdoings.

Castillo employs the 'fantastic rhetoric', a characteristics of magical realism, to show the dangers for a *mestiza* to lose connection with her cultural heritage. By using fantastic rhetoric, Fe's realistic death is depicted as something unusual and, to some extent, magical. Fe's way of doing things, which contrasts her mother, results in an unusual death than her sisters and fails to offer her any resurrection as Castillo writes, "Fe just died. And when someone dies that plain dead, it is hard to talk about" (148). Since Fe has severed her ties with her spiritual *mestiza* identity, she dies a permanent death and, unlike other sisters, is unable to visit the world after her death. By dissolving the boundaries between the real and the magical, Castillo attempts to show the significance of the *mestiza* heritage for Chicana women. She uses magical realist elements to (re)write myths, highlighting Chicana women, so that she can show the way they are treated negatively and brutally by, and in, American society.

Mexican Folk Healing and Close Connection with Nature

Although Caridad suffers terribly from the attack of *malogra*, she overcomes the physical and psychological wounds with the assistance and guidance of other female characters, and her deep connection with nature and Mexican folk healings, which starkly contrast the Western medicinal views of healing. Caridad's healing process, which contains multiple magical aspects, is largely due to the effort of Sofia and La Loca. Apart from her own healing, Caridad also assists Fe to come to terms with her trauma of separation with her boyfriend, where Fe magically stops screaming and becomes quiet. This non-Western healing method for both sisters plainly contrasts the situation of Caridad under Western medicinal practice. Caridad's healing process is itself a means of resistance against patriarchal society—it is the female bonding that has made her stronger than ever before. The ancient Mexican folk tradition, which is highly connected to the magical realist narrative, highlights the healer figure, 'the curandera'. Curanderas, which refer to a medicine woman dedicated to healing and assisting others and is intimately connected to nature or the natural world, use Christian, more specifically Catholic rituals, and indigenous practices to induce spiritual healing. This particular healing process comprises herbal treatment, baths, anointment, messages and spirituality. According to Castillo, "In terms of curanderismo, magic is directly related to the supernatural realm of our reality. However, for curanderas the supernatural is a reality based on the natural forces of the universe" (Castillo, "Brujas and Curanderas" 155).

In her *Massacre of the Dreamers*, an essay collection on Chicana agency and empowerment termed as *Xicanisma*, Castillo stresses on the association between *curanderismo* and the Americas: "We have unearthed the ways of our Mexic Amerindian ancestors preserved by our mestizo elders, most often, women, in the form of curanderismo" ("Brujas and Curanderas" 145). Castillo also suggests a self-healing method in order to recuperate "from the devastating blows [Chicanas] receive from society for having been born poor, nonwhite, and female in a hierarchical society" (153). Caridad's curative process emphasises rituals and the "construction of altars" (153), where her home-based ceremonies are closely associated with her spiritual life. Caridad's spiritual practices comprise works like cleaning the incense brazier, lighting white candles, and cleaning the altar. Kay Turner depicts home altars as "predominantly a women's tradition in a male-dominated Church" (Turner

315). However, he also claims that this marginalised folk practice "is denied any formal history by the institution" (Turner 316). Influenced by Doña Felicia, Caridad becomes a curandera where the transfer of healing power among women emphasises "the notion of a home-centered, healing, matriarchal, spiritual heritage" (Olmedo 10). Emphasising the use of natural medicine by women at home, Delgadillo considers home "a center of survival, recovery and self-knowledge" (903). She also says that "although these women feel the effects of a sexist, racist, and exploitative society, they also manifest the power to heal themselves and their communities through prayer, the application of natural remedios and action" (904). Magic and folk healing is thus a survival strategy for women and a strong blow against the authoritative society which aims to subjugate them.

Caridad's connection with nature is not only a way of healing but also of resisting patriarchy and other forces of nature. Living in a cave for over a year, Caridad develops an intimate connection with nature and forgets the society around her. The magical strength Caridad has demonstrated against the people who have come to take her back to society symbolises the strength of women when they are (re)connected with nature. Caridad's new-found strength, where she lifts a horse over her head, is so threatening for the patriarchal society that it makes the men apologise for mishandling her body: "[The] act of many men brought to their knees before the holy hermit, all begging forgiveness for their audacious attempt at manhandling her" (67). Caridad's magical connection with nature empowers her and "begins to deconstruct patriarchal tendencies to exploit women's bodies as well as the Earth's resources" (Holtzman 20). What connects women's body with nature is that both female bodies and Earth's surfaces are abused or mistreated by dominant structures such as patriarchy and consumerism. However, Caridad's close concern for, and association with, nature starkly contrasts the traditional capitalistic notion of the earth (both as land and women) to be utilised and oppressed. Holtzman argues again, "Castillo deconstructs this Western capitalistic system of exploitation by communicating how Caridad and the Earth's landscape are indispensable, and weren't created for patriarchal, economic progress" (21).

Like Catholicism, *curanderismo* and folk healing practices require strong faith. Doña Felicia's remedies for various physical and spiritual diseases—gastrointestinal obstruction, evil eye—address the potential healer as well as the reader and indicate an urgent oral discourse. Since the diseases are both physical and mystical, the healing ceremonies include magic as Sánchez says, "In Doña Felicia's remedies we find instructions such as rolling an egg in the sign of the cross on the stomach of a patient with 'empacho' and breaking it to discover where the obstruction is, or eating the meat of a black hen if a pregnant woman suffers from evil eye" (200). These rituals remind us of the African American healing practices in Gloria Naylor's *Mama Day* where hens and eggs are significant elements in healing process. These similarities between the two novels emphasise the acceptance of local lore and natural medicinal healing. Doña Felicia also teaches her healing power to Caridad, who seems to possess clairvoyance as after her holy restoration, she starts foreseeing the future and makes domestic prophecies such as Esperanza's arrival, the return of their dog and a number that will win a lottery and such. The youngest sister La Loca, who performs miracles and possesses telepathic communication with all animals, giants, spirits, and saints is a special type of curandera. When she falls ill, the family doctor Dr. Tolentino identifies that she is suffering from a disease incurable by Western medicine and suggests an alternative healing method he learnt from his Filipino mother. Dr. Tolentino's action shows the superiority of the Eastern healing system over the Western medical practices. His treatment of psychic surgery which requires unwavering faith and close association with religion, and which needs to be accompanied by prayers and completed with the help of sacred oil dissolves the border between physicality and spirituality and thus can rightly be considered magical realist:

> Doctor Tolentino dipped a cotton ball in a pan of warm water, and as he dripped the water on Loca's stomach with his right hand, his left hand made an opening through her flesh and disappeared right up to the wrist inside her stomach. [...] so fascinated was she to see the doctor's hand disappear into her body. She felt no pain [...]. (Castillo 183)

The contrast between the folk healing which assuages Loca's distress without causing any pain, and the Western healing method that Fe goes through, which involves cruelties and mistakes from the part of the hospital authorities, such as not removing a catheter from her collarbone to give chemotherapy, clearly shows the superiority of Eastern folk healing over the Western one and the way it empowers women. In order to aid La Loca, Doña Felicia shares her healing process with Dr. Tolentino and thus connects her native ancient herbal treatment with his psychic surgery he learnt from his mother's island.

Except for Fe, who was very much fond of American way of life, all three other sisters were able to communicate with their relatives after their death. The death of all four sisters represents the victimisation and systematic silencing of Chicana women. However, through the brutal fate of all the sisters and the rewriting of myths, Castillo attempts to show the way Chicanas can protest against evils like poverty, racial subjugation, and gendered violence inflicted by repressive cultures and institutions. By rewriting Chicana/o mythology from a female viewpoint, Castillo demonstrates the way magic and myth can be a subversive and transgressive means for protest and communal healing. By providing magical power to La Loca, Castillo also challenges the authority of the Catholic Church and advocates an alternative religious practice which is marginalised from both gendered and cultural perspectives. By emphasising the way Caridad's magical connection with nature makes her stronger both physically and spiritually, Castillo demonstrates female superiority over male. Castillo also shows the superiority of indigenous healing practices over Western medical system through *curanderismo* and, therefore, highlights female power and agency.

Part IV.
Questioning Racial and Gendered Supremacy and Empowering Women

Chapter 10

Healing Trauma of Sexual Abuse and Rejecting Patriarchal Authority in Gail Anderson-Dargatz's *The Cure for Death by Lightning*

Gail Anderson-Dargatz's *The Cure for Death by Lightning* deals with the trauma of the sexual abuse of Beth and her mother Maud. Here, trauma finds expression through the scrapbook of Maud, Beth's traumatic imagination, and animals, particularly the mythological Coyote figure. Maud's scrapbook and Beth's autobiography depict a family account of gendered violence and provide some sort of healing for both mother and daughter. It seems that it is her scrapbook and communication with her dead mother in the face of trauma that provide consolation to Maud. Again, although the scrapbook contains Maud's shocking memories of sexual abuse, Beth does not have any access to her accounts. Instead of becoming a vehicle for communication, the scrapbook separates Beth from surrounding female circle, and the spectral presence of her grandmother. The scrapbook thus represses its trauma and, at the same time, turns them into expression, encoding and hiding a cycle of sexual abuse by male family members. Just like the way the butterfly on the first page of Maud's diary is associated with her healing, the cure for death by lightning symbolises Beth's therapeutic journey. In the novel, both traumatic realism and magical realism converge in Beth's lightning arm to voice and thus to heal her trauma. Beth's lightning arm is supernaturally connected with her pain of sexual violence, resistance, and protection, performing what the scrapbook has done for Maud—silent witness and a defence mechanism. Beth's healing can be considered an act of imagination where she creates her own world and takes refuge there. One of Beth's ways of rewriting her trauma is through many of the animals occupying the space in the novel. Animals are metamorphosed from being abused to the symbols of healing.

The novel is set both in terms of Beth's personal experiences of sexual violence and of WWII. The narrative sheds light on a society undergoing changes regarding the economy and gender relations caused by the war. The novel focuses on the gendered and racial conflict over religious and geographical region and keeps raising troubling questions about the status of the settler-invader in Canada. It also evokes a landscape of mountain, forest, river, and bush, and emphasises the geographical and historical isolation of the region. The geographical immensity, along with the cultural variety and hybridity, which are considered to constitute the magical realist conditions of a region or nation, are also observed in Canada. The emphasis on local myths and folklores which are considered significant by Alejo Carpentier, is also prevalent in Native Canadian rituals and tales. Geoff Hancock clarifies that the Latin American magical realism itself might inspire the Canadian writers who are trying to find their own, authentic way of writing. He claims that "Canada is an invisible country in the same way that Colombia, Peru, Argentina, and Paraguay are invisible" (11). It is thus the role of magical realist authors to make the unseen reality visible, "to convince us that the marvellous is possible in a bland surface, and indeed inherent to the place" (10).

Scrapbook and Autobiography as Principal Methods of Healing

The novel opens with the scrapbook on the page, which covers the cure for death by lightning, Beth's father's cake recipes and the broken-winged butterfly. Although the scrapbook is, in general, a female form of writing, it goes beyond the generic border where Beth's repressed family trauma of sexual abuse is metamorphosed, partly through the butterfly with a broken wing. She later uses the scrapbook as evidence to write her own story, and by doing so, she sheds light on the sexual abuses narrated in her story and her mother's awareness about them. Beth explains that the scrapbook was her mother's "way of setting down the days so they wouldn't be forgotten. This story is my way. No one can tell me these events didn't happen, or that it was all a girl's fantasy. The reminders are there, in that scrapbook, and I remember them all" (Anderson-Dargatz 14). Beth's mother Maud's awareness of her trauma, which is mentioned in the scrapbook, works as a passive spectator to Beth's suffering from a series of trauma. Instead of giving Beth an access to her scrapbook, Maud basically hides it from her and thus detaches Beth from her (Maud's) female community. For Maud, it is the scrapbook and the conversation with her deceased mother which provides her with some sort of consolation and guidance during her traumatic periods. Entering the house, Beth finds Maud "sitting at the kitchen table, writing on one of the pages of her scrapbook, mumbling to [Beth's] dead grandmother" (86). By failing to protect Beth from her father's sexual desire, which is her responsibility as a mother, Maud proves herself no less despicable than John, Beth's father.

Herself being the victim of an incestuous sexual abuse, Maud fails to cope with Beth's trauma of sexual violence and isolates herself in the realm of the scrapbook and the imaginary communion with her deceased mother. Beth sadly admits that her "mother was no help, no help at all. She sat in her rocking chair, rocking and rocking, hanging on to her scrapbook, staring off at nothing. [Her] mother sat in her chair all that time, rocking, muttering, and [her] father didn't say a word about it" (Anderson-Dargatz 184-185). It is a photo of Maud with her parents that gives Beth a clue about Maud's own trauma(tisation):

> My mother wore a nurse's uniform and stood very tall over her own tiny mother. My grandmother was dressed in dark and lacy Victorian garb and looked very old and tired, but my grandfather, an engineer, looked quite dapper. He was smiling and had his hand around my mother's waist. Neither my grandmother nor my mother was smiling. ... My mother became the woman of the house then, making the meals and tending her mother and looking after her two younger sisters. As my grandmother became increasingly bedridden, my mother also became her father's escort to plays and concerts. She became his favorite of the three daughters. *He bought her silk stockings*, boxes of candy, and called her dear. (26; my emphasis)

The photograph can be strong evidence of the family legacy of sexual violence, where the reference to the silk stockings is particularly significant, which Maud ultimately includes in her scrapbook. Maud's father's buying stocking for her suggests that he does not see her as his daughter but rather from a sexual standpoint, considering that Maud's mother is bedridden and that she has to attend different events with her father. In other words, the act of buying stockings, in a way, sexualises the relationship between Maud and her father. Maud's scrapbook can be considered a text which hides trauma but at the same time transforms those traumatic events or memories into expression.

On the morning after her trauma of sexual abuse, Beth is awakened by Maud with a "butterfly kiss" (Anderson-Dargatz 86). Maud creates the butterfly as a gift for Beth: "It was made from petals of scarlet flax, and my mother's fingers breathed life into it. This was a child's game; it made me angry" (86). Maud's sense of trauma and desire of healing is symbolised by the torn-winged butterfly that keeps flying in the scrapbook and in the gift. Although Maud shows her understanding of Beth's sexual abuse and attempts to comfort her with a child's game, she fails to save Beth from the lust of John, suffering from the helplessness of being a silent witness to it. However, nowhere in the text is there any clear mentioning of Maud witnessing the rape of her daughter; it just hints at the possibility of the presence of Maud, symbolising Beth's assumption that both of them must have known what has happened with her. Maud seems to speak about her trauma only when she mutters incomprehensibly to her dead mother, who haunts her and whose apparition seems to be addressed in the narrative. Beth says, "My dead grandmother had taken over the rocker; it went on rocking all through dinner" (200). Maud's ability to commune with her dead mother blurs the border between the dead and the living and seems to suggest the comforting and guiding abilities of the dead. Again, the presence of the spectre of the grandmother suggests that Maud also suffered from sexual violence by her father. After her rape by her father, Beth leaves her room and sees the ghostly presence of her grandmother: "I followed my body [...] through the parlor and past my father, who slept in his chair by the gramophone as if he'd never entered my room. Over him, her face reflecting the dim light from my bedroom window, my grandmother watched him grimly" (166). The silent presence of the ghost refers to the family legacy of silence over sexual abuse.

To Maud, her scrapbook, apart from writing, is also a source of healing from trauma. The family saga of gendered violence is represented by nylons bought by John and later added by Maud to her scrapbook. Maud becomes enraged, knowing that her husband has purchased nylons for a "delighted and mortified" Beth since she never received any from him (Anderson-Dargatz 178). Being traumatised for some moments after learning about the nylons, Maud starts mumbling to her departed mother while rocking in her chair, "rocking and rocking, hanging on to her scrapbook, staring off at nothing" (184). Beth's attempt to comfort her mother goes in vain as "[her mother] looked through [her], like a stubborn child punishing the parent that punished her" (185). The fact that it is Maud, and not Beth, who is traumatised, indicates that Maud has been re-traumatised by Beth's trauma to such a high level that she begins to re-enact her past events. Through Maud's confession, "'My father gave me stockings too—silk stockings—while my mother went without'", a shared experience of sexual abuse is expressed (186). The closeness between Beth's knowledge of the nylons and her privileges—the torn-winged butterfly and the lightning arm, representing metamorphosis and cure—implies that the narrative she is creating mainly focuses on her healing process, leaving her trauma on the scrapbook. Maud's scrapbook can be considered her "private place", which everybody needs in the time of distress (Anderson-Dargatz 196). Beth's novel and Maud's scrapbook externalise their traumatic experiences and thus possess therapeutic feature.

Beth's Lightning Arm and the Field of the Flax as Healing Mechanisms

Just like the way the butterfly in the scrapbook is associated with Maud's trauma and healing, the cure for death by lightning mirrors Beth's therapeutic journey: Beth's lightning arm is a magical weapon for voicing and curing trauma. Apart from being raped by her father, Beth is also sexually victimised by a group of her classmates who provoke her by naming her "Dirty Beth" and calling her mother a "witch" who "talks to the Devil" and her father crazy (Anderson-Dargatz 87). Her lightning arm goes dead, marking the escalation of her trauma. When Beth is finally let to go after being taken to a deserted house and stripped of her clothing, she has the weird feeling of being followed by someone. Beth takes shelter in her imagination:

> [...] it seemed if I were to stay very still everything would stop. ... After some time like that, the hand on my lightning arm began to expand, spread out like a balloon, take on proportions much too big for my arm, big enough to hit back. ... I stared up at the blue forget-me-nots on the headboard of my bed and put myself there, in a stream full of them. (89)

As Beth does not have the physical strength to fight the boys who are bullying her, she imagines her lightning arm possesses the required strength to bounce back. In other words, Beth's imagination gives her some sort of strength which she unsuccessfully desires to have in her real life. Together with the calming blue flowers that give Beth comfort, her lightning arm extends imaginarily to save her from her attackers.

Not finding any comfortable environment at home, Beth runs into the velvet flax, but her attempt to console herself is prevented by a storm, ultimately sending her back home. Following Beth's failure to comfort herself through all real(istic) attempts, the story assumes a magical mood by changing the surroundings into violet flax:

> I pressed my face against the window and saw a rain begin to fall, so gently the raindrops seemed to float. Then I saw they weren't raindrops, they were flowers, violet flax, fluttering to the ground. In no time at all

> the rain covered the earth in flowers. I opened my window and crawled out onto the purple carpet, took my shoes off and paddled around in pools of flax. The fragrance was intoxicating. The clouds moved on, and still the violet flax drifted down from a blue sky. (Anderson-Dargatz 90)

Dropping flowers from the sky instead of rain, even when the cloud moves and the sky becomes blue, is a magical realist phenomenon. The fact that Beth fails to get rid of her trauma through realistic means and that she must resort to magical means clearly emphasises the role of magical realist elements in giving comfort to people and healing their trauma by creating a magical world for them to take refuge. Anne Hegerfeldt argues that "literalization is behind much of magic realism's magic, for many of the apparently fantastic events are based on a making-real of figures of speech, mental concepts, or psychological mechanisms" (56). Michelle Coupal argues, "[...] Beth's psychological defence mechanism of dissociating into the flowers of her headboard and field of flax is literalized into a therapeutic imaginary of healing pools of flax in a transformed world of blue" (152). By transforming Beth's sordid material world into one that is comfortable, beautiful and way removed from the trauma of her abuse, the purple flax provides Beth with a magical relief. It is thus, by creating a magical realist world through Beth's imagination, that Anderson-Dargatz enables her to get rid of her trauma of asexual abuse by her classmates. As Beth asserts, "With blue flax in my cupped hands, blue flax on my hair, my face, my dress, I looked over a world that was blue and as strange as a dream. The shame of nakedness in front of the kids at school seemed so far from this blue world" (91). When Filthy Billy was assessing the damage of John's old car, Beth imagines that she can fly—a clear indication of her desire of freedom: "It occurred to me that if I ran down that hill, I could fly. I spread my arms, and it felt like that: the air carried me" (92).

One of Beth's primary ways of imaginative rewriting of her trauma of sexual abuse is through animals. The death of Sarah, who was apparently killed by a bear, is described in sexual terms by Beth's brother Dan that she was "pulled apart from the crotch up" and that her thighs and nipples were partially devoured (Anderson-Dargatz 33). Throughout the novel, animals are graphically and disturbingly linked to sex or sexual violence. The old cat lifting the kittens foreshadows Beth's trauma and future human acts of sexual violence. By attempting to hide the kittens from her father and the cat, Beth makes a connection between the sexually predacious cat and her father. The instance of traumatic detachment takes place when Beth fails to save the kittens and look at the dead bodies in the bucket: "Then I removed myself and watched my hands take up a shovel, make a hole in the manure pile, and empty the foul water and the bodies of the dead kittens into it. Their bodies slid from the bucket like fish. I covered them over with manure, then followed myself to the barn, like a child following her mother" (49). Here, Beth is clearly a traumatised subject who is following an invisible mother (read unsympathetic and uncaring). The entire traumatic scene, which starts with the death of the kittens and reaches the climax with the rape of Beth, is later repeated in other events, including the torture of Gertrude, the cow, with the increase of John's sexual appetite and depravity. Beth's forced involvement in John's brutal treatment of Gertrude, the cow, metaphorically displaces her own sexual abuse, highlighting the way sexual trauma is recurrently foretold by and fantasised through animals. John's act of performing the operation to remove Gertrude's ovaries becomes an act of sexual torture. John's remark to Beth after showing her the cow's ovaries—"'You have these [...]. This is what makes you female'" (85)—suggests that Beth is featured in terms of her reproductive organs and that John can easily take from her the very thing that makes her female. The remark also strengthens the dehumanising and misogynistic side of sexual attack and suggests that Beth is more connected to animals than John is. The frequent sexualisation of animals, together with the recurring violence on Beth, disturbingly connects women with animals, representing Beth as some sort of meat to be consumed or an object to be sexually abused.

Whereas for Maud, the scrapbook works as a silent mediator for her trauma, it is the coyotes which are Beth's ways of imagining and arbitrating her unvoiced trauma. However, in neither of the circumstances, is trauma articulated but rather is experienced or reconstructed metaphorically in the scrapbook. Beth, therefore appositely emphasises healing through the scriptotherapeutic act of turning her concealed experiences into narratives. Quite significantly, the construction of Beth's storyline is emphasised in the final pages where she finds the healing source(s). Although her book will differ from her mother's one—"It would be a book of words, my words" (Anderson-Dargatz 253)—it will be a secured place for her to unleash her emotion. She can now comprehend her mother's magical communication with her departed grandmother as a healing act: "It was craziness, talking to a dead woman, but she spoke the words, got them out of her mouth, and that was what mattered" (253). Beth is determined to write down her thoughts on paper in order to end the history of traumatic hauntings in her family. Beth's ability to put her thoughts in writing provides her with the sense of healing and some sort of agency, having the courage to face her abusive and sexually pervert father:

"'You never touch me again [...]. Keep your goddamned hands off me. You're my father, for Christ's sake'" (256).

The Role of Native Coyote Figure

The Cure for Death by Lightning represents traumatic imagination, in particular through the use of the Native Coyote figure. Beth's trauma of sexual abuse, which she cannot utter and which Maud refuses to listen to, finds written expression through Maud's scrapbook and the Native Coyote figure, where Coyote is associated with the dichotomy between female victims and male victimisers. Fred Botting opines, "In keeping with Gothic conventions, Coyote's possession of the bush is initially aligned with the familiar binary opposition between helpless young women and male victimisers whose erotic and incestuous tendencies raise the spectre of complete social disintegration (5). When Beth is followed by a mysterious and threatening force, she states, "It could be anything: a man like the ones my mother's friend Mrs. Bell warned of, who would catch a girl in the bush and do unspeakable things to her" (Anderson-Dargatz 16).

In the scenes that precede Beth's rape by John, both the real and the mystical are frequently mentioned. After being approached by a young man at a social gathering, Beth runs towards home for safety where she notices a dying sheep whose sex organs are devoured by a coyote. However, the real coyotes which have predicted the sexual violence of Beth by her father are metamorphosed into spectral coyotes: "Though my mother must have been awake, he came into my room, came to my bed as a black faceless thing, with only the form of a man" (166). To adjust with the brutality of the event, Beth gives full attention to the blue flowers on the headboard and attempts to take an imaginary sojourn there: "I removed myself into the forget-me-knots painted on the headboard of my bed, and watched from there, leaving all the fear and anger in my body" (166). Apart from taking the imaginary resort, Beth also retaliates with her lightning arm to defend her. In addition, Beth's experience of the shocking remembrance of the scene—"[...] coyotes put their claws over my mouth. They lifted my nightgown. They rubbed their wet tails between my legs and over my belly. ... When they had their fill, the shadows sighed deeply, came together, and took the form of my father. He lifted his weight from my body and left the room" (233)—clearly shows her father's involvement in her being abused: coyotes thus metonymically symbolise John's sexual attack on Beth.

Magical realism emphasises multiple versions of reality and thus multiple ways of knowing the world, and the novel *The Cure for Death by Lightning* is keen on presenting more than one version of every traumatic event that takes place. Whereas in the official version, it is the bear which is responsible for the death of Sarah, Bertha's daughter persistently offers a more magical and grotesque view that "'That was a man that done the killing. Coyote come and took him over'" (Anderson-Dargatz 73) or stresses on the mysterious Coyote figure whose "body flitted back and forth between man and coyote, then the coyote dropped on all fours and cowered away" (240). The unofficial version of traumatic events involves the reference to the Coyote myth; however, concerning the official version with coyote, Macpherson opines, "Coyote is both a shape-shifting spirit who controls damaged men's behaviour, and a real animal who kills the helpless and the vulnerable, animal and human alike" (94). In these multiple ways to know the reality or the world, magical realism thus functions to question reality. Just like magical realism, the discourse of trauma also disrupts the uncomplicated understanding of a uniform psychological experience or reality. Anderson-Dargatz uses coyote figure as the manifestation of traumatic imagination—a way of voicing the inexpressible trauma of sexual abuse which exceeds our imagination. As Hegerfeldt suggests, "In supernaturalizing cruel events, the texts express a stunned incredulity about the state of the world, implying that the idea of such things actually happening exceeds—or should exceed—the human imagination" (61). The novel thus exposes the inability of realist narrative to represent trauma in a graspable way and advocates the subversive and penetrative aspects of magical realist narrative to do so.

Magical Realism, Canadian Gothic and Female Strength

Anderson-Dargatz equates the challenges posed by Beth's lesbian friend Nora, a Native girl, with the global threats to the Canadian nation-state. By constantly asking Beth to elope with her, Nora herself symbolises the possibility of women defying patriarchal constraints and invokes the subversive power of lesbian relationship. As their relationship continues to develop, an interesting shift is observed in the threatening phantom-like force where the coyote is associated with Nora. Aligning Nora with coyotes turns her phantom-like probably because, as opined by Castle, "to love another woman is to lose one's solidity in the world, to evanesce, and fade into the spectral" (32). Castle seems to be saying that, a lesbian relationship might reduce the acceptance of women in the male-dominated society, but it definitely provides them a magical bond by allowing them to go beyond the social restriction and poses a threat to the oppressors. In other words, a lesbian relationship provides women with agency and emancipation. The dual-threat Nora poses to the patriarchy and the Canadian society is manifested through her uncommon eyes: "Each of her eyes was a different color, one blue and one green. She was a half-breed, then" (Anderson-Dargatz 24). Beth later says that Nora "was Indian enough to be an outcast in town and white enough to be an outcast on the reserve" (93). Apart from her split identity, a mixture of native and white, Nora's two-coloured eyes also show her potential homosexual tendency, referred to by the Native North Americans as "two-spirit people" or "the eyes of two women in one face" (72). Nora can be the embodiment of female empowerment because of possessing more than one woman in her and of blurring the dress differences between men and women. She is considered a threat to both native and settler's community and thus is ridiculed and attacked by both communities.

The Cure for Death by Lightning draws an association between freakishness or the grotesque and female independence. Mary Russo considers the grotesque body as "the open, protruding, extended, secreting body, the body of becoming, process, and change. The grotesque body is opposed to the Classical body, which is monumental, static, closed, and sleek, corresponding to the aspirations of bourgeois individualism; the grotesque body is connected to the rest of the world" (Russo 62-63). Regarding the grotesque's potential to challenge the dominant authority or ideology, Abdullah says,

> The grotesque body resists containment, rather strives for and welcomes change; indeed, it cannot but change. [...] in the grotesque, one finds an avenue to challenge the norm, to establish meaningful social change, whether that be women's rights, gay rights, or the rights of other marginalized groups. It is confronting the hegemonic with the existence of the marginalized, often through somewhat fantastical means —it is for this reason that the grotesque fits snuggly within the multivalent category of magical realism. ("Fluids, Cages, and Boisterous Femininity" 115)

Beth notices that apart from Nora with two-coloured eye, several other women in Bertha's household are characterised by bodily grotesque. During the reader's first meeting with Bertha, Beth states that "Bertha had no husband and no son. Her house was a house of women" (Anderson-Dargatz 20). By demonstrating the female dominance in Bertha's house, the narrative poses a threat to the patriarchal notion of a family ruled by a man, providing agency to the native women. Beth goes on observing that "One of the daughters' daughter was pregnant, another had webbed fingers" (20) and that Nora' mother possesses "a man's voice" (109) and "an extra finger on her right hand" (109). The bodily grotesque of Bertha's female family members alienates them from other people, causes some sort of fear in those people, assists them to assert female rights, and ultimately results in female empowerment.

Both magical realism and the gothic can converge and form a unique world. Both modes challenge the rational approach to the reality presented in novels, contest a singular version of reality and a linear narrative progression, and advocate multiple versions of truth or reality. Lucy Armitt argues over the cooperation between the gothic and magical realism, stressing on the way magical realist novels, particularly Canadian ones, quite regularly share gothic settings—haunted houses and natural scenarios—and quite often combine traditionally extensive and invasive landscapes with "inevitably claustrophobic" gothic landscapes (Armitt 308). Armitt's one of the keys to the association between the gothic and magical realism is the uncanny as she opines that both modes show "a surprising narrative similarity" in terms of the travel into the mysterious and unconscious (308). Armitt's another key is the idea of transgenerational trauma or haunting. She argues that when the gothic and magical realism combines with each other, "we find a perfect territory for cryptonym, magic realism reminding us of the omnipresence of transgenerational haunting by giving it a shared cultural, political and mimetic sanction, while the Gothic continues to endow that presence with the sinister particularity of the nuclear family unit" (Armitt 315). Armitt thus emphasises the political side of magical realism that, in association with the gothic, politicises "the unconscious through transgenerational haunting" (307). In *The Cure for Death by Lightning*, both Maud and Beth's experiences of sexual abuse at the hands of their own fathers shed light on a shared culture of incest in a male-dominated society. This issue clearly aligns with the transgenerational haunting, combining magical realism with gothic elements.

Conforming to Gothic tradition, the dystopian, patriarchal family structure makes Beth feel suffocated at her home: '"It's so dark in here, I feel like I'm suffocating"' (Anderson-Dargatz 116). On the other hand, the utopian potential of Beth and Nora's friendship is evident in their finding a hideout in the forest, which was once owned by Bertha Moses. By clarifying that before belonging to her grandmother, the house was her "great-granny's house" (105), Nora indicates the house has been owned by the family for generations. Again, by demonstrating that the house has belonged to many of her female ancestors, Noria sheds light on female possession of the property and to some extent shows their empowerment. With its "opening into darkness at the center of [a] mound of dirt and weeds" (105), the layout of the house resembles female sex organ, emphasising female possession and control over their properties: house and genitalia. By telling Beth that her mother "'used to say the winter houses were safe like a mother's hug'" (108), Nora makes a significant association between the house and the female body. Goldman asserts that "the girls' discovery of the ancient, underground Native home [...] affirms the [...] potential for escaping and radically revising the structure of the mainstream, patriarchal family" (27). The fact that the winter house is passing through the maternal lines and that it now belongs to Nora is a strong blow against patriarchy.

It is the combination of magical realism, the grotesque, Canadian gothic and the uncanny that allows Anderson-Dargatz to give her female characters the necessary strength to fight their gendered violence and, to some extent, ethnic marginalisation. Beth's lightning arm and the field of the flax provide her with imaginary healing. Again, it is through different animals, particularly female ones, that Beth comes up with an imaginative rewriting of her trauma of sexual abuse. Magical realism in the novel also provides the author with the required scope to come up with alternative versions of events which starkly contrast the official, patriarchal version. Anderson-Dargatz also emphasises the bodily deformity of some female members of a Native family and the lesbian tendency of a Native girl, Nora, connects both phenomena with female independence, and advocates a female-oriented family and society, providing a strong blow against a patriarchal and racist society. Last but not least, the novel emphasises the role of deceased family members in healing female trauma of sexual violence, which is evident from the communication between Maud and her dead mother.

Chapter 11

Challenging White History and Emphasising Female Solidarity in Gloria Naylor's *Mama Day*

African American author Gloria Naylor's *Mama Day* focuses on female empowerment through the supernatural power and magical healing ritual of a black character, Mama Day, who floats on the border between the natural and the supernatural. Through Mama Day's magical 'fertility rite' which helps Bernice to conceive, Naylor shows the way women heal other women, and thus emphasises female empowerment. By giving the African American inhabitants of the fictional Willow Springs, a woman-centred island controlled by a woman with magical power, a voice, Naylor attempts to create an entire world for the black people, devoid of many of the facts or facets of the racial history of the US. Again, through the depiction of the matriarch Sapphira Wade, who has the ability to draw magical power from nature and who is believed to be a divine woman, Naylor seems to question the reality based on written evidence and advocates an alternative oral reality, which is subjective. Naylor shows the way the Willow Springers defend themselves against the White exploitation, Western education system, and the loss of cultural memory through their oral tradition and the fostering of the memory of the past.

Although the novel starts with a collective prologue, it contains two distinct parts: one occurs in New York, a megacity, and the other in Willow Springs, an unmapped island inhabited by mostly black people. By juxtaposing two different, even contradictory, worldviews—one is realistic, and the other is magical—Naylor creates a liminal space, emphasising the plurality of worlds, spaces, and heterogeneity. This liminal space takes apart the difference(s) between the real and the supernatural, giving access to a space where the unspeakable can be spoken and the unrepresentable can be represented. In the novel, through the first-person discourse between Cocoa and George, who reminisce about their early lives together, we are provided with two versions of their stories, particularly the action-packed summer in Willow Springs. It becomes clear only at the end of the story that we are following a narrator,

George, who has been dead for many years. The dialogue between George and Cocoa shows a conflict between a male and female tradition and between a rational and spiritual worldview. The magical Willow Springs, which is unmapped and unchartered, is connected to the mainland by a bridge which needs to be rebuilt by the inhabitants of the island following every storm: "[…] Willow Springs ain't in no state. […] the only thing connects us to the mainland is bridge–and even that gotta be rebuilt after every big storm" (Naylor 4). The reader is provided with the family tree of the Day family, beginning with Sapphira Wade, the founder of Willow Springs, and going down to Mama Day "springing from the seventh son of a seventh son" (6) and Cocoa, Mama Day's grandniece. The reference to the postscript of the family tree: "'God rested on the seventh day and so would she.' Hence, the family's last name" (1) indicates that Sapphira possesses celestial status and is compared with God. She is described as a woman of incredible powers:

> She could walk through a lightning storm without being touched; grab a bolt of lightning in the palm of her hand; use the heat of lightning to start the kindling going under her medicine pot: depending upon which of us takes a mind to her. She turned the moon into salve, the stars into a swaddling cloth, and healed the wounds of every creature walking up on two or down on four. It ain't about right or wrong, truth or lies; […]. (3)

In the novel, both an inner and an outer frame can be distinguished, juxtaposing the modern city world represented by New York with the natural, mythical, and magical world of Willow Springs.

In *Mama Day*, Naylor emphasises the notions of land and genealogy. Willow Springs is geographically situated between Georgia and South Carolina; however, it belongs to neither of the states. It is a secluded world which is literally untouched and thus uncorrupted by American civilisation, where the slave culture has sustained. The act of locating Willow Springs within the islands where black identity and African tradition survived as these places are inhabited for centuries by the successors of the African and Barbadian slaves and on the edge of things without any map or location, refer to the magical realist technique of establishing an alternative, autonomous world where any magical event is possible. The fact that the land gives the former slaves some sort of refuge from white conventions and exploitations and the chance to recover their own identity and traditions and to present an alternative to white history adds a political connotation to the place and a political flavour to the text.

Empowering Women through Magical Healing Practices or Rituals

The prevalent supernatural context of Willow Springs and the matriarchal Day family demonstrate female dominance. In Willow Springs, George serves more as a caregiver to Miranda, Abigail, and Cocoa. Nevertheless, Cocoa's potential ally, Miranda, and the malevolent villain, Ruby, have more influence on Cocoa's life than George has. George's logic and rationality fail to save Cocoa, whereas Miranda's mystic power restores Cocoa's health from Ruby's lethal spell. Therefore, the magical realism incorporated in *Mama Day* empowers the female characters to depict their impact on each other as a collective. Nesrin Yavaş talks about the use of magical realism in *Mama Day* to re-conceptualise the collective past to "empower black women through temporal and cultural changes" (71). Again, the idea of female consciousness is quite crucial to formulate solidarity based on common experiences and oppression. As a result, the myth of Sapphira Wades' contribution in emancipating her predecessors, Miranda and Abigail, by resisting slavery in the past has indirectly affected Cocoa's life. Miranda and Abigail have witnessed the misfortune of the women who were born before Cocoa in the Day family. Their acknowledgement of the past misery solidifies their bond with Cocoa, and they consider securing a better future for her. In addition to Miranda's contribution in shaping the future of the women in Day family, she serves as a healer and shaman in her community. Miranda's alliance with Bernice indicates that she uses healing properties to aid the women of Willow Springs.

Cocoa's life in the rational world is mainly guided by George, whereas Miranda can efficiently assist her when she stays amidst the mysticism of Willow Springs. The myth of Sapphira Wade, the unreal atmosphere, and the powerful female shamans provide Willow Springs with a spiritual quality. The magic realist setting of Willow Springs allows the medicine women to exert authority over the men in the community. According to Bowers, when magic realism is perceived "from the position of the 'other' and consider that it brings into view non-logical and non-scientific explanations for things, [then] the transgressive power of magical realism provides a means to attack the assumptions of the dominant culture and particularly the notion of scientifically and logically determined truth" (65). So, the matriarchs of the Day family challenge male domination by asserting their control over George. Additionally, Miranda's ability to salvage Cocoa despite George's non-performance accentuates her contribution in Cocoa's retrieval.

In the novel, it is through the characters' connection with each other that Naylor depicts the picture of female unity and empowerment. It is through

Mama Day's magical healing abilities where she was influenced by her ancestor Sapphira Wade, that she is able to relieve the torment of other black women. Magic or magical healing power is thus empowering for women. Khaleghi opines that Sapphira "represents women oppressed because of their strength and sexuality. Because of her refusal to accept the role of a slave and because of her knowledge of nature and female sexuality, she was given the title 'witch'. As midwife, mother, matriarch, and archetypal Mother, Sapphira embodies maternality" (135). A worthy descendent of Sapphira Wade and her black master, Bascombe Wade, Mama Day receives strength and knowledge of nature from her and plays multiple roles in the Willow Springs community. As a liminal character, Mama Day (also known by the name Miranda) transgresses the border between the magical and the real, and between the past and the present. As a conjurer and shaman, she can control the forces of nature with the movement of her walking stick and forecast the arrival of natural calamities. However, the supernatural aspects of her character do not have their origin only in a magical past: her "timeless experience of Willow Springs" as Benito et al. would call it, "her communion with nature, reflected in her acute sense and perception of all aspects of the movements, sounds and changes in nature are also part of her mysterious, supernatural powers" (140). As Naylor writes, "A wave over a patch of zinnias and the scarlet petals take flight. ... Winged marigolds follow them into the air. ... A thump of the stick: morning glories start to sing" (146-147). She also uses magic and healing practices in the service of her community, particularly to its female members. Because of her therapeutic achievements and healing power, she is acknowledged and respected by Dr. Smithfield, a local doctor, albeit reluctantly. Again, her status as a communal leader is endorsed by the Willow Springs inhabitants. Finally, apart from having the power to foresee what will happen around her, Miranda also has the ability to comment on the demoralised world of America. All these aspects of her character make her a powerful woman who is also a source of agency and empowerment for the female characters of her community.

Mama Day, who can be considered an Earth-Mother figure, is greatly respected by her own community in Willow Springs because of her wisdom and knowledge of human nature and is considered a community leader. In an interview with Angels Carabi, Naylor herself emphasises the role of female leaders in black community:

> For various reasons, I am drawn to this sense of community. ... Besides, family and class community is my communal history as a black American. Our survival today has depended on our nurturing each

> other, finding resources within ourselves. The women in Robinsonville, Mississippi, who dealt with herbs, [...] weren't just magical women. They had a definite medical purpose, because you could not depend on the outside hospitals to take care of your needs. So people grew up within a community that birthed you and laid you away when you died. Community is what I know and what I feel most comfortable with. (Carabi 114)

Naylor's statement regarding her belief in a community and the significance of women dealing with herbs and natural medicines is quite clearly reflected in the novel *Mama Day*. Sapphira Wade's courage and the urge for freedom win the freedom of the slaves of Bascombe Wade; Mama Day also helps the community people with her medicinal knowledge. Although the inhabitants of Willow Springs are provided medical care from a university-educated doctor, they still depend on her: a feat which shows the superiority of women over men and the local healing rituals over Western empirical cure system. Mama Day's superb medical knowledge also earns her respect from the Western doctor: "Although it hurt his pride at times, he'd admit inside it was usually no different than what he had to say himself–just plainer words and a slower cure than them concentrated drugs. And unless there was just no other choice, she'd never cut on nobody" (Naylor 80-81). Critics like Amy Levin argue that the idea of a community leader has its origin in African culture. Levin points out that "the vision of the women's leadership can be traced to West African women's traditions" (70) and that "surreal elements in novels may be read as signs of an African presence, while the mother figures may be viewed as expressions of a conception of female authority derived from West African women's traditions" (71).

Tucker opines that Naylor intends to restore in her novel the conjure women figure, a figure which is mainly found on the margin of folklore and are thus not considered reliable (174). The conjure women in *Mama Day* is linked to traditions, rituals and myth, which form the shared imagination of the community. According to Sánchez, "Conjurers [...] were supposed to be closer to their African roots than other more acculturated slaves and, therefore, used their psychic abilities and second sight to hold the communities together" (82). Mama Day, who continues the legacy of Sapphira's practice of the conjure women, serves as the basis for spiritual revival for the people of her island. Tucker also interestingly connects Mama Day with Yoruba "trickster figure Esu-Elegbara" (181), which is an adept figure in the magical or mythical barrier that distinguishes the magical or supernatural from the real or natural. Regarding

Esu-Elegbara, Henry Louis Gates states, "In Yoruba mythology, Esu is said to limp as he walks precisely because of his mediating function: his legs are of different lengths because he keeps one anchored in the realm of the gods while the other rests in this, our human world" (6). Just like Esu, Mama Day is also in continuous movement with her stick, hobbling a bit because of her rheumatism. Associated with the universal process of creation and destruction, she functions as a bridge between the mundane Western world, and the holy and magical African world.

Elizabeth Hayes argues that Miranda skilfully practices "intuitive thinking" or "connected knowing", something that is severely criticised by the rationalists of the post-enlightenment period (179). Miranda's knowledge of the future events, which is certainly impressive, is always shown in a matter-of-fact manner without the slightest doubt from any of the Willow Springs inhabitants. When Miranda tells her sister Abigail that Cocoa will travel by plane and not by train as she mentioned in the letter, Abigail does not doubt her clairvoyance but rather considers them as facts. It is interesting to notice that Abigail does not consider planes as natural for the fact they are the technological products that have the power to fly, a gift given only to birds by nature. Miranda's intuitive knowledge reaches the next level, where she is able to foresee future tragedies, both manmade and natural. It is through the changes in nature that she understands what will happen, although she cannot change them. By implying the fact that Miranda's knowledge is validated by nature itself, Naylor distinguishes her clairvoyance from any type of black magic. Naylor has quite clearly distinguished Mama Day's healing ability from Dr. Buzzard's voodoo practices and Ruby's medicinal knowledge that is directed towards killing. Miranda's magic, which has its origin in her instinct, herbal knowledge, and clairvoyance, goes beyond the world of rationalism and explanation. For example, it is her sprinkling of magical powder in Cocoa's letter sent to George, following a job interview, which helps her draw his attention and is therefore responsible for initiating their love relationship. Although George notices the powder in his fingers, he has no idea about its impact on him. Although both George and Cocoa seem to be attracted to each other from the beginning, the magical powder of Mama Day is a push behind their unification. This scene also suggests the way women help other women through magical means.

The magical rituals and healing practices Mama Day performs on other women heal their wounds: the healing act provides women some sort of agency and empowerment. A particular magical scene occurs where Mama Day performs a "fertility rite" on Bernice, who visits her to become pregnant. She takes Bernice to the old house of the Day family, which is a mystical place "where flowers can be made to sing and trees to fly" (Naylor 134). The entire ritual is narrated in some sort of detached language, which makes the reader to doubt if it is reality or imagination. The narrator's statement—"In the morning she can tell herself it was all a dream" (135)—increases the dreamlike environment of the ritual. The ordinary event of an elderly woman stitching a blanket on a rocking chair becomes cryptic since the environment turns threatening. Bernice's approaching to the house is described as:

> Moving through the bush, guided by the starlight that glints off the two pair of eyes waiting and rocking, both unblinking. One pair cradled low in the lap of the other, soft rumbles vibrating its feathered throat. One pair humming a music bom before words as they rock and stroke, forefinger and thumb, gently following the path of feathers, throat, breast, and sides. The right-hand stroking, the left hand cupping underneath the tiny egg hole that sucks itself open and closed, open and closed. (134)

The assumption that Mama Day is holding a chicken suggests the well-known connection between hens and voodoo, and indicates some sort of sacrificial ritual. In the seeming otherworldly ritual, Bernice feels Mama Day's hands in her body and doubts that "[...] it can't be human hands no way, making her body feel like this" (135). As Naylor describes,

> She ain't flesh, she's a center between the thighs spreading wide to take in ... the touch of feathers. Space to space. Ancient fingers keeping each in line. The uncountable, the unthinkable, is one opening. Pulsing and alive—wet—the egg moves from one space to the other. A rhythm older than woman draws it in and holds it tight. (135)

The fact that the chicken lays one more egg as Bernice fails to eat the freshly laid one is completely magical, as we know, a single chicken lays one egg a day. Although readers are not given any rational explanation of the magical healing ritual, they are later informed of the birth of Bernice's baby. Through her magical ritual, where she shows the female power of creation, Mama Day aids Bernice in conceiving a child and thus be empowered. Regarding Mama Day's role behind Bernice's conceiving the child, Sánchez writes, "Miranda possesses extraordinary powers usually associated with Mother Nature and the Life Force.

Hens and eggs as symbols of fertility acquire a sacral dimension within an animistic universe and will play an essential role in George's final trial" (87-88).

The death of Bernice's child and her act of taking the dead body to 'the other place' so that it can be resurrected by the rituals of Mama Day highlights the magical aspects of the novel. The community's doubtless acceptance of her conduct starkly contrasts George's disbelief. Instead of trying to understand the native's way of life, George attempts to grasp the issue in terms of his understanding of the world in New York. The fact that Willow Springers have air conditioning system, and student bank accounts shows the touch of modernity in their lives but, at the same time, makes Bernice's faith in resuscitating her baby more magical. As George writes, "If this was reality, it meant I was insane, and I couldn't be— and she couldn't be, because I had met that woman. ... No, this was the stuff of dreams. I spoke because I needed to hear the reality of my own voice" (Naylor 247). When Miranda realises that it is Ruby's magical tricks which are responsible for Cocoa's fatal illness, she straightaway understands that she will need to go beyond just herbal medicine to protect Cocoa as she tells Abigail, '"we ain't talking about this world at all"' (257). Miranda's revenge on Ruby, which involves spilling silvery powder around Ruby's house creates a storm where it is stated in a nonchalant manner that the lightning "hits Ruby twice, and the second time the house explodes" (261). Neither the reader nor the inhabitants of Willow Springs have the slightest doubt that it is Miranda's magical power and the act of summoning a lightning storm that is responsible for Ruby's house burning.

Questioning Western Empirical Reality and Advocating an Alternative Oral Reality

Black women are neglected and absent in the official white version(s) of slavery, and just like any white historian, George attempts to replace Sapphira's story by that of her white master, Bascombe Wade. George's intention to marginalise the story of Sapphira culminates in the act of romanticising the master-slave relationship. George even considers her ungrateful and dangerous, who did harm to her master. He was dissatisfied for not being able to place the history of Willow Springs to the dominant masculine framework; his questions about Bascombe Wade were answered with the stories of Sapphira Wade, something that makes him confused and even more dissatisfied: "Who exactly was he? And I got the same legend. The unnamed slave woman. The deeds to Willow Springs. The vigil by the ocean bluff. Except that you told me that woman had been your grandmother's great-grandmother" (209). However, George aims to use her empirical instrument to find out the reality behind the perceived myth of Sapphira. Although many versions of the story of Sapphira remain among the Willow Springs inhabitants and nobody except the narrator remembers her name, everybody undoubtedly believes in her spiritual healing power, a feat which stresses on the fact that it is possible for a community to know its history even if it is unspoken. It is worth mentioning that characters in *Mama Day* have conceptions and misconceptions not only of each other but also of reality itself because of the oral traditions of their culture. Because of their emphasis on oral telling of stories, characters like Cocoa are always aware of the family history and tradition without suffering from any kind of identity crisis. It also shields them against exploitation and the intrusion of foreign education.

The novel *Mama Day* is a complex text which includes multiple voices where Naylor's technique of using a shifting first-person narrative provides more than one point of view and advocates multiple versions of truth and reality. As Cocoa mentions, "[W]hat really happened to us, George? You see, that's what I mean—there are just too many sides to the whole story" (Naylor 298). By commenting on reality and truth and advocating multiple versions of reality, the novel emphasises the key features of oral descriptions: they are retold, allowing inclusions and exclusions, and thus giving multiple versions of reality or events. Sánchez argues that Naylor maintains the oral aspect of the novel using "Black English vernacular" (71). She explains, "The speech of the inhabitants of Willow Springs, and particularly of Mama Day, follows morphological and syntactical structures characteristic of Black English" (71). The sentence—"But ain't a soul in Willow Springs don't know that little dark girls, hair all braided up with colored twine, got their '18 & 23's coming down when they lean too long over them back yard fences"— can be a good example of the adoption of this style (Naylor 3). Gates opines that the employment of Black English dialects along with multiple voices turns the novel into a "speaking text", a text that emphasises the demonstration of black voice in a written narrative (xxv). In the tradition of 'speaking text' or 'talking book', language and signifying practices meaning making behaviours people get involved following rules of formation and interpretation aim to destabilise imposed (dominant) discourse. Gates argues that the language and signifying practices are strategies of the employment of black metaphorical language, "the figurative difference between the literal and the metaphorical, between surface and latent meaning" (82). A good example can be the dates 18 and 23 which in Willow Springs convey different meaning depending on the situation, having various symbolic applications: the birth of a child ("won't be no 'early 18 & 23's' coming here for me to rock"); using somebody while making a deal ('"tried to 18 & 23 him"'); or a dreadful summer storm ("we had that '18 & 23 summer' and the bridge blew down") (4).

Throughout the novel, George's rational mindset starkly contrasts Mama Day's instinctive one: a necessary contrast to place magical events in a realistic setting. George symbolises rationalism and patriarchy established by Western society. During the game of poker with the natives, George's behaviour with them conveys his lack of respect towards local culture and indicates his failure to understand Willow Springs and to be integrated there. Mama Day's idea of reality differs strongly from that of George. When Cocoa becomes seriously sick due to the conjuring of Ruby, her survival cannot be ensured by the Western empiricist mindset of George, but rather requires unshakable faith in Mama Day's instructions which he denies. When Dr. Buzzard advises that George meets Mama Day on 'the other place', his reaction echoes the Western notion of a self-made man, emphasising his rational mind and individualism in overpowering any obstacles: '"We're going to be fine. I believe in myself"' (Naylor 281). Dr. Buzzard suggests George to let go his male, rational and Western ideas of self, and enter the magical, mythical, and female-centred world of Willow Springs. When George meets Mama Day for advice and later considers them as sheer metaphors, she, seeing his misapprehension, says, "Metaphors. Like what they used in poetry and stuff. The stuff folks dreamed up when they were making a fantasy, while what she was talking about was *real.* As real as them young hands in front of her" (283). George also considers Mama Day's, ritual, which goes against his empirical and individualistic mindset, "mumbo-jumbo" (283). However, eventually, he is forced to follow her instructions:

> "I can't believe you're saying this—this is your way?"
>
> "It's the only one I got."
>
> "Then I'll find my own."
>
> "I pray to God you don't."
>
> "And I came to you for help—"
>
> "I'm giving it to you."
>
> "All that walking for this—this mumbo-jumbo? (283)

It is in the chicken coop, which symbolises female productiveness and, therefore, female empowerment, where George's rationalism and male-dominant attitude are tested. Mama Day wants George to leave the documents of Bascombe Wade and the walking stick of John-Paul in the coop, both of which symbolise male domination. The walking stick, a miraculous thing in the hands of Mama Day, becomes a symbol of male supremacy in George, who kills the hen, symbolising nothing: "There was nothing there—except for my gouged and bleeding hands. Bring me straight back whatever you find. ... Could it be that she wanted nothing but my hands?" (288). Unable to realise that it is hands that Mama Day requires, and thus to enter the female-centred magical world of Willow Springs, George experiences a fatal heart attack. His demise symbolises the superiority of indigenous belief of the inhabitants of Willow Springs over the rationalistic Western worldview, considering myth and magic as the sources of female empowerment. George's death takes place due to his attempt to rationalise all the events and to maintain logical and empirical borders between worlds (Western and native, earthly and spectral), whereas Mama Day wants him to dissolve such borders.

The concept of death is quite imperative in understanding *Mama Day*, which is based on the communication between Cocoa, a living person, and George, a living dead. In the African context, the interaction between the dead and alive is considered a fact, and, in the novel, the narrator never doubts the authenticity of this type of conversation or the connection between the mortal and the spectral world. While walking together across the family lands in Willow Springs, Cocoa hears the hushed murmurs from the graves, uttering, "you'll break his heart" (Naylor 215), but George fails to do so due to his rational mindset. Again, on another occasion, when George hears the words, "*Waste. Waste.*" (238) coming from the grave of Bascombe Wade, he (mis)reads them as the sound produced by tree in the air. It is the rational aspects of his mind that do not allow him to admit any probability of having a connection with the dead. However, having continuous communion with the demised, Miranda can hear Sapphira Wade's "long wool skirt passing", Bascombe Wade's "thread of heavy leather boots" (114) and her father's instruction to "*look past the pain*" (273). She also communicates with George and Abigail after their death. George's rationalistic outlook prevents him from seeing things beyond what logic and rationalism permit him to do, limits his outlook and thus does not allow him to accept the existence of multiple versions of reality. On the contrary, Miranda and Willow Springs inhabitants' connection with the world of spirits and emphasis on orality helps them to come up with a marginalised version of reality which the dominant discourse wants to suppress or erase.

The notion of death is associated with the African understanding of time and space. The Western idea of sequential progression of time is contrasted with the

African concept of time, where there is no concept of future time since future actions have not taken place and thus are unable to form time. John Mbiti opines that the African notion of time moves "backward" rather than "forward":

> Time has to be experienced in order to make sense or to become real. … Outside the reckoning of the year, African time concept is silent and indifferent. ... Each year comes and goes, adding to the time dimension of the past. Endlessness or 'eternity' for them is something that lies only in the region of the past. (17)

Magical realist writing questions established perception of time and space, and advocates alternative one(s), and the novel *Mama Day* plays with the concept of time. By situating himself in the future time, in 1999 (relating to the publication of the novel), the collective narrator describes events that took place in the past, in 1985. Time in the novel, which is intertwined with space, is experienced in opposite manner in New York—Western concept of time which is linear—and in Willow Springs—African concept of time which is fragmented and mythical. Even the narrative pace is also different in both mentioned places: the steady rhythm of New York is replaced by a slow rhythm once the plot shifts to Willow Springs where time seems to be at a standstill: "Time don't crawl and time don't fly; time is still. You do with it what you want: roll it up, stretch it out, or here we just let it lie" (Naylor 155). For George, the place seems eternal— "It all smelled like forever" (167)—and after crossing the bridge, he finds himself in an unknown and mythical world, full of local people and devoid of rationality: "The closeness of all this awed me—people who could be this self-contained. Who had redefined time. No, totally disregarded it" (209). Naylor's upholding the mythical and non-linear progression of time is a great response to the Western outlook of the world, and a way of upholding Native cultures and rituals.

Missy Dehn Kubitschek opines that the novel *Mama Day* suggests an alternative means of structuring the world, which "creates a working nurturance for both men and women" (88). Though outwardly, George cannot create this "working nurturance", his passing away makes it possible for Cocoa to survive. Although the reader is not provided with any justification behind Cocoa's magical healing, it is suggested that George dies for her, a phenomenon that goes against our logical understanding of the world. George understands this only after his physical demise and thus sheds his rationalistic and individualistic attitude: "But I want to tell you something about my real death that day. I didn't feel anything after my heart burst. As my bleeding hand slid gently down your arm, there was total peace" (Naylor 289). George's death also goes beyond the understanding and the expectations of the reader, who are surprised to learn that they have been following a narrator who died fourteen years ago. Interestingly, the death of the character George overlaps with the final involvement of the narrator George; his role as a narrator comes to an end after he himself describes his own death. Therefore, the borders between life and death and between fiction and reality vanish. Quite skillfully, Naylor does not let the demise of the character and narrator diminish the magical aspects of the novel: Cocoa's conversation with George goes on and on.

Chapter 12

Conclusion

If female marginalisation and/or victimisation are considered normal by a patriarchal society, there will be no change in their wretched condition. Authors who, regardless of their gender, feel and protest against female victimisation want to give a literary representation of their victimisation and thus create consciousness against the victimisation need to swim against the current. Their writing, on the one hand, creates concern among people and, on the other hand, infuriates a large section of society. It is the desire to give a voice to women in their multifarious victimisation which connects magical realism with feminism and forms the term magical feminism. Giving a literary representation of women's victimisation and traumatisation requires high imagination and a sense of empathy. Magical realism provides authors with the necessary means to explore female victimisation and to penetrate the rigid shell of trauma, and helps them to bring it to light, which is not possible by a traditional, realist narrative. In the literary representation of traumatic events, mimetic realism depicts those events the way they already are, and thus frightens and repels the readers, rather than making them empathise with victims. Magical realism, on the other hand, conceals traumatic events under the mist of myth, mystery, magic, and imagination and represents the events in a more accessible way. In doing so, this technique makes the reader understand the suffering of victims, and thus empathise with them. The use of myth, magic, and local belief, culture and tradition gives women the strength to defy patriarchal oppression and enables them to achieve agency and, to some extent supremacy. It is also used by authors as a survival technique and a means of consolation for oppressed women.

Female oppression and victimisation is a widespread phenomenon. Patriarchal society's abominable attitude towards women is primarily responsible for this victimisation. Society cannot think of women as independent and able to go on their own. It very much loves to see women subservient to men and are victimised by them. Again, during any war, genocide or political violence, women are victims of institutional violence. Besides gendered violence, women are also victims of social, cultural, political, racial, and ethnic violence. This research project has discussed female oppression in different countries across the Americas and pointed out that despite having geographical distance and social and cultural differences, women in these nations have suffered from multifarious sources of oppression. The study has also shown that the history of the Americas is as much of political and social violence as it is of female victimisation. Here, one noteworthy aspect which the book has highlighted is that the oppression of women is pervasive in Western societies and that it is pretty much a colonial issue. Female marginalisation does not occur in indigenous societies where women have been considered important and equal to men. The white invaders/colonisers tried to inflict the notion of 'female oppression' in Native societies in the Americas as some sort of colonial mechanism to break the foundations of their culture and society. The study has also highlighted the role of magical realism in providing an alternative picture of female marginalisation. It has shown the way female authors across the Americas have voiced against female oppression and attempted to provide agency and empowerment to those women by using magical realist technique and/or narrative.

The project has divided the entire issue of female oppression and the authors' use of magical realism in a female context into four parts. Whereas the notion of gendered victimisation is present in all the parts, the analysis also exposes diverse factors behind, and in context of, female victimisation. By including the novels, *The House of the Spirits* and *The Inhabited Woman*, the first part has shown the way magical feminist authors attempt to question and challenge dictatorial regime, and topple patriarchy. In *The House of the Spirits*, Isabel Allende has portrayed the political violence in Chile through female clairvoyance, given women a place in male history, and emphasised their empowerment. Allende demonstrates the way Chilean women survived the volatile time of dictatorship through female bonds and the assistance of their deceased female family members. By connecting women from different generations and employing the notion of collective memory, Allende thus creates a legacy of norm-defying women, some sort of female force, who fought both political and patriarchal oppression, and shows the potential of female history to surpass male history. It is through magic and clairvoyance, Allende provides Chilean women, particularly four generations of del Valle family, an alternative means of communication, and enables them to rewrite male history from a female perspective, incorporating female experiences and viewpoints. By contrasting Alba's voice/narrative, which represents female agency and empowerment, with Esteban's one, which emphasises male supremacy, Allende seems to be upholding a female and a more compassionate version of history. Magical realism in this novel is not only used from a feminine standpoint but also from a political one. However, although Allende upholds the female voice, she also recognises the significance of reason and the male perspective.

It is the magical transmission of female resistance to patriarchy, colonial power, and dictatorship, and female emancipation and empowerment from one generation to the others, which is emphasised in Gioconda Belli's *The Inhabited Woman.* By focusing on the character of Lavinia, her involvement in national politics, and her magical connection with Itzá, a revolutionary woman from the past, Belli not only enables her to embark on a journey of self-discovery but also creates an alternative, female-oriented history of Nicaragua, which has completely been excluded from traditional male history. Belli thus emphasises the significance of collective memory through magical realism in re-establishing the connection between past and present and restructuring or reforming a nation. By allowing the spirit of Itzá to enter the body of Lavinia, and showing the way the spirit of one woman instils revolutionary zeal into another woman from another generation and guides her, Belli shows female involvement in male-dominated politics, and their agency and emancipation, and emphasises the legacy of resistance to oppression and marginalisation. Itzá, thus can be considered the representation of female potential, which has been repressed but is exposed and materialised when she is connected with Lavinia. Lavinia's association with other female warriors creates a web of female bonding and mutual assistance during political and gendered violence, and thus creates a collective female resistance and voice.

The second part, which has discussed resistance towards colonisation and assertion of female identity through magical realism, includes the novel *Shark Dialogues,* set in Hawaiian context, and *Tracks,* set in Native American context. The study has attempted to show the way Kiana Davenport relates female victimisation as well as their empowerment with their cultural and political, more specifically (post/neo)colonial, contexts through magical realism in *Shark Dialogues* where she resorts to their local belief and myth. Quite interestingly, Davenport equates geographical land with female body, and colonial invasion of the land with physical and sexual oppression of women and, therefore, severely criticises colonial and phallocentric discourses. Besides demonstrating the disastrous consequences of cultural and environmental destruction on women, Davenport also highlights their resistance to both colonial and patriarchal constraints. By describing colonial invasion, and socio-political history of Hawaii from a female perspective, Davenport creates an alternative and, more specifically, feminised version of Hawaiian history. It is, therefore, by connecting magical realism with the socio-political history of Hawaii, Davenport gives the marginalised women a voice, and enables them to come up with their own version of history. It is also by incorporating magical elements in the story, she comes up with the notion of marginality, represented by the character of Pono, who possesses ancient native knowledge. Pono's anguish represents the collective suffering of her own people at the destruction of native culture. Her shamanistic healing and supernatural power and her communication with her dead ancestors have enabled her to fight both patriarchal and colonial oppression.

It is the same sense of oppression that we find in Louise Erdrich's *Tracks* although this time it is against white subjugation from an ethnic standpoint, showing the way Native American people were deprived of their land and property by white people. She also shows the way Native American culture is polluted by white culture, turning male Natives against their female counterparts, and thus tearing down the fabrics of established Native culture which has always exhibited gender equality. Erdrich provides the women with magical power and enables them to fight both patriarchy and white oppression. Unlike many other prominent magical realists, Erdrich employs magical realism not by incorporating magical realist elements from local culture and tradition but through her language and diction. She thus may not be considered a quintessential magical realist author. Erdrich equips her female character Fleur with magical means so that she can avenge her rape, and challenge and attack white culture or any colonial instrument or agent that aims to destroy her native culture. Fleur's lonely battle against patriarchy and white invasion provides the novel with a political tone, and thus establishes the proposition that magical realism is firmly anchored in social, cultural, and political reality. Interestingly, Erdrich includes the carnivalesque to assist magical realism in tackling dominant power structure.

The third part of the book project, which has dealt with the potential of magical realism to protest cultural invasion, and to criticise the tradition of male politics, contains the novels *Dreaming in Cuban* and *So Far from God*. *Dreaming in Cuban*, written by Cuban American writer Cristina García, emphasises the development of female awareness and identity, and connects it with Fidel Castro's regimes, its impact on the non-conformists, and their subsequent dislocation. By depicting Cuban national history through female protagonists, García includes female experiences and enables women to come up with an alternative and marginalised (read feminised) version of history. Again, by magically connecting Cuban women, particularly three generations of del Pino women, irrespective of their geographical distance and ideological difference, García creates a female bond in the brutal male world and empowers them. She also shows the role of deceased family members behind female survival and empowerment, who appear in the midst of reality and guide women during their struggle. Lourde's supernatural encounter with her dead father enables her to come out of her trauma of being raped by Castro revolutionaries and helps her to mitigate many of the misunderstandings with her mother. By stressing on the experiences of Pilar, the third generation of del Pino family, and including her migrant outlook, García also provides an outsider perspective into the story. Again, by inserting metaphors from different Santeria rituals and goddesses, Yemayá goddess, phoenix cycles, and the appearance of ghosts, García enables her female characters to recreate themselves and to overcome any kind of victimisation. Female empowerment on an individual level is also paralleled with female supremacy on a collective and/or national level.

It is the same desire for women to find a place in the male narrative and male politics, which is addressed in Chicana author Ana Castillo's *So Far from God*, connecting the novel's magical realist character(s) and/or elements with social and political realities. Castillo shows the damaging influences of US cultural invasion on the Chicanas but at the same time shows female defiance to patriarchal constraints, and their agency and empowerment by (re)creating *mestiza* myth. Castillo scathingly criticises the brutal patriarchal forces that attack and deform Caridad, which considers her sexual freedom a threat for it, and demonstrates the failure of Western medicine in healing her and emphasises the role of local ritual and magical healing, which comes from women around her. By contrasting the local healing system, which is also connected with harmonious relation with nature, with Western medicinal practice, she not only shows female supremacy over male but also proves the way local healing is more capable than Western medicine. To rephrase, through the differences in medical practices, Castillo stresses both gendered and political protest. Castillo also shows the way both the female body and nature is abused by oppressive structure, and thus unleashes a strong criticism of both patriarchy and capitalism. By rewriting the myth of La Llorona and La Malogra and magically connecting Sofia's youngest daughter, La Loca, with them, she enables her to predict the future and to be powerful; she, at the same time, attempts to question the superficial patriarchal understanding of Chicana issues.

The fourth and final part, which has analysed the way magical realism challenges and criticises racial and gendered oppression, and provides necessary means for female empowerment, includes *The Cure for Death by Lightning* and *Mama Day*. Set during WWII and in the Shuswap region, Canada, Gail Anderson-Dargatz's *The Cure for Death by Lightning* brings to light the sexual oppression of both Beth and Maud (Beth's mother) by their fathers and, with this, a culture of incest where women are victimised, and the domination of aboriginal population by the White. By combining magical realism, Canadian gothic, and the grotesque, Anderson-Dargatz has shown female empowerment and emancipation. Anderson-Dargatz shows the way Beth saves herself from the local boys who attack her sexually through the magical means of her lightning arm. By exposing the lesbian tendency of Beth's indigenous friend Nora and her reckless invitation to Beth to elope with her, Anderson-Dargatz has demonstrated the potential of women to defy patriarchy through the subversive power of lesbianism. Because of possessing two-coloured eyes, which shows her potential lesbian tendency, and of dissolving the male and female dress codes, Nora represents female emancipation and agency. Again, by showing the female dominance in Nora's house, and highlighting their bodily grotesque, Anderson-Dargatz enables them to voice out, to assert their right, and to be empowered.

Gloria Naylor's *Mama Day* not only shows the solidarity and mutual healing among black women and thus their empowerment but also highlights the way black people in Willow Springs overcome their racial marginalisation through the help of black lore, rituals, and other magical means. The herbal healing practices of Mama Day, who carries the legacy of the myth of Sapphira Wade, enable her to relieve the suffering of black women and provides her with some sort of psychological and spiritual supremacy over evil women and even over men. Again, her control over nature itself equips her with certain instruments to control natural forces and to foresee any natural calamities. Moreover, by attempting to restore the figure of conjure women, a magical realist figure that is not considered reliable but is respected, feared, and othered by an oppressive patriarchal society, Naylor enables her to revive the spirituality of the people of Willow Springs. Naylor also connects Mama Day with a Native trickster figure, showing her potential to bridge both African and Western worlds. By contrasting the Willow Springers' unshaken faith on Mama Day's magical prophecy and all the supernatural events with George's logical, Western way of seeing things with doubt, Naylor shows the uniqueness of Native worldview, and provides an alternative (read Native and female) reality.

It can quite clearly be stated that magical feminism is of the women, for the women, and by the women. The study has clearly shown the multifarious victimisation of women in different American countries and the role of magical realism in challenging all kinds of subjugation and giving women emancipation. The study has also shown the way magical feminist authors from different American nations have collected magical realist elements from diverse sources, and employed those elements from different perspectives, although the notion of gender has constantly been there. Magical realism has constantly shown its potential in fighting oppression, and in exposing deep-rooted trauma of female oppression. It has also contrasted both Native (victimised) and Western (victimiser) worldviews and questioned a singular version of truth and reality. By providing the marginalised (here the women) a space in nationalist male history/narrative, magical realism has enabled their voice to be heard and liberated.

Works Cited

Abdullah, Abu S. "Speaking the Unspoken: Rewriting Identity Loss and Memory of Slavery through Magical Realism in Toni Morrison's *Beloved.*" *English Language and Literature Studies*, vol. 5, no. 3, 2015, pp. 25-32. https://doi.org/10.5539/ells.v5n3p25.

---. Rewriting Rural Community and Dictatorial History through Magical Realism in Márquez's *One Hundred Years of Solitude.*" *Journal of Language and Cultural Education*, vol. 3, no. 2, 2015, pp. 55-65. https://doi.org/10.1515/jolace-2015-0014.

---. "Fluids, Cages, and Boisterous Femininity: The Grotesque Transgression of Patriarchal Norms in Angela Carter's *Nights at the Circus.*" *Journal of Language and Cultural Education*, vol. 5, no. 2, 2017, pp. 114-122. https://doi.org/10.1515/jolace-2017-0022.

---. "Heavy Silence and Horrible Grief: Reconstructing the Past and Securing the Future through Magical Realism in Joseph Skibell's *A Blessing on the Moon.*" *Ostrava Journal of English Philology*, vol. 12, no. 1, 2020, pp. 29-44. https://doi.org/10.15452/ OJoEP.2020.12.0003.

---. "Reconstructing Personal Identity and Creating an Alternative National History: Magical Realism and the Marginalised Female Voice in Gioconda Belli's *The Inhabited Woman.*" *The Palgrave Handbook of Magical Realism in the Twenty-First Century*, edited by Richard Perez and Victoria A. Chevalier, Switzerland: Springer Nature, 2020, pp. 281-196.

---. *Traumatic Experience and Repressed Memory in Magical Realist Novels.* New Castle: Cambridge Scholars Publishing, 2020.

Adams, Jenni. *Magic Realism in Holocaust Literature: Troping the Traumatic Real.* UK: Palgrave Macmillan, 2011.

Ahmad, Mumtaz, and Kaneez Fatima. "Female Identity and Magical Realism in Native American and Afro American Women Writing: A Comparative Analysis of Louise Erdrich's Tracks and Tony Morrison's Beloved." *Scholedge International Journal of Multidisciplinary & Allied Studies*, vol. 4, no. 11, 2017, pp. 108-115. https://doi.org/10.19085/JOURNAL.SIJMAS041102.

Aldama, Frederick L. *Postethnic Narrative Criticism: Magicorealism in Oscar "Zeta" Acosta, Ana Castillo, Julie Dash, Hanif Kureishi, and Salman Rushdie.* Austin: U of Texas P, 2003.

Allen, Paula G. *The Sacred Hoop: Recovering the Feminine in American Indian Traditions.* Boston: Beacon Press, 1992.

Allende, Isabel. *La casa de* los *espíritus. 1982. Plaza & Janés, 2014.*

---. *The House of the Spirits.* Translated by Magda Bogin, New York: Bantam, 1986.

---. "Writing As an Act of Hope." *Paths of Resistance: The Art and Craft of the Political Novel*, edited by William Zinsser, Boston: Houghton Mifflin, 1999, pp. 41-63.

Alvarez-Borland, Isabel. "Displacements and Autobiography in Cuban-American Fiction." *World Literature Today*, vol. 68, no. 1, 1994, pp. 43-49. *JSTOR*, https://doi.org/10.2307/40149843.

Anderson-Dargatz, Gail. *The Cure for Death by Lightning*. 1996. Toronto: Vintage, 1997.

Anzaldúa, Gloria. *Borderlands/La Frontera: The New Mestiza*. San Francisco: Aunt Lute, 1987.

Armitt, Lucie. "The Magical Realism of the Contemporary Gothic." *A Companion to the Gothic*, edited by David Punter, Oxford: Blackwell, 2000, pp. 305-315.

Bakhtin, Mikhail. *Rabelais and His World*. Translated by Hélène Iswolsky, Bloomington: Indiana UP, 1984.

Bal, Mieke. "Introduction." *Acts of Memory: Cultural Recall in the Present*, edited by Mieke Bal, et al., Hanover: Dartmouth College, 1999, pp. vii-xvii.

Barker, Chris. *The SAGE Dictionary of Cultural Studies*. UK: SAGE Publications, 2004.

Barrios, Flor F. *Blessed by Thunder: Memoir of a Cuban Girlhood*. Seattle: Seal Press, 1999.

Barnet, Miguel. "La Regla de Ocha: The Religious System of Santería." *Sacred Possessions: Vodou, Santería, Obeah, and the Caribbean*, edited by Margarite Fernández Olmos and Lizabeth Paravisini-Gebert, New Brunswick: Rutgers UP, 1996, pp. 79-100.

Beckwith, Martha. *Hawaiian Mythology*. Honolulu: Hawai'i UP, 1970.

Bellamy, Maria R. *Bridges to Memory: Postmemory in Contemporary Ethnic American Women's Fiction*. Charlottesville: U of Virginia P, 2015.

Belli, Gioconda. 1988. *La Mujer Habitada*. Buenos Aires: Emecé Editores S.A., 1992.

---. *The Inhabited Woman*. Translated by Kathleen March, USA: Curbstone Press, 1994.

Benito, Jesús, et al. *Uncertain Mirrors. Magical Realisms in US Ethnic Literatures*. Amsterdam: Rodopi, 2009.

Berry, Jan. "Whose Threshold?: Women's Strategies of Ritualization." *Feminist Theology*, vol. 14, no. 3, 2006, pp. 273-288. https://doi.org/10.1177/0966735006063769.

Bhabha, Homi. *The Location of Culture*. London: Routledge, 1994.

Botting, Fred. *Gothic*. New York: Routledge, 1996.

Bowers, Maggie A. *Magic(al) Realism*. London and New York: Routledge, 2004.

Butler, Judith, and Athena Athanasiou, editors. *Dispossession: The Performative in the Political*. Cambridge: Polity Press, 2013.

Caminero-Santangelo, Marta. "The Pleas of the Desperate: Collective Agency versus Magical Realism in Ana Castillo's *So Far from God*." *Tulsa Studies in*

Women's Literature, vol. 24, no.1, 2005, pp. 81-103. http://dx.doi.org/10.2307/20455212.

Can, Taner. *Magical Realism in Postcolonial British Fiction: History, Nation, and Narration.* Stuttgart: *ibidem*-Verlag, 2015.

Carabi, Angels. "An Interview with Gloria Naylor." *Conversations with Gloria Naylor*, edited by Maxine Lavon Montgomery, Jackson: U of Mississippi P, 2004, pp. 111-122.

Carpentier, Alejo. "The Baroque and the Marvelous Real." *Magical Realism: Theory, History, Community*, edited by Lois P. Zamora and Wendy B. Faris, Durham & London: Duke UP, 1995, pp. 89-108.

---. "On the Marvelous Real in America." Translated by Tanya Huntington and Lois P. Zamora, *Magical Realism: Theory, History, Community*, edited by Lois P. Zamora and Wendy B. Faris, Durham & London: Duke UP, 1995, pp. 75-88.

Castillo, Ana. *So Far from God.* New York: W. W. Norton & Company, 1993.

---. "Brujas and Curanderas: A Lived Spirituality." *Massacre of the Dreamers: Essays on Xicanisma*, edited by Ana Castillo, Albuquerque: U of New Mexico P, 1994, pp. 145-161.

Castle, Terry. *The Apparitional Lesbian.* New York: Columbia UP, 1993.

Chanady, Amaryll B. *Magical Realism and the Fantastic: Resolved Versus Unresolved Antinomy.* New York & London: Garland, 1985.

---. "Cultural Memory and the New World Imaginary." *Colonizer and Colonized*, edited by Theo D'Haen and Patrick Krus, Amsterdam: Rodopi, 2000, pp. 183-192.

Chasteen, John C. *Born in Blood and Fire: A Concise History of Latin America.* New York: W.W. Norton & Co., 2001.

Cheyfitz, Eric. "Introduction." *The Columbia Guide to American Indian Literatures of the United States Since 1945*, edited by Eric Cheyfitz, New York: Columbia UP, 2006, pp. vii-x.

---. "The (Post)Colonial Construction of Indian Country: U.S. American Indian Literatures and Federal Indian Law." *The Columbia Guide to American Indian Literatures of the United States Since 1945*, edited by Eric Cheyfitz, New York: Columbia UP, 2006, pp. 1-124.

Chidester, Phil. "May the Circle Stay Unbroken: *Friends*, the Presence of Absence, and the Rhetorical Reinforcement of Whiteness." *Critical Studies in Media Communication*, vol. 25, no. 2, 2008, pp. 157-174. https://doi.org/10.1080/15295030802031772.

Chrisler, Joan C., and Maureen C. McHugh. "Waves of Feminist Psychology in the United States: Politics and Perspectives." *Handbook of International Feminisms: Perspectives on Psychology, Women, Culture, and Rights, edited by* Alexandra Rutherford, Rose Capdevila, Vindhya Undurti and Ingrid Palmary, New York: Springer Science + Business Media, 2011, pp. 37-58.

Coltelli, Laura. "Louise Erdrich and Michael Dorris." *Winged Words: American Indian Writers Speak*, edited by Laura Coltelli, Lincoln: U of Nebraska P, 1990: 41-52.

Condé, Maryse. *I, Tituba, Black Witch of Salem.* Translated by Richard Philcox, New York: Ballantine Books, 1994.

Cook, Barbara J. "La Llorona and a Call for Environmental Justice in the Borderlands: Ana Castillo's *So Far from God.*" *Northwest Review,* vol. 39, no. 2, 2001, pp. 124-133.

Cooper, Brenda. *Magical Realism in West African Fiction: Seeing with a Third Eye.* London and New York: Routledge, 1998.

Corrigan, Lisa M. "After the Revolution: Cuban Women's Healing Practices and Knowledge Spaces." *Advances in the History of Rhetoric,* vol. 11-12, no. 1, 2008, pp. 103-131. https://doi.org/10.1080/15362426.2009.10597382.

Coupal, Michelle. "Storied Truths: Contemporary Canadian and Indigenous Childhood Trauma Narratives." PhD Dissertation, University of Western Ontario, 2013. https://ir.lib.uwo.ca/etd/ 1274/. Accessed 17 March 2021.

Cupples, Julie. "Between Maternalism and Feminism: Women in Nicaragua's Counter-Revolutionary Forces." *Bulletin of Latin American Research,* vol. 25, no. 1, 2006, pp. 83-103. doi:10.1111/j.0261-3050.2006.00154.x.

Dandavati, Annie G. *The Women's Movement and the Transition to Democracy in Chile.* New York: Peter Lang, 1996.

Davenport, Kiana. *Shark Dialogues.* New York: Plume Books, 1994.

de Beauvoir, Simone. 1949. *The Second Sex.* Translated by Constance Borde and Sheila Malovany-Chevallier, London: Vintage, 2010.

Delbaere-Garant, Jeanne. "Psychic Realism, Mythic Realism, Grotesque Realism: Variations on Magic Realism in Contemporary Literature in English." *Magical Realism: Theory, History, Community,* edited by Lois P. Zamora and Wendy B. Faris, Durham & London: Duke UP, 1995, pp. 249-263.

Delgadillo, Theresa. "Forms of Chicana Feminist Resistance: Hybrid Spirituality in Ana Castillo's *So Far from God.*" *Modern Fiction Studies,* vol. 44, no. 4, 1998, pp. 888-916. https://doi.org/10.1353/MFS.1998.0108.

D'haen, Theo. "Magical Realism and Postmodernism: Decentering Privileged Centres." *Magical Realism: Theory, History, Community,* edited by Lois P. Zamora and Wendy B. Faris, Durham & London: Duke UP, 1995, pp. 191-208.

Dickens, David R., and Andrea Fontana. "Postmodernism in the Social Sciences." *Postmodernism And Social Inquiry,* edited by David R. Dickens and Andrea Fontana, UK: Routledge, 1994, pp. 1-24.

Du Bois, William E. B. *The Souls of Black Folk.* Harmondsworth: Penguin, 1989.

Dyhouse, Carol. *Glamour: Women, History, Feminism.* London: Zed Books Ltd, 2010.

Earle, Peter G. "Literature as Survival: Allende's *The House of the Spirits.*" *Contemporary Literature,* vol. 28, no. 4, 1987, pp. 543-554. https://doi.org/10.2307/1208317.

Echevarría, Roberto G. "Isla a su vuela fugitiva: Carpentier y el realismo mágico." *Revista Iberoamericana,* vol. 40, no. 86, 1974, pp. 9-63.

Edwards, Justin D. *Postcolonial Literature.* New York: Palgrave Macmillan, 2008.

Erdrich, Louise. *Tracks.* 1988. New York: Harper Collins, 2004.

Espinosa, Aurelio M. "New-Mexican Spanish Folk-Lore." *The Journal of American Folklore,* vol. 23, no. 90, 1910, pp. 395-418. https://doi.org/10.2307/534325.

Farganis, Sondra. *Situating Feminism: From Thought to Action.* UK: SAGE Publications, 1994.

Faris, Wendy B. "Scheherazade's Children: Magical Realism and Postmodern Fiction." *Magical Realism: Theory, History, Community,* edited by Lois P. Zamora and Wendy B. Faris, Durham & London: Duke UP, 1995, pp. 163-190.

---. *Ordinary Enchantments: Magical Realism and the Remystification of Narrative.* Nashville: Vanderbilt UP, 2004.

Felman, Shoshana. "Women and Madness: The Critical Phallacy." *Feminisms: An Anthology of Literary Theory and Criticism,* edited by Robyn R. Warhol & Diane P. Herndl, New Brunswick: Rutgers UP, 1997, pp. 7-20.

Fernández, Alina. *Castro's Daughter: An Exile's Memoir of Cuba.* New York: St. Martins, 1999.

Flores, Angel. "Magical Realism in Spanish American Fiction." *Magical Realism: Theory, History, Community,* edited by Lois P. Zamora and Wendy B. Faris, Durham & London: Duke UP, 1995, pp. 109-117.

Foreman, Gabrielle. "Past-On Stories: History and the Magically Real, Morrison and Allende on Call." *Feminist Studies,* vol. 18, no. 2, 1992, pp. 369-388. https://doi.org/10.1515/9780822397212-017

Frick, Susan R. "Memory and Retelling: The Role of Women in *La casa de los espíritus.*" *Journal of Iberian and Latin American Studies,* vol. 7, no. 1, 2001, pp. 27-41. https://doi.org/10.1080/713678895.

Friedman, Susan S. "Identity Politics, Syncretism, Catholicism, and Anishinabe Religion in Louise Erdrich's *Tracks.*" *Religion & Literature,* vol. 26, no. 1, 1994, pp. 107-133. *JSTOR,* https://www.jstor.org/stable/40059588.

Gandhi, Leela. *Postcolonial Theory: A Critical Introduction.* New York: Columbia UP, 1998.

García, Cristina. *Dreaming in Cuban.* 1992. New York: Ballantine Books, 1993.

Gates, Henry L. Jr. *The Signifying Monkey. A Theory of African American Literary Criticism.* Oxford: Oxford UP, 1988.

Gedi, Noa, and Yigal Elam. "Collective Memory—What Is It?" *History and Memory,* vol. 8, no. 1, 1996, pp. 30-50. *JSTOR,* https://www.jstor.org/stable/25618696.

Goldman, Marlene. "Coyote's Children and the Canadian Gothic: Sheila Watson's *The Double Hook* and Gail Anderson-Dargatz's *The Cure for Death by Lightning.*" *Australasian Canadian Studies,* vol. 24, no. 2, 2006, pp. 15-44.

Gordon, Rebecca. "Earthstar Magic: A Feminist Theoretical Perspective on the Way of theWitches and the Path to the Goddess." *Social Alternatives,* vol. 14, no. 4, 1995, pp. 9-11. https://search.informit.org/doi/10.3316/IELAPA.960302490. Accessed 27 August 2020.

Grosz, Elizabeth. *Volatile Bodies: Toward a Corporeal Feminism.* Bloomington: Indiana UP, 1994.

Guenther, Irene. "Magic Realism, New Objectivity, and the Arts during the Weimar Republic." *Magical Realism: Theory, History, Community,* edited by Lois P. Zamora and Wendy B. Faris, Durham & London: Duke UP, 1995, pp. 33-73.

Halbwachs, Maurice. *The Collective Memory.* Translated by Francis J. Ditter and Vida Yazdi, New York: Harper & Row, 1950.

Hart, Patricia. *Narrative Magic in the Fiction of Isabel Allende.* London: Associated UP, 1989.

Hart, Stephen M. "Magical Realism: Style and Substance." *A Companion to Magical Realism,* edited by Stephen M. Hart and Wen-chin Ouyang, UK: Tamesis, 2005, pp. 1-13.

Hayes, Elizabeth T. "Gloria Naylor's *Mama Day* as Magic Realism." *The Critical Response to Gloria Naylor,* edited by Sharon Felton and Michelle C. Loris, Connecticut: Greenwood, 1997, pp. 177-186.

Hancock, Geoff. "Magic Realism." *Magic Realism: An Anthology,* edited by Geoff Hancock, Toronto: Aya Press, 1980, pp. 7-15.

Hegerfeldt, Anne C. "Contentious Contributions: Magic Realism Goes British." *Janus Head: Journal of Interdisciplinary Studies in Literature, Continental Philosophy, Phenomenological Psychology, and the Arts,* vol. 5, no. 2, 2002, pp. 62-86. https://philpapers.org/asearch.pl?pub=1383. Accessed 21 July 2021.

---. *Lies that Tell the Truth: Magic Realism Seen through Contemporary Fiction from Britain.* Amsterdam: Rodopi, 2005.

Holland-Toll, Linda J. "Bluestockings Beware: Cultural Backlash and the Re/Configuration of the Witch in Popular Nineteenth Century Literature." *Femspec,* vol. 6, no. 2, 2005, pp. 37-58.

Holtzman, Emily. "Indispensable Lives: Magical Realism and Postcolonial Resistance in Ana Castillo's So Far from God and Junot Díaz's The Brief Wondrous Life of Oscar Wao." BA Thesis, University of Missouri-Columbia, 2015. https://hdl.handle.net/10355/45473. Accessed 17 November 2020.

Hubata-Ashton, Rachel. "Isabel Allende's *The House of the Spirits*: Examining Magical Realism as It Bears Witness to Life." BA Thesis, Midlands Technical College, South Carolina, 2012. http://www.collegepassport.org/edu/ed/english/Stylus/Bonner/2012HUBATAASHTON_Bonner.pdf. Accessed 15 November 2021.

Hutcheon, Linda. *A Poetics of Postmodernism: History, Theory, Fiction.* New York & London: Routledge, 2000.

Indriyanto, Kristiawan. "Hawaii's Ecological Imperialism: Postcolonial Ecocriticism Reading on Kiana Davenport's *Shark Dialogues.*" *International Journal of Humanity Studies,* vol. 2, no. 2, 2019, pp. 123-133. https://doi.org/10.24071/ijhs.2019.020202.

Jacobs, Beverley. "International Law/The Great Law of Peace." MA Thesis, University of Saskatchewan, 2000. http://hdl.handle.net/10388/etd-07042007-083651. Accessed 11 January 2023.

Jenainati, Cathia, and Judy Groves. *Introducing Feminism: A Graphic Guide.* UK: Icon Books Ltd, 2007.

Jenkins, Ruth Y. "Authorizing Female Voice and Experience: Ghosts and Spirits in Kingston's *The Woman Warrior* and Allende's *The House of the Spirits.*" *MELUS*, vol. 19, no. 3, 1994, pp. 61-73. https://doi.org/10.2307/467872.

Khaleghi, Mahboobeh. "Female Leadership in Gloria Naylor's Novels: Bloodmothers, Othermothers, and Community Othermothers." *Journal of Social Sciences*, vol. 26, no. 2, 2011, pp. 131-138. https://doi.org/10.1080/09718923.2011.11892889.

Kristeva, Julia. *Powers of Horror: An Essay on Abjection.* Translated by Leon S. Roudiez, New York: Columbia UP, 1982.

Kubitschek, Missy D. "Toward a New Order: Shakespeare, Morrison, and Gloria Naylor's *Mama Day.*" *MELUS*, vol. 19, no. 3, Fall 1994, pp. 75-90. https://doi.org/10.2307/467873.

Kunjakkan, Karanvil A. *Feminism and Indian Realities.* New Delhi: Mittal Publications, 2002.

Lanza, Carmela D. "Hearing the Voices, Women and Home and Ana Castillo's *So Far from God.*" *MELUS*, vol. 23, no. 1, 1998, pp. 65-79. https://doi.org/10.2307/467763. *JSTOR*, https://www.jstor.org/stable/467763.

Lara, Irene. "Sensing the Serpent in the Mother, Dando a luz la Madre Serpiente: Chicana Spirituality, Sexuality, and Mamihood." *Fleshing the Spirit: Spirituality and Activism in Chicana, Latina, and Indigenous Women's Lives*, edited by Elisa Facio and Irene Lara, Tucson: U of Arizona P, 2014, pp. 113-134.

Leal, Luis. "Magical Realism in Spanish American Literature." *Magical Realism: Theory, History, Community*, edited by Lois P. Zamora and Wendy B. Faris, Durham & London: Duke UP, 1995, pp. 119-124.

Levin, Amy K. "Metaphor and Maternity in *Mama Day.*" *Gloria Naylor's Early Novels*, edited by Margot Anne Kelley, Florida: UP of Florida, 1999, pp. 70-88.

Lorber, Judith. *The Variety of Feminisms and Their Contributions to Gender Equality.* Bibliotheks Und Informations system Der Universität Oldenburg, 1997.

Lorde, Audre. "Uses of the Erotic: The Erotic as Power." *Sister Outsider: Essays and Speeches*, edited by Audre Lorde, New York: The Crossing Press, 1984, pp. 53-59.

Lyons, Paul. "Reviewed Work(s): *Shark Dialogues* by Kiana Davenport." *Mānoa*, vol. 7, no. 1, Summer, 1995, pp. 265-267.

Márquez, Gabriel G. *One Hundred Years of Solitude.* Translated by Gregory Rabassa, Kolkata: Penguin Books India, 1996.

Macpherson, Heidi S. "Coyote as Culprit: 'Her-story' and the Feminist Fantastic in Gail Anderson-Dargatz's *The Cure for Death by Lightning.*" *History, Literature, and the Writing of the Canadian Prairies*, edited by Alison Calder and Robert Wardhaugh, Winnipeg: U of Manitoba P, 2005, pp. 87-100.

Mallory, Devona. "Magical Realism as a Tool of Empowerment in Selected Women's Novels." PhD Dissertation, Illinois State University, 2008. ProQuest. https://www.proquest.com/openview/30ee71d9c4688b387d6dad2b9940c31d/1?pq-origsite=gscholar&cbl=18750. Accessed 23 September 2020.

Mardorossian, Carine M. *Reclaiming Difference: Caribbean Women Rewrite Postcolonialism.* Charlottesville: U of Virginia P, 2005.

Martínez, Danizete. "Teaching Chicana/o Literature in Community College with Ana Castillo's *So Far from God.*" *Rocky Mountain Review*, vol. 65, no. 2, 2011, pp. 216-225. https://doi.org/10.1353/RMR.2011.0016.

Martinez, Nelly Z. "The Politics of the Woman Artist in Isabel Allende's *The House of the Spirits.*" *Writing the Woman Artist: Essays, Poetics, Politics, and Portraiture*, edited by Suzanne W. Jones, Philadelphia: U of Pennsylvania P, 1991, pp. 287-306.

Matus, Jill. *Toni Morrison.* Manchester & New York: Manchester UP, 1998.

Mbiti, John S. *African Religion and Philosophy.* London: Heinemann, 1969.

Meyer, Doris. "'Parenting the Text': Female Creativity and Dialogic Relationships in Isabel Allende's *La casa de los espíritus.*" *Hispania*, vol. 73, no. 2, May 1990, pp. 360-365. https://doi.org/10.2307/342815. *JSTOR*, https://www.jstor.org/stable/342815.

Morace, Robert A. "From Sacred Hoops to Bingo Palaces. Louise Erdrich's Carnivalesque Fiction." *The Chippewa Landscape of Louise Erdrich*, edited by Allan Chavkin, Tuscaloosa and London: The U of Alabama P, 1999, pp. 36-66.

Morales, Aurora L. *Medicine Stories: History, Culture and the Politics of Integrity.* Cambridge: South End Press, 1998.

Morrow, Colette. "Queering Chicano/a Narratives: Lesbian as Healer, Saint and Warrior in Ana Castillo's *So Far from God.*" *The Journal of the Midwest Modern Language Association*, vol. 30, no. 1-2, 1997, pp. 63-80. https://doi.org/10.2307/1315427.

Mrak, Anja. "The Intersections of Magical Realism and Transnational Feminism in Cristina Garcia's *Dreaming in Cuban.*" *Interactions: Ege Journal of British and American Studies*, vol. 23, no. 1-2, 2014, pp. 179-190. *Gale Academic OneFile*, https://gale.com/apps/doc/A363103646/AONE?u=anon~110f6049&sid=googleScholar&xid=4e0bd72c. Accessed 28 Apr. 2021.

Naylor, Gloria. *Mama Day: A Novel.* New York: Open Road, 1988.

Nora, Pierre. "Between History and Memory: *Les Lieux de Mémoire.*" *Representations*, no. 26, 1989, pp. 7-24. https://doi.org/10.2307/2928520. *JSTOR*, https://www.jstor.org/stable/2928520

Olmedo, Rebeca R. "Women's Earth-Binding Consciousness in *So Far from God.*" *Label Me Latina/o*, vol. 2, Fall 2012, pp. 1-22. https://labelmelatin.com/wp-content/uploads/2012/09/Womens-Earth-Binding-Consciousness-in-So-Far-from-God.pdf. Accessed 15 June 2021.

Olmos, Margarite F. "Women's Writing in Latin America: Critical Trends and Priorities." *Searching Women in Latin America and the Caribbean*, edited by Edna Acosta-Belén and Christine E. Bose, Oxford: Westview Press, 1993, pp. 135-152.

Otero, Gerardo, and Janice O'Bryan. "Cuba in Transition? The Civil Sphere's Challenge to the Castro Regime." *Latin American Politics and Society*, vol. 44, 2002, pp. 29-57. https://doi.org/10.2307/3176994. *JSTOR*, https://www.jstor.org/stable/3176994.

Owens, Louis. *Other Destinies: Understanding the American Indian Novel.* Norman: U of Oklahoma P, 1992.

Pérez Jr., Louis. *Cuba: Between Reform and Revolution.* Oxford: Oxford UP, 1988.

Perez, Domino R. *There was a Woman: La Llorona from Folklore to Popular Culture.* Austin. U of Texas P, 2008.

Peterson, Nancy J. "History, Postmodernism, and Louise Erdrich's *Tracks.*" *PMLA*, vol. 109, no. 5, 1994, pp. 982-994. https://doi.org/10.2307/462966. *JSTOR*, https://www.jstor.org/stable/462966.

Pettersson, Inger. "Telling it to the Dead: Borderless Communication and Scars of Trauma in Cristina García's *Dreaming in Cuban.*" *Journal of Literary Studies*, vol. 29, no. 2, 2013, pp. 44-61. https://doi.org/10.1080/02564718.2013.777143.

Plummer, Elizabeth P. "Mermaids, Monsters, and Madwomen: Voices of Feminism and Feminine Consciousness." PhD Dissertation, Pacifica Graduate Institute, 2003. ProQuest Dissertations and Theses Database. https://www.proquest.com/docview/305232354/abstract. Accessed 29 August 2022.

Porter, Joy. "Historical and Cultural Contexts to Native American Literature." *The Cambridge Companion to Native American Literature*, edited by Joy Porter and Kenneth M. Roemer, Cambridge: Cambridge UP, 2005, pp. 39-68.

Quintana, Alvina E. *Home Girls: Chicana Literary Voices.* Philadelphia: Temple UP, 1996.

Reid, Alana. "The Erotic Union of Marxist and Feminist Thought in Gioconda Belli's *La Mujer Habitada.*" *Letras Femeninas*, vol. 36, no. 2, 2010, pp. 61-81. *JSTOR*, https://www.jstor.org/stable/23022102.

Rimstead, Roxanne. "Introduction: Double Take: The Use of Cultural Memory." *Cultural Memory and Social Identity*, Special Issue: *Essays on Canadian Writing*, no. 80, 2003, pp. 1-14.

Rocha, Ana C. Gomes da. "Narratives of Women: Gender and Magical Realism in Postcolonial Texts." PhD Dissertation, Departamento de Línguas e Culturas, Universidade de Aveiro, 2012. http://hdl.handle.net/10773/10506. Accessed 11 April 2021.

Rodriguez, Ralph E. "Chicana/o Fiction from Resistance to Contestation: The Role of Creation in Ana Castillo's *So Far from God.*" *MELUS*, vol. 25, no. 2, 2000, pp. 63-82. https://doi.org/10.2307/468219

Rushdie, Salman. *Midnight's Children.* London: Vintage, 2006.

Russo, Mary. *The Female Grotesque: Risk, Excess and Modernity.* New York and London: Routledge, 1994.

Rzepa, Agnieszka. "Feats and Defeats of Memory: Exploring Spaces of Canadian Magic Realism." PhD Dissertation, Adam Mickiewicz University, 2009. https://repozytorium.amu.edu.pl/bitstream/10593/1265/1/Rzepa_2009_Feats_And_Defeats_of_Memory.pdf. Accessed 11 December 2021.

Sáez, Elena M. "The Global Baggage of Nostalgia in Cristina Garcia's *Dreaming in Cuban.*" *MELUS*, vol. 30, no. 4, 2005, pp. 129-147. https://doi.org/10.1093/melus/30.4.129.

Sánchez, Maria R. Noriega. "Magic Realism in Contemporary American Women's Fiction." PhD Dissertation, Department of English Literature, University of Sheffield, 2001. https://etheses.whiterose.ac.uk/3502/. Accessed 10 November 2021.

Santos, Maria, and Barbara A. Engel. "Women in the Nicaraguan Revolution." *Frontiers: A Journal of Women Studies*, vol. 7, no. 2, 1983, pp. 42-46. *JSTOR*, https://doi:10.2307/3346284.

Schultermandl, Silvia, and Sebnem Toplu. "A Fluid Sense of Self: The Politics of Transnational Identity in Anglophone Literatures." *A Fluid Sense of Self: The Politics of Transnational Identity*, edited by Silvia Schultermandl and Sebnem Toplu, Vienna: LIT Verlag, 2010, pp. 11-24.

Sheffield, Carrie. "Voices from the Political Abyss: Isabel Allende's *The House of the Spirits* and the Reconstruction and Preservation of History and Memory in 1970s Chile and Beyond." *Proteus: A Journal of Ideas*, vol. 19, no. 2, 2002, pp. 33-38.

Simpkins, Scott. "Sources of Magic Realism/Supplements to Realism in Contemporary Latin American Literature." *Magical Realism: Theory, History, Community*, edited by Lois P. Zamora and Wendy B. Faris, Durham & London: Duke UP, 1995, pp. 145-160.

Slemon, Stephen. "Magic Realism as Postcolonial Discourse." *Magical Realism: Theory, History, Community*, edited by Lois P. Zamora and Wendy B. Faris, Durham & London: Duke UP, 1995, pp. 407-426.

Smith, Kathryn M. "Female Voice and Feminist Text: *Testimonio* as a Form of Resistance in Latin America." *Florida Atlantic Comparative Studies Journal*, vol. 12, no. 1, 2010-2011, pp. 21-37. https://home.fau.edu/peralta/web/facs/testimonioresistance.pdf. Accessed 16 August 2021.

Soto, Francisco. "Reinaldo Arenas: The 'Pentagonía' and the Cuban Documentary Novel." *Cuban Studies*, vol. 23, 1993, pp. 135–166. *JSTOR*, https://www.jstor.org/stable/24487022.

Spencer, Stephen. "Memory and The Convergence of Cultures in Kiana Davenport's *Shark Dialogues.*" *Review of International American Studies*, vol. 2, no. 2, 2007, pp. 8-18. https://www.journals.us.edu.pl/index.php/RIAS/article/view/575. Accessed 26 April 2022.

Spindler, William. "Magic Realism: A Typology." *Forum for Modern Language Studies*, vol. 29, no. 1, 1993, pp. 75-85. https://doi.org/10.1093/FMLS%2FXXIX.1.75.

Sternbach, Nancy S. "Re-membering the Dead: Latin American Women's 'Testimonial' Discourse." *Latin American Perspectives*, vol. 18, no. 3, 1991, pp. 91-102. *JSTOR*, https://www.jstor.org/stable/2633742.

Stirrup, David. *Louise Erdrich*. Manchester: Manchester UP, 2010.

Tankersley, Caleb. "Magical Resistance: Louise Erdrich's Use of Magic Realism in *Tracks* and *The Plague of Doves*." *Proceedings of the Eleventh Native American Symposium*, edited by Mark B. Spencer, USA: Southeastern Oklahoma State University, 2015, pp. 20-34. https://www.se.edu/native-american/wp-content/uploads/sites/49/2019/09/AAA-NAS-2015-Proceedings-Tankersley.pdf. Accessed 23 June 2022.

Taylor-Guthrie, Danille, editor. *Conversations with Toni Morrison*. Jackson: U of Mississippi P, 1994.

Trask, Haunani-Kay. *From a Native Daughter: Colonialism and Sovereignty in Hawai'i*. Honolulu: U of Hawai'i P, 1999.

Tucker, Lindsey. "Recovering the Conjure Woman: Texts and Contexts in Gloria Naylor's *Mama Day*." *African American Review*, vol. 28, no. 2, 1994, pp. 173-188. https://doi.org/10.2307/3041991. *JSTOR*, http://www.jstor.org/stable/3041991?origin=JSTOR-pdf.

Turner, Kay F. "Mexican American Home Altars: Towards Their Interpretation." *Aztlán: A Journal of Chicano Studies*, vol. 13, no. 1, 1982, pp. 309-326. https://www.ingentaconnect.com/contentone/csrc/aztlan/1982/00000013/f0020001/art00017. Accessed 26 March 2021.

Valdés, María E. de. *The Shattered Mirror: Representations of Women in Mexican Literature*. Austin: U of Texas P, 1998.

Velie, Alan. "The Trickster Novel." *Narrative Chance: Postmodern Discourse on Native American Indian Literatures*, edited by Gerald Vizenor. Albuquerque: U of New Mexico P, 1989, pp. 121-139.

Walter, Robert. "Pan-American (Re)Visions: Magical Realism and Ameridian Cultures in Susan Power's *The Grass Dancer*, Gioconda Belli's *La Mujer Habitada*, Linda Hogan's *Power*, and Mario Vargas Llosa's *El Hablador*." *American Studies International*, vol. 37, no. 3, 1999, pp. 63-80.

Warnes, Christopher. *Magical Realism and the Postcolonial Novel: Between Faith and Irreverence*. UK: Palgrave Macmillan, 2009.

Wells, Kimberly A. "Screaming, Flying, and Laughing: Magical Feminism's Witches in Contemporary Film, Television, and Novels." PhD Dissertation, Texas A&M University, 2007. https://oaktrust.library.tamu.edu/handle/1969.1/6007. Accessed 19 June 2021.

Womack, Craig S. *Red on Red: Native American Literary Separatism*. Minneapolis: U of Minnesota P, 1999.

Yavaş, Nesrin. *In the Tracks of an Oxymoron: Magical Realism*. Izmir: Ege UP, 2021.

Yuval-Davis, Nira. "Belonging and the Politics of Belonging." Patterns of Prejudice, vol. 40, no. 3, 2006, pp. 197-214. https://doi.org/10.1080/00313220600769331.

Zamora, Lois P., and Wendy B. Faris. "Introduction: Daiquiri Birds and Flaubertian Parrot(ie)s." Magical Realism: Theory, History, Community, edited by Lois P. Zamora and Wendy B. Faris, Durham & London: Duke UP, 1995, pp. 1-11.

Zobaie, Ola A. Kareem. "Magical Realism in Contemporary Novels Beloved and Wise Children: Feminist Reading." MA Thesis, Karabuk University, 2022. http://acikerisim.karabuk.edu.tr:8080/xmlui/handle/123456789/1799. Accessed 23 December 2023.

Index

D

E

F

G

H

T

U

V

W

X

Y

www.ingramcontent.com/pod-product-compliance
Lightning Source LLC
Chambersburg PA
CBHW050447280326
41932CB00013BA/2270

9798881901103